Practical Software Measurement

Practical Software Measurement

Bob Hughes
School of Information Management, University of Brighton

The McGraw-Hill Companies

London • Burr Ridge, IL • New York • St Louis • San Francisco • Auckland • Bogotá • Caracas
Lisbon • Madrid • Mexico • Milan • Montreal • New Delhi • Panama • Paris • San Juan • São Paulo
Singapore • Tokyo • Toronto

Published by
McGraw-Hill Publishing Company
SHOPPENHANGERS ROAD, MAIDENHEAD, BERKSHIRE, SL6 2QL, ENGLAND
Telephone: +44(0) 1628 502500
Fax: +44(0) 1628 770224
Web site: http://www.mcgraw-hill.co.uk

British Library Cataloguing in Publication Data
A catalogue record for this book is available from the British Library

ISBN 007 709459 X

Library of Congress cataloguing in publication data
The LOC data for this book has been applied for and may be obtained from the Library of Congress,
Washington, D.C.

Author's Web site address: http://www.mcgraw-hill.co.uk/hughes

Publishing Director: David Hatter
Produced by: Steven Gardiner Ltd
Typesetting: Mouse Nous, Cross-in-Hand
Cover: Hybert Design

The **McGraw·Hill** *Companies*

Printed in Great Britain at the University Press, Cambridge
1   2   3   4   5   CUP   4   3   2   1   0

Contents

Preface

Thou shalt not have in thy house divers measures, a great and a small.

But thou shalt have a perfect and just weight, a perfect and just measurement shalt thou have: that thy days may be lengthened in the land which the Lord, thy god, giveth thee.

Deuteronomy Chapter 25 Verses 14–5
Authorized Version of Bible

'This trifling matter, I said, of distinguishing one and two and three. I mean in sum, number and calculation. Is it not true that every art and science must necessarily partake of them?'

Plato's Republic
Translated by Paul Shorey

To me, the reasons why measurement should be used in the management of information technology and information systems (IT/IS) and software engineering development are clear-cut, both for practitioners and researchers. If we believe in management, then we must believe that making a decision in one direction rather than another is going to make a real difference that could affect the chances of an organization being a success in its sphere of activity. If it truly does make a difference then that difference must be perceptible and if it is perceptible then it is likely to be measurable. As the quotation from Deuteronomy (which is echoed in Magna Carta) illustrates, fair measurement has always been needed in trade and commerce. The movement in IT/IS towards the measuring of software size in function points, despite the objections of many academics, demonstrates that this is still the case where that business concerns the newer technologies.

In order for discipline areas to be detailed, theories need to be developed. There needs to be some way of testing the truth of these theories, for example about the efficacy of particular techniques. This invariably requires measurement.

Yet measurement is often dismissed. Taking measurements for their own sake is clearly absurd. In Iain Banks' novel *The Wasp Factory*, the villain of the piece continually does this ('See that door over there? It's eighty-five inches, corner to corner'). Quantifying can also be difficult – as one colleague in industry wanted to know: how do you put a money value on redecorating the reception area to you building? Making a good impression on visitors is important, but how important? While these points are conceded, to rule measurement out of hand in all situations relating to the management of IT/IS seems to be resigning ourselves to uncertainty and ignorance.

In colleges and universities, the teaching of quantitative methods seems to be becoming more difficult. In fact, I sometimes get the impression that many teachers, outside the core mathematical and scientific subjects, are giving up on quantitative approaches. One of the aspirations of this book is to assist in the re-invigoration of the teaching of quantitative methods on IT/IS courses and software engineering courses by using measurement to link quantitative techniques to the practical concerns of IT/IS and software engineering development.

Where this book differs in approach from other books on this subject is in the recognition that measurement has to be based firmly on a qualitative understanding of the systems under scrutiny. Although software measurement theorists often seem to stress the need for measurement to be built on sound models of the underlying systems, in practice there is a tendency to look for correlations between the inputs and outputs to systems without any real understanding of the processes by which those inputs might be transformed into outputs. This book also avoids excessive analogies between the measurement of IT/IS and software development and its products and measurement in the physical sciences. Fundamentally IT/IS and software engineering development is a human activity system, and measurement techniques that have a sound foundation in the social sciences are almost always more appropriate.

This book has emerged partly from a general interest in software project management, as evidenced by the book on the subject written in collaboration with my colleague, Mike Cotterell, and partly from my research work on the practical problems of software effort estimation, which eventually led to a PhD. I am by no means a natural statistician and I am grateful to colleagues such as Keith Parramore, Graham Winstanley and Dave King at the University of Brighton and especially to Martin Shepperd of Bournemouth University for the assistance they rendered me when I was getting to grips with software measurement. Despite the heated debates that one comes across over such matters as functional size measurement, I have found the 'software measurement community' to be an extremely friendly and supportive one. Among many who have been helpful I would like to particularly single out Barbara Kitchenham of Keele University who has provided warm encouragement to many fledgling researchers in software measurement.

My research involved extensive work in a real industrial environment that I have labelled the 'XYZ organization' in this book. Alan Cunliffe and Franklyn Young-Martos were my industrial collaborators and I owe them much gratitude for the opportunities they gave me.

David Longstreet, Darrel Ince and Tracy Hall reviewed the original proposal and made some useful comments. Tracy also commented on drafts of some of the chapters. David Hatter and the team at McGraw-Hill have kept up the momentum of the book's progress. My thanks go to all of these.

Finally, I would like to record my appreciation of the forbearance of Heather, Katherine and Tom. Their names have been borrowed in Chapter 2, but as well as being empirical and numerical relations they are family relations of mine as well.

Bob Hughes
University of Brighton

Chapter 1

Why software should be measured and how we can begin to do this

---

OBJECTIVES

In this chapter you will learn about:

☐ why measurement should be an important part of software development

☐ some of the pitfalls associated with measurement

☐ how measurement can assist in evaluating the effectiveness of software

☐ some basic concepts used in software measurement

1.1 Why software measurement is important

To what extent do software developers really need to concern themselves with software measurement? The truth is that not all software engineers are convinced that software measurement is necessary or even useful. One software engineering authority was famously known to have declared that 'software metrics is crap'. In the United Kingdom, one of the father figures of software engineering argued that the only software metric that he needed to be aware of was the binary one indicating whether a piece of program code was correct or not. The implication was that this correctness could be established through a formal logical proof.

The view of the software measurement community is that in order to resolve most of the issues concerning the best way to conduct software development, measurement of some kind must be the basis for establishing the truth. Many practitioners in various sections of the computing industry would like to think that their 'profession' (if it really is such) is based on engineering disciplines. One of the hallmarks of an engineering discipline is its rational, scientific foundation. Francis Crick, along with James D. Watson, one of the discoverers of the structure of DNA, has commented that it has been said that any subject that has 'science' in its name is unlikely to be one. At the time cognitive science was being teased, but computer 'science' would not be unscathed if its alleged scientific basis were carefully analysed. One social scientist analysed discussions between computer scientists at a conference about the merits of different programming languages. It will not come as a surprise to many that

> *computer science ... does not proceed in quite the simple fashion of clear paradigms and rational argument that might be imagined from a characterisation as 'hardcore science'.*

> (Robinson 1994)

Hugh Robinson also noted the use by computer scientists of assertions that lacked supporting justification and which also seemed to contradict each other:

> *... the contradictory nature was commented on ... and in question sessions the contradictions were the subject of direct questions. What is interesting is that both such comments and direct questions never led to any significant debate or marshalling of evidence for or against a position. It was sufficient for the protagonists to reaffirm their (contradictory) positions, in a way that is akin to reaffirming opinions rather than facts.*

Norman Fenton and Shari Pfleeger (1997) have noted the scanty evidence upon which many of the 'principles' of accepted software engineering practice have been based. For example, the use of flowcharts to document software designs and algorithms has been frowned upon by instructors in programming for years. Typical is the comment cited by Fenton from Martin and McClure (1985), *'flowcharts should be avoided as a form of program documentation'*. Yet a study by Scanlan (1989) found that flowcharts – if they were properly structured – took significantly less time to comprehend than the equivalent pseudocode.

Not only the academic community is lacking in rational support for its assertions. Peter Keen (1981) surveyed research on decision-making and noted that it was possible to overestimate the extent to which information systems were used to support decision-making by managers. Indeed, under pressure, managers tended to discard information, and to avoid bringing in outside expertise.

> *Almost every descriptive study of a complex decision process suggests that the formal analysis of quantified information is, at best, a minor aspect of the situation ... Negotiations, ... habit, rules of thumb and 'muddling through' have far more force. This may seem an extreme assertion but there is little empirical evidence to challenge this.*

> (Keen 1981)

A case in defence of managers can certainly be made: they often have to make decisions in complex situations where there are time pressures that prevent a careful analysis and where in any case all the relevant information that would be helpful is not available.

At this point let us marshal the arguments in favour of using measurement. It is suggested that measurement can assist:

- understanding;

- objectivity;

- communication;

- effective prioritization;

- prediction.

Each of these will now be considered in turn.

Understanding. It is traditional at this point to quote Lord Kelvin and we will follow that tradition:

> *When you can measure what you are speaking about, and express it in numbers, you know something about it; but when you cannot measure it, when you cannot express it in numbers, then your knowledge is of a meagre and unsatisfactory kind.*

(quoted in Shepperd 1995)

Reading the quotation, it should be noted that while Lord Kelvin was suggesting that a sound and accurate understanding of a phenomenon ought to lead to the ability to express that understanding quantitatively, it does not follow that measurement will automatically lead to understanding. However, attempts at meaningful measurement usually require observation of the subject under investigation and/or the conduct of experiments which may allow a better understanding to emerge.

Objectivity. The need for the objectivity that measurement can provide can be seen particularly in relation to the quality of software products. In IT there has been the growing awareness that attention needs to be given not only to functional requirements (that is, what the software will do), but also to quality requirements (how well the software will be designed and built). However, user demands, for example, for 'user-friendliness' will founder unless there is a way for this quality to be quantified so that the requirement can be effectively incorporated in contracts. Moves towards 'out-sourcing' and 'service level agreements' have made this an increasingly pressing concern.

Communication. This is associated with the need for objectivity noted above. Middle-ranking managers in large organizations are going to find it difficult to get an accurate picture of what is actually going on in their areas of responsibility simply by resorting to 'management by walking around'. At some point, direct experience and face-to-face communication will need to be supplemented by the production, at lower levels, of management information about work in progress and its analysis by higher levels of management. The setting up of this kind of management information system will inevitably lead to the requirement for some kind of measurement.

Lord Kelvin (born William Thompson), British physicist, professor at University of Glasgow 1846–1899.

Lord Kelvin did not always get his quantitative thinking correct: he miscalculated the age of the Earth based on how long it would have taken to cool to its current temperature.

Effective prioritization. Qualitative approaches to systems analysis, design and construction can be quite effective, but there is a danger in ignoring quantitative and measurable factors. One aspect of this is the need to use measurement to establish the cost-effectiveness of any proposed system and another the need to quantify the use different parts of the system will experience as a factor in systems design and construction.

However well designed and constructed a new IT-based system might be it will not be regarded as a success if it is not cost-effective – the costs involved in its construction must not exceed the value of the benefits that will accrue with its eventual operation. The designer must therefore be aware of the potential development effort needed to implement particular features and this will require assessment of the 'work content' of that feature.

Vilfredo Pareto, Italian economist and sociologist, 1848–1923.

One characteristic of systems is sometimes referred to as the 80/20 or Pareto Principle: the bulk of the processing in a system (say 80%) tends to be executed by a relatively small proportion (say 20%) of the total set of procedures, the remaining procedures dealing with minority cases and exceptions. The designer or manager of a system must ensure that the main attention is focused on that small proportion of procedures of real importance. Usability, processing efficiency and even reliability will be of more importance for these heavily used parts of the system.

Prediction. Effective planning and management depend upon a knowledge of the likely consequences of proposed actions – for example the likely increase in the failure rate of the system when it becomes operational if system testing is curtailed. This has to be based on measurement data from past projects.

1.2　Difficulties and pitfalls in the measurement approach

A book on software measurement is bound to be very positive about the merits of a more measurement-based approach to software project management. However, it would be misleading to suggest that measurement is without difficulties, such as:

- rigour of the methods involved;

- narrowness of the applicability of findings;

- uncertainty of 'success';

- danger of 'political' misrepresentation;

- adoption of indicators as targets.

Let us look at each of these in turn.

Rigour of methods. Effective measurement depends on the correct application of key techniques including experimental design and statistical analysis. These 'rigorous' procedures should be transparent. Interested parties should be able to examine the processes undertaken and, where necessary, identify any possible limitations or flaws – this can even include simple arithmetic slips on occasion.

Having flaws pointed out can be embarrassing, say, to a manager who may be perhaps trying to promote a more rational and objective approach to decision-making. More 'qualitative' and intuitive ways of justifying decisions do not have quite this potential for embarrassment.

Narrowness of the applicability of findings. Results found in one environment might not be applicable in another. You might, for example, have worked hard finding out the software coding productivity of a department in thousands of lines of code per month. Yet when you use those findings to predict the coding effort for a new project in a different department, you may find that the productivity findings are just not transferable. Mangers often become aware that established researchers seem to contradict each other. For example, Belady and Lehman (1979) showed that as a software system evolves it loses structure and thus becomes more time-consuming to change. Other work by Basili and Turner (1975), however, discovered that in some cases the structure of software could actually be improved by maintenance work over a period of time. Similarly, while some researchers have suggested that development productivity will fall as the system to be built increases in size (for example, Boehm 1981, Albrecht and Gaffney 1983), others have found that productivity can actually be better with larger systems (for example, Bailey and Basili 1981; Kemerer 1987; Marwane and Mili 1991). The manager may be justified in wondering just who to believe. In fact, the conclusions could all be correct – *but for particular environments.* We see this as an argument in favour of conducting your own measurements: not as one for ignoring measurement altogether.

Uncertainty of success. Measurement is normally carried out as part of an investigation to answer some question. In software development, for example, the question might be whether a software engineering technique improves reliability. Because of any of a number of good reasons the outcome of the analysis of measurement data collected could be simply inconclusive. If this happens to you then you are in good company (see Pfleeger *et al.* [1994], for example), but this could be a blow if you are a missionary for measurement who is trying to persuade a sceptical management of its merits.

Danger of political misrepresentation. The people carrying out measurement projects often have higher management as their clients. These clients will have their own agenda and results appearing to support a course of action they wish to pursue might be eagerly seized upon and publicized. In the process, the real significance of the results may be distorted.

Adoption of indicators as targets. Sometimes you may not be able to measure a particular quality directly. Instead one or more **indicators** (or **surrogates**) of the relative presence or absence of the quality might be measured. For example, 'thousands of lines of code per month' might reasonably be used as an indicator of productivity in a particular environment. If word gets around that project teams or even individuals are being judged by this indicator, then the temptation will be to write verbose code rather than compact code to implement particular system features. People will start to work to the indicator rather than the proper objectives.

Talking of embarrassment, as a new database analyst I once wrote a report on machine performance with calculations based on an hour having 360 seconds.

1.3   Some preliminary examples of measurement

We will now look at some of the basic ideas of software measurement by means of three examples based on exercises that readers, if they wish, may attempt.

Before proceeding, it is stressed that the scope of term 'software measurement' will be fairly widely drawn in this book. It will include not just the measurement of the internal components of software code of which a software developer would be aware, but will also take into account, in quantitative terms, the external features of software of which the users would be aware. In fact we will introduce some of the initial measurement concepts using examples based on the external attributes of software before exploring the more technical field of internal software measurement in later chapters.

The first example is where the performance of a spell-checker is to be evaluated. This is followed by an exercise that attempts to measure the effectiveness of a check-digit algorithm while the final example deals with the evaluation of Web search engines.

One of our aims is to make the reader an active participant in the progress of the text that follows. We do this by means of self-assessment questions and exercises. We would like to reassure you that while it would be gratifying if you read every word in the book from cover to cover, the book has been designed to allow sections to be skipped. One irritation that the writer has experienced when reading technical computer science literature has been that a pre-existing knowledge of the particular notations or techniques that are referred to has been assumed. Even where you have previously been in contact with the technique, unless you use it on a day-to-day basis, it is easy to forget its details. This is particularly the case with the statistical techniques associated with software measurement. We have attempted to remedy this by including sections, where appropriate, explaining the relevant supporting technique. Where readers are already familiar with the technique then they are welcome to skip over that section.

1.4   Example 1 Evaluating a spelling-checker

Exercise 1.1 Qualities of a spelling-checker   What qualities would you look for in a spelling-checker?

A desirable feature in a spelling-checker would clearly be its effectiveness in detecting incorrect spelling. If you have used a spelling-checker you will know that another desirable feature is that it should not identify words that are in fact correct as incorrect. Most spelling-checkers will, when they detect what they regard as an incorrect word, attempt to suggest a correct spelling – sometimes a totally different word to the one that was meant. Thus the ability of the spelling-checker to suggest the correct word in a high proportion of cases could be taken as another desirable quality.

EXAMPLE 1 EVALUATING A SPELLING-CHECKER 7

A software writer might at this point object that the qualities identified above do not relate solely to the spelling-checker as an effective piece of software but also depend upon the dictionary that is used. The designers of the software could have written an excellent piece of code but have been let down by the poor construction of the dictionary. This raises the question of the **system boundary**. Circumstances can be envisaged where the task might be to evaluate the quality of the spelling-checker algorithm regardless of the dictionary used. However, in the current context, we adopt the end-user's viewpoint – users of a word processing package would tend not to distinguish between the spelling-checker algorithm and the dictionary it uses – it is just one 'package' to them.

Given the desirable qualities in a spelling-checker that have been identified in Exercise 1.1, how might we carry out evaluations to see to what extent a particular spelling-checker has the desired qualities?

Exercise 1.2 Evaluating qualities of a spelling-checker

The use of questionnaires would evaluate what people thought was the relative presence or absence of the quality in the spelling-checker but would not be measuring the quality directly – different people would have different opinions. Although sometimes it would be important to measure people's perceptions, for example, when devising marketing plans, usually it is better to try to take direct measurements.

If you have access to a word-processing package with a spelling-checker, obtain, or create for yourself, a document which has not been previously machine-checked. Run the spelling-checker on the document and count the instances where the checker has spotted an incorrect word, the cases where a word is flagged as incorrect when it is in fact acceptable, and the cases where the correct spelling of an incorrect word is wrongly suggested. Also obtain a word-count for the document.

Table 1.1 shows the sort of results that you might get.

Exercise 1.3 Practical evaluation of a spelling-checker

The trial will have raised many practical points. The number of incorrect spellings identified depends not just on the spelling-checker's processing but also on the number of misspellings actually in the document. If the document had been

Table 1.1 *Sample results of a spelling-checker trial*

Incorrect spellings identified	18
Correct words wrongly rejected	1
Incorrect suggestions	3
Words in document	845

written by someone who was a good speller and an accurate typist, then a much lower figure would be expected. We can see that the result has stemmed from a specific spelling-checker processing a specific document typed by a particular person.

In measurement terminology we can say we have three **entities** involved: a spelling-checker, a document and a document writer. Each entity had a number of characteristics or **attributes**: for example, *document length* (in words) is an attribute of the entity *document*.

Exercise 1.4 Identifying attributes

What might be attributes of the entities *spelling-checker* and *document writer*?

Strictly speaking we should distinguish between the **attribute** which is the characteristic in general terms (such as *document length*) and a **metric** (such as *document length in words*) which will be some number and an associated unit that will reflect the current state of the attribute. For *document length*, alternative metrics might be *number of characters* or *number of paragraphs*.

The number of errors found in a document is not an attribute solely of a single document or the spelling-checker but of them both together. In fact you could envisage *number of errors* as an attribute of another entity called spelling-checker trial which is related to a particular document and to a particular spelling-checker. This could be expressed in the entity-relationship model (ERM) in Figure 1.1.

1.5   Entity-relationship models (ERMs)

The reader familiar with ERMs may wish to skip this section.

Data modelling is a technique by which the things about which information is held in an information system are identified. These things are called **entity types**. In a payroll system, for example, an important entity type would be an *employee*. The term entity type refers to the entity as a generality: an actual example of the entity, for example, 'David Pressman' would be called an **entity occurrence**.

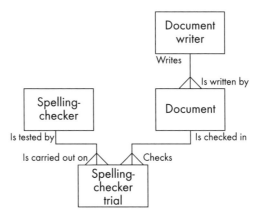

Figure 1.1 *An entity-relationship model.*

Each entity type may have a number of **attribute types**. The attributes of the entity type *employee* might be *payroll number, name, address, date of birth*, *salary grade, department code*. As in the case of entity types and entity occurrences, attribute type refers to the attribute in general terms (what format it is in, the maximum length etc.) while an actual example of the attribute, for example the *date of birth* attribute of the entity occurrence for David Pressman being '4th January 1972', is referred to an **attribute occurrence**.

Data modellers tend to use the term attribute in a slightly different way to measurement theorists. Data modellers refer to any item of data as an attribute. If it was decided to hold *number of characters, number of words* and *number of paragraphs* for each document, then these, according to data modellers, would all be attributes of the entity *document*. Measurement theorists tend to use the word attribute to denote a more conceptual idea of a characteristic or property of an entity such as *length* with *number of characters, number of words* and *number of paragraphs* as **metrics** which attempt to capture that characteristic through a measurement.

Only some data attributes are measurement related. Some like *payroll reference, name* and *address* would not relate to measurement as such. Each entity type will need either a single data attribute or a group of data attributes that **uniquely identify** each occurrence of that entity. For the *employee* entity type, the *payroll reference* would be different for each employee and would distinguish that occurrence of the entity from others. These data attributes are known as **keys**.

Some entity types may be related to others. For example, in the payroll system the entity type *employee* might have a **relationship** with another entity type called *department*. This might be important because different departments might be paid on different days. The relationship between *employee* and *department* would be a **many-to-one** relationship. An employee would belong to only one department, but a department would have many employees. We call the entity type at the 'one' end, the **parent** entity in the relationship and the entity at the 'many' end, the **child** entity. A many-to-one relationship will normally mean that the child entity at the many end will have as one of its data attributes the value of the key data attribute of the parent. For example, *employee* will need to have a *department code* (if *department code* were the key of *department*) as a data attribute to show to which department it belonged. This would be called a **foreign key** – it is not the 'native' key of *employee* but it refers to the key of some other entity type.

One-to-one relationships are also possible but are relatively rare: if a relationship is one-to-one, you have to ask carefully whether you are not really dealing with one combined entity type.

The other possibility is that the relationship between two entity types is **many-to-many**. Logically there is no problem with this: in the payroll case it might be that in fact an employee could do work for several different departments and hence there could be a many-to-many relationship between *employee* and *department*. In practice there are complications in recording the details of many-to-many relationships and so the usual thing is to add a new linking entity type which breaks the many-to-many relationship into two one-to-many relationships (see Figure 1.2).

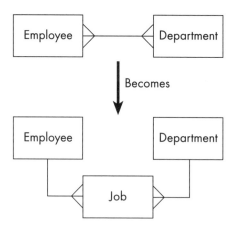

Figure 1.2 *Introducing a link entity type.*

This illustrates how a link entity introduced to split and remove a many-to-many relationship may often turn out on further consideration to be an entity in its own right.

A final consideration is that a relationship may be **optional** or **mandatory**. For example, it might be the case that a *job* entity cannot exist unless it is attached to an occurrence of the *employee* entity but an *employee* might not have to carry out any jobs as such. Optional relationships are shown by broken lines, see Figure 1.3.

1.6   Measuring spelling-checker effectiveness

To resume our main theme. The number of errors found by a spelling-checker in a trial relates not just to a particular spelling-checker but also to a particular document. We can validly make comparisons between the results from different spelling-checkers as long as we use the same document in each trial. This is known as controlling the variables in the experiment. Where we have data which relates to different documents as well as different spelling-checkers then things start to get a bit tricky.

Is the figure of 18 errors correctly identified relatively high or low? One obstacle to making a judgement here is that not all documents are of the same size. You would certainly expect a document of 8450 words to have more errors than another with 845 words. A fairer comparison might be to compare error **rates** – the number of errors found in each document per thousand words. In the example above this

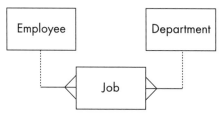

Figure 1.3 *Optional and mandatory relationships.*

would be 18/845×1000 that is, 21.3 errors per thousand words. One way of looking at this is to think that the maximum number of errors in an 845 word document is 845 if all the words were misspelled – the error rate is effectively comparing the actual number of errors with the maximum possible. Similarly, when it comes to incorrect alternative spellings being suggested, the maximum possible incorrect alternative spellings would depend on the number of incorrect words detected.

With the data presented in Table 1.1, what would be the error rate for the suggested correct spellings when an incorrect word has been found?

Exercise 1.5 Error rate for suggested corrected spellings

For the spelling-checker, the maximum number of errors that could be correctly found would depend on the number of actual errors in the document, something that we might not know for sure. A way round this problem is **error-seeding**: purposely putting some errors into the document. Say I put six spelling mistakes into the document on purpose and out of the 18 errors found according to Table 1.1, only three of the six seeded errors are included. Not only does this mean that half of the seeded errors were not found, but it suggests many more genuine errors have been missed: in fact doubling the 18 to 36 might be realistic.

One advantage of a measurement approach coupled to practical experimentation is that it can highlight aspects of the question that might not otherwise be considered. You might, for example, have noticed that in Table 1.1 only a single instance of words being incorrectly rejected was recorded. The results in Table 1.1 did in fact come from a real trial and what emerged there was that many proper nouns were being incorrectly identified as being wrong. On reflection, it would seem to be rather unfair to count, say, the place names in a guide to the ancient Mayan sites of central America as being incorrectly rejected. The definition of the metric 'correct words wrongly rejected' was therefore amended to 'correct words (less place names) wrongly rejected'. There is no problem with changing the way things are counted as long as it is done consistently. Problems would occur if some trials had been conducted using the old definition and others using the new and the results were not distinguished. More formally we might state that we need to use uniform and consistent **measurement protocols**.

Associated with the problem of place names is that of technical terminology. If the spelling dictionary was based on the most frequently used words in standard English usage how would the performance of the spelling-checker vary if, for example, the document were an article to be submitted to a medical journal? We have commented that as long as the same document is used with different spelling-checkers then the comparison of performance may be valid. However, a particular spelling-checker could have been designed especially for use with medical literature, but be poor in other technical fields. This illustrates how the results of the trial and the measurements that emerge will depend very much upon the context of the trials.

You might therefore decide to conduct trials to compare the performance of the spelling-checkers on a number of different documents from different sources. An example of the sort of results that might be obtained are shown in Table 1.2.

Table 1.2   *Second sample document*

Incorrect spellings identified	3
Correct words wrongly rejected	10
Incorrect suggestions	1
Words in document	240

Jeffery S. Poulin (1997) notes someone making this kind of mistake at IBM – showing that it can happen to the best of us!

The error rate for this document would be $3/240 \times 1000$ or 12.8 errors found per thousand words. How can we combine these results with those of the previous trial? It would be tempting simply to take the average of the two rates, that is $(21.3+12.8)/2$ or 17.05 errors per thousand words. However, this would be incorrect because the original 21.3 and 12.8 errors per thousand word error rates originally related to two different sized documents: by averaging them, the smaller document is allowed to exert an unduly large influence on the results. It would be rather like averaging the average number of camels per head for Saudi Arabia and the United States. Rather, the words in each document should be added together and then the error rate recalculated using the data in Table 1.3.

Table 1.3   *Combining error rates*

Document	Words	Errors
1	845	18
2	240	3
Combined	1085	21

$$\text{combined error rate} = 21/1085 \times 1000$$
$$= 19.35 \text{ detected error per thousand words}$$

Effectively, the two documents have been treated as if they were one large document.

This illustrates the need to consider carefully the method by which the metric values relating to a lower level entity such as *trial* can be aggregated to produce metrics that are applicable to a higher level entity such as *spelling-checker*.

Exercise 1.6 Information lost by aggregation

What information has been lost by creating a combined error rate?

EXAMPLE 2 EVALUATING A CHECK DIGIT ALGORITHM 13

Treating the two documents as one aggregate can lose important information. For example, the designers of the spelling-checking algorithm might be considering starting the checking process by reading each word into a separate cell of an array in computer memory. They might wish to know the largest document (in words) that they are going to have to process. For timing purposes they could also wish to have an idea of the most common size for a document. To answer these questions, **descriptive statistical data** such as the **mean, standard deviation, mode** and **median,** would be of use.

These terms will be explained in Chapter 2.

So far we have looked at the **external attributes** of the spelling-checker. The measurements of these external attributes have involved executing the spelling-checker on some actual documents. This could be of use to someone thinking of acquiring such software, but would not be of great use to the developer of such software. For a start, the spelling-checker and its dictionary would have to be built before such trials could be conducted. This is late for the designers of the package: they would like an indication of the performance of particular design options for the spelling-checker during its development. This requires examination of the **internal attributes** of the software that are likely to lead to desirable values for the relevant external attributes. Consider the work of the dictionary compilers. They will not be able to identify which documents will be spelling-checked using the package. What they could do is find what the most commonly used words are in the English language and make sure that they are in the dictionary. It may be assumed that a form of the Pareto principle applies to language: that a relatively small number of words make up a majority of written text and that after this there are diminishing returns. Adding extra words to the dictionary gradually makes less and less of an impact on the percentage of words that will be accepted in normal text. This notional percentage coverage could therefore be regarded as an internal attribute.

1.7 Example 2 Evaluating a check digit algorithm

This next example deals with how we might measure the effectiveness of a check digit method. A check digit is appended to a reference number used within a system to identify a particular occurrence of a type of record. The check digit is calculated from the other digits in the number when the reference numbers are originally distributed. When a number is subsequently input to the system, an algorithm checks to see if the value of the digit is compatible with the remaining digits in the number: if not, the digits have been incorrectly input.

An example of a reference number would be an account number which is used to identify an account in a banking system.

1.7.1 The modulo-11 check digit

The modulo-11 method works as follows. It is not essential to understand this and this explanation can therefore be skipped, but a familiarity with how it works might help understand some of the later parts of this section.

Assume that there is a six digit reference number to which a check digit is to be appended. As an example take the reference number 265643. Each digit is multiplied by a pre-specified weighting: these could be 7, 6, 5, 4, 3, 2 (the weightings used must be the same for every occurrence of the reference number). An important desirable characteristic of the weightings is that adjacent digits should have different values as shown in Table 1.4.

Table 1.4   *First stage of the check digit calculation*

Reference number digits (d)			2	6	5	6	4	3
Weightings (w)			7	6	5	4	3	2
$d \times w$			14	36	25	24	12	6

The products of the multiplications are then summed, in this case, to give 117.

The result of this addition is then divided by 11 – hence the name 'modulo-11 check digit' – and the remainder is extracted, for example $117/11 = 10$ remainder 7. Finally this remainder, if it is not zero, is subtracted from 11 to give the check digit, for example $11-7=4$. If the remainder was zero, then the check digit would be zero. If result was 10, this would have been appended to the reference number as X.

To check a reference number, each digit, apart from the check-digit, is multiplied by the corresponding weighting used in calculating the check-digit and the products are summed. The check-digit is added to the sum. If the result is divisible exactly by 11 then the check-digit test is passed. In the example above, the sum of the products is 117 and the check-digit value is 4 which added together make 121 which is divisible by 11. Now say that the third digit from the left, 5, was misread as 6 the resulting calculation would be as shown in Table 1.5.

Table 1.5   *Checking a check-digit*

Reference number digits (d)			2	6	6	6	4	3
Weightings (w)			7	6	5	4	3	2
$d \times w$			14	36	30	24	12	6

The sum of the products would be $14+36+30+24+12+6$ that is, 122 which with the check digit added would be 126 which would not be divisible by 11.

As the check-digit can have a value of 0–9 or X, that is, one of eleven settings, and there are potentially 999,999 different reference numbers, there will be many different combinations of digits that can generate the same check-digit value. The check-digit check does not therefore give a complete guarantee that garbled reference numbers will be detected.

EXAMPLE 3 EVALUATING WORLD WIDE WEB SEARCH ENGINES 15

In what proportion of cases could the check-digit check be expected to accept erroneously a garbled reference?

Exercise 1.7 Check-digit effectiveness

The estimate of how often check-digits for different numbers are likely to coincide is based on what might be called an *internal* attribute of the check-digit algorithm.

A 'user' of the check-digit system, ignorant of how it works, might wish to carry out a practical test on the actual errors people make. To illustrate this point, the reader may wish to conduct the following experiment.

Get a volunteer to listen to a list of 24 six-digit numbers with check-digits. A list of such numbers is given below in Table 1.6. After each number is read out, the volunteer is to write the number down. You should make sure you read each number only once.

Exercise 1.8 Reference number transcription exercise

At the end of the exercise, check the numbers in the volunteer's list. Where the number has been transcribed incorrectly, work out whether the check-digit check would have detected the mistakes.

Table 1.6   *Twenty-four random numbers plus check-digits*

5357020	7998945	4203410	0884847
4212657	0459062	0974838	2702231
0071692	7316267	5067332	6616119
4207904	536129X	0605794	9142576
0339032	5629306	3075869	9623833
3835626	0533904	2184931	0492388

What should emerge (it is hoped!) from this exercise is that when human beings make transcription errors, the types of error made tend to be rather limited. Typically, a single digit is miscopied, or two adjacent digits are switched. The check digit is designed to catch these most commonly occurring errors. Its effectiveness in detecting garbled references as an *externally measured* attribute in a particular context is much better than the internal attribute measurement might suggest.

1.8   Example 3 Evaluating World Wide Web search engines

The final example of how measurement might be used in an IT environment evaluates the effectiveness of different World Wide Web search engines. A pertinent question might be which is the best search engine for a particular user. For the sake of brevity we will restrict our attention to keyword searches where the seeker after information specifies certain key-words which in combination, it is hoped, will identify the Web pages which hold information about the topic of interest. For example they might be interested in '*software*', '*measurement*' and '*quality*' and specify these as keywords.

An effective search engine might be regarded as one that identifies as many relevant sites as possible. Information retrieval specialists (see Salton and McGill 1983, for example) use a metric which captures this called **recall percentage**.

$$Recall\ percentage = (number\ of\ relevant\ references\ reported)/$$
$$(number\ of\ relevant\ references\ in\ database) \times 100$$
$$(Equation\ 1.1)$$

Note that the metric counts the number of *relevant* references. As anyone who has tried to retrieve information in this way will know, one of the problems is that many references will not be relevant. An ornithologist interested in obtaining information about the species *grus grus* (that is, cranes) was annoyed to be given references to load-lifting equipment. Measurement specialists are keen to avoid subjective judgements, but it can be seen that what is regarded as relevant depends on the individual concerned – a mechanical engineer might have been delighted with some of these references.

We might have a problem knowing what all the correct references (however defined) are in the 'database', in this case the World Wide Web. This is a similar problem to knowing all the possible incorrect spellings in a document, but raised to a more severe level of difficulty where possible relevant locations may be anywhere on the globe. We could attempt to use a similar approach to that used when evaluating a spelling-checker and actually 'seed' relevant references and then check whether the search engine had actually found them. We would not necessarily need to have actually set themselves up ourselves, but could have found out about them by some other means.

This leads to the consideration of a method of estimating the size of population of valid references based on a suggestion by Tom Gilb for estimating the number of errors in a piece of software. Two different search engines could be used to identify which locations are relevant to a particular query. The findings from the two search engines are then analysed and references that are clearly irrelevant are discarded. Of the remainder, the number of references that are common to both are identified. It might be hoped that if a large proportion of the finds are common to both then this indicates that most of the relevant finds have been picked up. If there are many valid references that only one search engine has picked up then this suggests that there are many references that have yet to be identified. One major assumption upon which this is based is that the two search engines are substantially different and independent of one another. If one were really the other with a different name then you would expect them to produce the same references.

EXAMPLE 3 EVALUATING WORLD WIDE WEB SEARCH ENGINES   17

In any case the theory has been quantified as follows. There will be three sets of valid references:

N1   the number of valid references detected by search engine A;
N2   the number of valid references detected by search engine B;
N12 the number of common references detected by both search engines A and B.

   The Venn diagram shown below in Figure 1.4 below illustrates the relationship between the three sets of references:

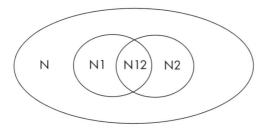

Figure 1.4   *Venn diagram showing the relationship between N1, N2, and N12.*

N, an estimate of the total valid references, may then be calculated thus:

$N = (N1 \times N2)/N12$ (Equation 1.2)

   For example, search engine A might find 30 references and search engine B might find 20 of which 15 are common to both. An estimate of the total number of valid references might therefore be calculated thus:

$N = 30 \times 20/15 = 40$

   A massive 'health warning' needs to be issued in relation to this approach: the result is only an estimate! The assumption upon which it is based is that both search engines are distinct and independent has already been noted.

Exercise 1.9

In order to carry out this exercise you will need access to three World Wide Web search engines. Select three fairly narrow topics for which you might want to seek information and choose the combination of keywords to be searched upon. Try out the keywords using the three search engines.

   (i)   Identify the search engine which produces the most valid matches.
   (ii) If the three search engines are identified as X, Y and Z, work out the N estimate (see above) for the combinations XY, XZ and YZ. To what extent do the *N* estimates for each combination match?
   (iii) Calculate the recall percentage for each of the three search engines.

If we wish simply to compare search engines, the counts of valid matches made by each of the search engines might give us enough information. However, recall percentage tells us is the extent to which it might be possible to improve the effectiveness of a searching mechanism.

The big problem with search engines is not always that they fail to access enough valid references, but that these valid references are swamped by references that are not relevant, as we saw earlier with the 'crane' example. Information retrieval specialists have tried to quantify this phenomenon by defining a quality of **retrieval precision**. This is defined thus:

$$Retrieval\ precision\ percentage = (number\ of\ valid\ references\ reported)/$$
$$(total\ references\ reported) \times 100$$

(Equation 1.3)

For example, if 300 references were reported of which 60 were relevant, then the retrieval precision percentage would be $60/300 \times 100 = 20\%$. Good precision might be at the cost of poor recall and *vice versa*. The two quality attributes are thus said to be **competitive**. If two quality attributes tend to go together then they would be said to be **complementary**. The third possibility is that the two quality attributes are in fact **indifferent** to each other.

Exercise 1.10   Using the data gathered for Exercise 1.4, calculate the retrieval precision percentage for the three search engines.

1.9   Conclusions

In this Chapter, we have tried to use practical exercises to draw out and illustrate the following:

- how it is possible to use measurement to identify the degree to which a software product has particular qualities of interest to us;

- the difference between an **attribute** which is a characteristic of an **entity** and a **metric** which indicates the nature and/or strength of that attribute, usually by means of some number, often in conjunction with a unit;

- if the metric is accurate as an indicator of the relative presence or absence of the attribute then it may earn the right to be called a true **measurement**;

- the metric may be manipulated to show how the value for the metric relates to the maximum possible value that it could have;

- when it is necessary to combine metric values for different occurrences of the same entity type, care must be taken to ensure that metric values are aggregated in a way that is valid;

- aggregation of the values for a particular attribute, while valid, can lose important information about the range of values that exist for that entity – summary statistics such as the mean, median, and mode may be able to summarize this kind of information;

- attributes may be **external** ones apparent to the users of the software;

- usually, these external attributes would be measured by actually executing the software: thus the values of the metrics collected would be influenced not only by the nature of the software, but also by the context in which the trial was conducted;

- **internal** attributes are those that would be apparent to the developer of the system while it was being designed and constructed;

- pairs of quality attributes may be **competitive**, where the presence of one will tend to be at the detriment of the other; **complementary**, where the presence of one quality will tend to be accompanied by the presence of the other, or **indifferent** to each other.

The reader might have noticed that with each of the three examples above things have rarely been 'cut-and-dried': various questions about the nature of what was being tested and how it could be effectively measured were raised. Some were trivial, but others were more serious. In the view of the writer, this is one of the strengths of the empirical approach – that by actively engaging with the problem being studied, a richer picture of the real issues involved is obtained. (This argument is similar to the one advanced in favour of early prototypes in software development.) This means that often experiment and/or measurement can raise more questions than it appears to answer. This invariably seems to be the case with the production of any type of management information: having produced results, the task remains of finding out what the figures really mean.

'Empirical – originating in, based, or relying on observation or experiment rather than theory', *Longman's Concise English Dictionary,* 1985.

1.10 References

Albrecht, A. J. and Gaffney, J. E. (1983), 'Software function, source lines of code and development effort prediction: a software science validation', *IEEE Transactions in Software Engineering,* 9(6) 639–648.

Bailey, J. W. and Basili, V. R. (1981), 'A meta-model for software development resource expenditures', *Proceedings of 5th Int. Conference on Software Engineering,* 107–115.

Basili, V. R. and Turner, A. J. (1975), 'Iterative enhancements: a practical technique for software development', *IEEE Transactions in Software Engineering*: 1(6), 390–396.

Belady, L. A. and Lehman, M. M. (1979), 'The characteristics of large systems' in Wegner, P. (ed), *Research Directions In Software Technology,* MIT Press, Cambridge, MA, 106–138.

Boehm, B. W. (1981), *Software Engineering Economics,* Prentice-Hall, Englewood Cliffs, NJ.

Crick, F. (1988), *What Mad Pursuit: A Personal View Of Scientific Discovery,* Penguin Books, Harmondsworth, 47.

Fenton N. E. and Pfleeger, S. L. (1997), *Software Metrics: A Practical and Rigorous Approach,* International Thomson Computer Press, London.

Gilb, T. (1977), *Software Metrics,* Winthrop Publishers, Cambridge, MA.

Keen, P. G. W. (1981), 'Information systems and organizational change', *Communications of ACM*: 24(1), 24–33.

Kemerer, C. F. (1987), 'An empirical validation of software cost estimation models', *Communications of ACM*: 30(5), 416–429.

Martin, J. and McClure, C. (1985), *Diagramming Techniques For Analysts And Programmers,* Prentice-Hall, Englewood Cliffs, NJ.

Marwane, R. and Mili, A. (1991), 'Building tailor-made software cost model: inter-mediate TUCOMO', *Information and Software Technology*: 33(3), 232–238.

Pfleeger, S. L., Fenton, N. and Page, S. (1994), 'Evaluating software engineering standards', *IEEE Computer*, September, 71–79.

Robinson, H. (1994), 'What paradigms do for us: evidence and argument in computing'. In Davies, M. J. and Tully, C. J. *Proceedings of the 6th ISTIP (Information Systems Teaching – Improving the Practice),* University of Hertfordshire, 117–121.

Salton, G. and McGill, M. (1983), *Introduction To Modern Information Retrieval,* McGraw-Hill, New York.

Scanlan, D. A. (1989), 'Structured flowcharts outperform pseudocode: an experimental comparison', *IEEE Software*, September, 28–36.

Shepperd, M. J. (1995), *Foundations of Software Measurement,* Prentice-Hall, Hemel Hempstead.

1.11 Additional questions

1. An organization has an internal PC help-desk which assists users who have problems running standard off-the-shelf software on their PCs. The organization decides to out-source the help-desk facility to an external company. How might the organization measure the effectiveness of this facility after out-sourcing?

2. A manager of a software development team is interested in collecting information about the size (in Lines of Code) of software modules and how long they took to write as this will help in estimating the effort needed to develop new modules. These modules are written in a variety of languages. The manager is also interested in the number of faults found in the operational versions of the modules and how long it has taken to remedy each fault. Draw up an entity-relationship model (ERM) that represents the information the manager requires, identifying the data attributes of each entity type.

3. A software development team uses a methodology which requires that an ERM be developed representing the database for each information system (IS) that it develops. The manager of the team believes that the size of the ERM for a potential computer-based IS can be used to judge the amount of effort needed to develop the IS, and wants to collect data to test out this idea. To do this, ERM diagrams themselves need to be subjected to measurement. What would be the data attributes of ERMs that might be used to indicate the 'size' of an ERM?

4. A test is carried out to see whether the age or gender of data inputters has any effect on the accuracy and speed of data input to an IT system. Each of 100 subjects will be given a list of 100 account numbers, each of which has a check-digit. They will be asked to type in as many of the numbers as possible within a predefined period of time. The number of account numbers each subject can input and the number of incorrect numbers input will be counted by the system and these figures will be subsequently analysed. Draw up an ERM for the data that will be needed and identify the data attributes needed for each entity on the ERM.

5. I am system testing some software. In order to judge the effectiveness of the testing process, I leave 20 known errors found at inspection time in the code. In the first week of testing, I find 15 errors of which five are among the known errors. Estimate the number of errors left in the software.

6. Classify each of the following as relating to either internal or external attributes of a software module:
   (a) average response time when an operator types in a certain command,
   (b) number of lines of code,
   (c) number of comment lines,
   (d) number of different operator warning messages,
   (e) number of coding errors,
   (f) number of failures during one month's operational running.

7. Draw up an ERM for the data needed to evaluate the recall and precision of different Web search engines. List all the attributes for each entity on the ERM.

8. After inputting certain keywords to a Web search engine, 17 valid references are found but it is known by other means that 56 valid references exist on the Web. Calculate the recall percentage. If in addition to the 17 valid references identified by the search engine, 100 irrelevant references were found, what would be the retrieval precision?

9. Using Web search engine A, 50 relevant references are found, while Web search engine B finds 30. Ten of these finds are common to both. Estimate the number of relevant references that exist on the Web to the keywords.

10. Which of the following pairs of data attributes relating to software modules are likely to be complementary, which are likely to be conflicting and which indifferent to one another?
    (a) Number of lines of code and number of compilation error messages.
    (b) Number of lines of code and the hours of development effort.
    (c) Number of hours of system testing and number of errors in the operational system.
    (d) Execution speed of a software module and the number of hours of development effort.
    (e) Months of experience of the developer who wrote the code and the hours of development effort.

Chapter 2

How to ensure that software measurements are valid

OBJECTIVES

Having completed this chapter, you will be able to:

- [ ] identify valid measurement systems

- [ ] document the processes, products and resources that are used by the execution of a development life-cycle

- [ ] distinguish between fundamental and derived measurements

- [ ] associate a measurement with the appropriate scale type

- [ ] understand the operations that can be validly carried out on measurements belonging to each scale type

- [ ] understand the Goal/Question/Metric (QGM) approach to planning measurement exercises

---

2.1   The nature of measurement

Measurement is a purposeful human activity. Measurements do not exist until someone actually collects them. Before anyone has thought to measure anything, what exists is the awareness of objects that have **attributes** or **properties**. Here we are using the term 'attribute' to represent some quality or property we might perceive in an entity. It could be something which is easily recognized like height or weight, in which case the meaning of the word 'attribute' is quite close to that understood by data modellers, or it could be something more difficult to pin down like the complexity of a piece of software. Although many writers in the field use the term 'attribute' in this latter context, see Kitchenham *et al.* (1996) for example, to avoid confusion we will use 'property' to convey the same meaning.

To be able to measure a property we need to be able to say that one instance of the object of interest can have the property to a greater or lesser extent than another, or that at least in one case the thing has the property or it does not. Also there should be general agreement among people about these judgements. In one family I know, when the children were young there was intense interest about whether the younger brother was going to end up taller than his elder sister and later on, whether he would go on to be taller than both his parents. Judgements as to the relative size of each member of the family could be made fairly easily (albeit not without some contention in marginal cases) without the use of formal measurement using a tape measure.

One requirement of a good measurement system is that the relationships between the measurement values obtained for each object should be consistent with the perceptions of the properties of those objects that existed beforehand. For example, if it is perceived that Tom is taller than his mother, Heather, and his sister, Katherine, who is about the same height as her mother, then measurement taken with a tape measure ought to give Tom a height in centimetres which is greater than the number of centimetres recorded as the height of Katherine or Heather. Moreover the number of centimetres recorded for Heather and Katherine ought to be the same. This is in accordance with what is known as the **representation condition**.

2.2   The representation condition

This stipulates that for a proper measure, the relationships between the empirical observations must also hold for the measurements of those observations. Formally the way this is expressed is by the identification of a set of objects in the real world. As an example let us take Heather, Katherine and Tom. This set of objects is called *C*. Then the different relationships that we are interested in that can exist between the objects in set *C* are listed in a second set that will be identified as set *R*. In the case of Heather, Katherine and Tom the relationships might be 'taller than', 'as tall as' and 'shorter than'. <*C,R*>, the set of objects and the set of possible relationships that can exist between the objects is called an **empirical relation model**.

We can now map this empirical model onto a **numerical relation system**. The set *N* is a set of numbers that relate to a particular aspect of Heather, Katherine and Tom, in this case their heights. If we are thinking in terms of centimetres then these numbers might be 166, 166 and 176. We can then list the relations that can exist between the numbers, that is <, = and >. This list of operations we can refer to as set *P*. For the representation condition to apply, the objects in *C* need to be associated with numbers (or symbols) in set *N* and the empirical relations in set *R* matched with the numeric relations in set *P* in such a way that all the relations are preserved – see Tables 2.1 and 2.2.

Table 2.1 *An empirical relation system*

	Heather	Katherine	Tom
Heather	As tall as	As tall as	Shorter than
Katherine	As tall as	As tall as	Shorter than
Tom	Taller than	Taller than	As tall as

Table 2.2 *A numerical relation system*

	166	166	176
166	=	=	<
166	=	=	<
176	>	>	=

In a shared database application, users complain that when a report is requested, if option A is taken rather than B, the response time seems to be longer. However, option C seems to be completed more quickly than either A or B. The software support staff analyse execution times and find that in their test environment the average execution times are:

Exercise 2.1 Comparing an empirical and numerical relation model

Option	Time (seconds)
A	19
B	20
C	23

Draw a table showing the users' perception of the response times and a second one showing the numerical relations found by the support staff. Do the discrepancies necessarily mean that the users' perceptions are wrong? Why could it be that the average execution time is not a satisfactory measure of the users' experience of the system?

2.3   Relating measurements to attributes

The properties that are important for an entity will depend on the viewpoint of the observer at a particular point in time. There could be confusion where the properties of interest to different observers are overlapping yet distinct. For example, to both a user of a help-desk and the manager of one, 'speed of problem resolution' is important. However, from the point of view of users, the time that is important is that from the moment where they make the telephone call to the moment they are notified of the solution to the problem. A help-desk operation that is well-staffed would be in a good position to be effective according to this measure, but this might be at the expense of help-desk staff being under-employed between calls. The manager might wish to utilize fewer staff more fully, even if this means that some callers are in a queue for some time waiting to be dealt with. Indeed, in some cases users might hang up and try again later. For the manager 'speed of problem resolution' would still be a matter of concern, but only from the point that the call is actually answered.

Thus, when reading about the effectiveness and validity of a particular measurement, always pay careful attention to the **purpose** of the measurement. This will have a big influence on the way that the property in question is perceived and hence on the 'validity' of its measurement. An example of this is the Henry–Kafura Information Flow Measure (Henry and Kafura 1981) that involves multiplying the fan-in to a module (that is, the number of other modules that call the module in question) with the fan-out from that module (that is, the number of other modules that the module in question calls). Kitchenham *et al.* (1990) have criticized this on the grounds that fan-in and fan-out refer to two separate properties. Fan-in refers to the degree of reuse made of the module while fan-out refers to the number of modules controlled by the module. This is certainly true if one is primarily interested in the software structure as a whole of which the module is a component. However, if one is concerned with the potential internal complexity of just the module in question then each pair of fan-in and fan-out instances implies the possibility of a connecting path within the module that converts an input into an output. This potential number of input-output paths seems to be a plausible indicator of the potential complexity of the module.

Experts in this field have pointed out to the author that a stick dropped in the centre of a stream is likely to move more quickly than one near the bank and that this introduces an element of skill for more mature participants.

Just because a 'measurement' technique can produce a numeric score in a particular situation does not mean that the result is a true measurement unless it can be related in some way to a pre-existing property. For example, Katherine and Tom, when they were very young might have played 'pooh-sticks' (Milne 1928) and counted each time each of them won. Although the number of wins may, at the time, have seemed quite important, as a measurement of anything it was meaningless.

One group of measurement theorists (Kitchenham *et al.* 1995) has gone as far as to say that any definition of an attribute that implies a particular measurement scale is invalid. This seems a little harsh. The same group give 'length' and 'correctness' as examples of the properties of software modules. In practice, it seems difficult to imagine how you could judge empirically that one module was longer that another without considering the number of lines of code in some way, or correctness without taking account of the number of errors.

Traditional scientific and engineering activity has been concerned with the properties of physical entities and there has been an attempt to bring engineering principles into software development (for example, see Shaw 1990; Basili and Musa 1991) – indeed one of the earliest attempts at software measurement even referred to 'software physics' (Gordon and Halstead 1976). The attempt has not been a complete success. The problems with extending the traditional engineering paradigm to software development were most notably recognized by Brooks (1987) who argued that software differed from other engineered artifacts on four counts:

- **complexity** – software is perhaps more complex in relation to construction effort than other human constructs. This increases non-linearly in relation to the size of software leading to problems with communication, comprehension and validation.

- **conformity** – much of the complexity identified above is forced upon software by the human institutions and systems with which it has to interface because software is expected to fit in with its environment rather than vice versa. The conventional engineer deals mainly with the laws of physical science that appear to have a logic and rationality because the physical laws are manifested consistently and predictably. Human-made systems on the other hand are often illogical, inconsistent and unpredictable.

- **changeability** – software is constantly under pressure to change as it is embedded '*in a cultural matrix of applications, users, laws and machine vehicles*' which is always changing.

- **invisibility** – '*software*', according to Brooks, '*is invisible and unvisualizable*'. This suggests that measurement frameworks that are heavily reliant on analogies with physical measurements such as temperature, weight and height need to be examined with care.

Software development is an intensely human and even social activity, as Gerry Weinberg pointed out as early as 1971 in his seminal book *The psychology of computer programming*. Barry Boehm in developing COCOMO (Boehm 1981), a software development effort model which will be discussed in some detail later, and which seems in many ways to adopt the engineering paradigm, accepted that the major influence on productivity would be the capability of the development staff. Although the engineering approach to measurement is often advocated, it seems likely that software measurement will find more useful models in the social than physical sciences.

One advantage of a more social science orientation will be the recognition that the activity of measurement will itself influence the process and products being observed. This is particularly the case with software estimation where Abdel-Hamid and Maddick (1986), for example, have explored the influence of estimated effort on actual project performance. Measurement practices will also be influenced by cultural and organizational factors – particularly in relation to the properties that people wish to measure. It has, for example, been demonstrated that there are wide differences in accounting practices that can be traced back to cultural differences (Hofstede 1991).

Analogies from physical science are often unhelpful in relation to software and, we contend, often actually harmful.

The properties of physical objects can be sensed and experienced in a direct way. As I pick up the mug of tea on my desk, I can feel the weight of the mug and also its warmth. In the case of the artifacts of software engineering, researchers have addressed themselves to properties such as 'structuredness', 'complexity' and 'maintainability' which are not so easy to experience in a direct way. Not all software developers would rank software modules in a uniform way according to their perception of these candidate properties. This means that many putative software measurements will fail at the first test of measurement validity.

'Maintainability' can be loosely seen as the ease with which a software component can be altered. There might be indicators which suggest the presence of the property such as, in the case of maintainability, 'maintenance productivity', but this does not in itself measure maintainability. There may be other properties that contribute to maintainability such as 'self-descriptiveness', but direct measurement of property of maintainability seems impossible.

Software developers in the business of maintaining software could very well comment that one way of structuring code seems to be more complicated than another. This might be because they find its takes longer to understand what code structured in a certain way is designed to achieve. A user of a software application might comment after experiencing two or three 'crashes' that the software seems to be unreliable. It is easy in these circumstances to start talking about a thing called 'complexity' or 'reliability'. What has happened is that particular types of phenomenon have been selected and stressed. It is natural to speak as if they were manifestations of some underlying property, but this needs to be recognized as being speculative. The tendency to treat what is really an abstract idea as if it were a material thing is known as **reification**. An inherent danger of this process is that it may lead to what has been called the 'fallacy of misplaced concreteness' (*Whitehead*, 1926).

Nobody has ever seen reliability. It would be nice if it could be bottled and sprinkled over software in development. Does this mean that we cannot discuss reliability? Well, interestingly enough, physical scientists have similar problems with, for example, objects like sub-atomic particles. These cannot be seen directly. What can be done is to see to what extent the observed behaviour of matter is consistent with the existence of such particles. The sub-atomic particles in question are **hypothetical constructs**. As Hugh Coolican (1994) comments 'they will survive as part of an overall theory so long as the amount they explain is a good deal more than the amount they contradict'.

Thus the properties of reliability, complexity and, as we will find later, software size, are all really hypothetical constructs.

Exercise 2.2 Consequences of and contributions to 'user friendliness'

(i) How can the consequences of the quality of 'user friendliness' in a software application be assessed?

(ii) How can the factors that contribute to 'user friendliness' in software applications be assessed?

The process of formulating and testing hypothetical constructs is part of a wider activity of trying to understand and explain the 'real world'. As noted previously one aspect of this is abstracting from the real world those elements that appear to be important to a particular viewpoint.

Bush and Fenton (1990) have proposed that the software development process can be described in terms of **processes**, **products that** are created by some processes and may be used by other ones, and **resources which** are items used by a process, excluding the products of other processes. This does not mean that variables of other types of entity cannot be validly measured in a software development environment.

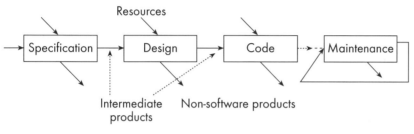

Figure 2.1 *A simplistic life-cycle model (from Bush and Fenton 1990).*

These three entity types can be used to construct various life-cycle models – see Figure 2.1 for example. One reservation about this type of model that arose during our own attempt to apply it has been that it implies a fairly self-contained system with little in the way of information flows to and from the environment. In fact the information that is used by a process to create a particular product comes not only from previous products but also from the environment. In one place we referred to this as the 'waterfall in a tropical thunderstorm' model (Hughes, 1994). Among other things this means that the potential size of the final system may grow (or occasionally shrink) during development as a result of additional information.

Draw up a diagram, similar to Figure 2.1 that portrays the following life-cycle model.

If the users of a software application wish that it be modified to include a new feature, they formulate a request for change. A business analyst will interview the users and draw up a change requirement which is passed to an analyst-programmer who will examine the program code of the existing application and assess the extent of the changes that will need to be made to the code. The analyst-programmer will produce an estimate of the effort needed to implement the change. If the estimate is acceptable to management then the amendment is made and the revised application is released to the users for preliminary acceptance tests. This may result in bug reports from the users to the programmers who will need to correct the errors. At some point, an authorization to make the revised software operational will need to be given.

Exercise 2.3
Representing a life-cycle model

2.4   Fundamental and derived measurements

Fundamental measurements and **derived** measurements need to be distinguished. These are sometimes referred to as **direct** and **indirect** measurements (see, for example, Bush and Fenton 1990).

Fundamental measurements use a single attribute. In the example of the help-desk that we referred to earlier, an attribute of particular enquiry would be 'resolution time'. As this involves one attribute, this would be classified as a fundamental measurement. To measure the effectiveness of the help-desk as a whole, 'average resolution time' might be calculated. This calculation would require two figures, total resolution time and the number of queries resolved, both of which are attributes of the help-desk operation as a whole. The result of this calculation would be a derived measurement.

The difference between a fundamental and a derived measurement relates to the method of measurement and is not implicit in the property being measured. In physics, density can be either a fundamental or a derived measurement depending on how it is measured (Roberts 1979). Indeed, in our help-desk example, it could be argued that resolution time is a derived measurement as it is the difference between the time an enquiry was received and the time the problem was resolved. Bush and Fenton use lines of code as an example of a derived measurement as, they state, it is calculated as number of carriage returns less the number of blank lines. It is not impossible to imagine someone counting lines of code while ignoring spaces and in this case lines of code would appear to be a fundamental measurement.

The key issue here is that if a measurement is derived it needs to be even more carefully examined to see if it does genuinely measure some attribute of some entity.

Often the purpose of a derived measurement is to create normalized measurements. A measurement value such as the number of unresolved calls for a help-desk being 10 may have a different significance where the help-desk is dealing with 200 calls a day than where it is dealing with 20 calls a day. In this case the percentage of calls unresolved would be a more useful measurement.

Exercise 2.4 Derived and fundamental measurements

Which of the following will require derived measurements and which fundamental ones?

(i)   the fault density of a software module

(ii) development effort for a module

(iii) software development productivity

(iv) operational reliability

2.5 Categorizing scales of measurement

2.5.1 Scale types

The type of scale that is appropriate for each measurement needs to be identified. To illustrate this we will use examples from an experiment where a group of 20 software developers are asked to develop individually computer programs based on the same specification. The group is divided into four sub-groups each of which will use a different programming language. The time that each individual takes to complete a working and error-free program will be measured.

The types of scale involved will include:

- **Nominal.** This is where each instance of the entity type of interest can be classed as belonging to a certain category, for example, programmers can be classified according to the programming language they are employing. Some claim that this is not really measurement at all.

- **Absolute.** An absolute measure is essentially a count. For example we could count the number of programmers using each programming language. Each instance of the entity type of interest has to be regarded as being exactly equivalent to every other instance.

- **Restricted ordinal.** The instances of the entity type are placed into bands depending on the degree to which they possess some property. The bands are not necessarily of equal width. For example, account might need to be taken of the degree to which programmers are experienced in the programming language that they are using. They might therefore be placed in bands as in Table 2.3.

Table 2.3 *Experience bands*

Experience (months)	Category
<6	Trainee
6–17	Improver
18–35	Experienced
>35	Expert

- **Unrestricted ordinal.** Once the experiment is complete the order in which each programmer finished the task can be recorded.

- **Interval.** This scale measures the differences between different instances. For example we might say that Wendy completed her programming task seven hours ahead of Franklyn who was just 30 minutes ahead of Ali. We might note that the difference between Wendy and Franklyn was much greater than that between Franklyn and Ali.

• **Ratio.** Times of task completion are recorded for each programmer measured from a zero point when he or she started.

The scales nominal, ordinal, interval, and ratio can be perceived as being in an ascending order of precision. A more precise measurement in terms of scale type can be transformed a less precise type, but not vice versa. For example, if we know the completion times of all the programmers (ratio scale), then we can work out an order of completion times (ordinal) but not vice versa.

In this context, students in the United Kingdom may wish to ponder the accuracy of GCE 'A' level points as a method of deciding who should be given a place on a university course.

One approach to measuring the size of software that will be described in more detail in a later chapter is **function points**. This approach has been criticized as the calculation of function points involves inadmissible transformations from one scale type to another (Abran and Robillard 1994). Originally, function point analysis required the categorization of, as one example, input transactions as being either 'simple', 'average' or 'complex'. This classification looks very much like a 'restricted ordinal' measurement. A score is then assigned to the transaction of either 3, 4 or 6 depending on the classification. It can be seen, incidentally, that according to this measurement scale the largest input transaction would only be measured as twice the size of the smallest. These scores were then totalled and the results were aggregated with similarly derived total scores for other system characteristics. The final overall function point count for the application was then treated as an interval scale. The generation of restricted ordinal measurements which were then treated as being on an interval scale was clearly moving invalidly from a less precise scale type to a scale type which would be assumed to be more precise.

Exercise 2.5
Identifying scale types

Table 2.4 provides the fault densities, in faults per thousand lines of code (kloc), for a number of modules.

(i)   Put these into ascending order of fault density and identify the modules with the greatest and least fault densities. What scalar type would be the order of fault densities?

(ii) Find the module which is at the mid-point of the ordered list. Calculate the difference between the fault density of this module and the module with the largest fault density or the module with the smallest fault density. What scalar types would these differences be?

(iii) If you had to classify these modules as having 'high', 'medium' or 'low' fault densities where might you define the boundaries for each of the categories? What would be the scalar type of the categories thus formed?

2.5.2 Discrete versus continuous scales

Some measurements that can be taken have to be an exact number by their very nature. For example, if we are counting the number of lines of code in a software module, then we would expect the result to be an exact number: you would not

Table 2.4 *Module fault densities*

Module	Faults/kloc
a	3.5
b	1.2
c	7.5
d	1.3
e	4.5
f	2.3
g	2.1

expect there to be any half-lines. With **discrete** scales of measurement, each possible value is entirely separate from the next. Absolute scales can only be discrete.

Ordinal scales would normally be discrete. However, where two or more instances of an entity type have been given an equal ranking, for example, 'equal third', then they are treated as sharing however many ranks there are instances with the same value. Thus, if there are three instances sharing third position, ranks 3, 4 and 5 are being shared. By convention the **median** of the shared ranks is allocated to all the equal-valued instances. The median position is half the sum of the highest and lowest rank numbers, so that in the example of three instances sharing third position, the rank that would be given to each of the three would be (5+3)/2, that is 4. It can be seen that if an even number of instances share the same position the resulting shared ranking would end in .5 – two instances sharing second place would both be allocated the rank 2.5.

Another way of distinguishing variables is between nominal scales which are **categorical** and are used simply to put each instance of a particular entity type into one of several categories, and other types of scale which can said to be **measured**.

Interval and ratio scales can be either continuous or discrete.

2.5.3 Scale types and valid comparisons

Scalar types are important for several reasons. First, they govern the types of comparison that can be made between different instances of the same type of entity.

With **nominal scale** measures, such as programming language or the application type of a computer system (for instance, payroll, accounting, order processing), a particular instance can only be said to belong to a particular category or not. We cannot say that it half belongs, although in real life sometimes we would like to do this. Of course, we may be able to get around this problem of intermediate or indeterminate classifications by adding other categories to cope with them.

With **ordinal scale** measures, we can say that one instance of the entity type of interest has some attribute to a greater or lesser extent than some other. For example, where modules have been ranked in order of the number of failures they have had during operational running we can say that one module has had more failures than some other.

With **interval scales**, as well as saying that Wendy was a faster software developer than Franklyn, we can also say that the difference in completion time between Wendy and Franklyn was greater than that between Franklyn and Ali.

With **ratio scales** which have a recognized zero point we can go on and say, for example, that Wendy completed the programming task in 70% of the time that Ali took.

Table 2.5 summarizes the allowable comparisons:

Table 2.5   *Allowable comparisons*

Scale	Allowable comparisons
Nominal	Equals
Ordinal	Equals, is more than
Interval	Equals, more than, difference between w and x equals (is more than) difference between y and z
Ratio	Equals, more than, difference between w and x equals (is more than) difference between y and z, w divided by x equals (is more than) y divided by z

2.5.4 Scale types and statistical operations

The average or mean is the sum of values for a variable divided by the number of occurrences. Excel has the AVERAGE function to calculate this value.

Scale types are also important because they dictate the statistical operations that can be validly carried out on a measured variable. As we will see in a moment, the **mean** is only a suitable indicator of the central tendency with interval or ratio measurements. In some cases, even these could lack certain other characteristics that are needed to allow the calculation of a valid mean. Where there is ordinal data, then the **median**, which we have already come across, would be the most appropriate way of characterizing the central, or most typical value, for the variable. In the case of absolute counts, the **mode** may be identified, which is the category which has the highest number of instances belonging to it.

Associated with the median are the terms **quartile, decile and percentile.** If the median is effectively the cut-off value between the top half and the bottom half of a set ordered on the variable in which we are interested, the first quartile is the cut-off value for the top 25%, the second quartile is the same as the median and the third quartile is the cut-off value for the bottom 25%. Decile and percentile have similar meanings but refer to 10% and 1% bands respectively.

There is a pecking order where 'higher level' scale types can use the 'lower level' indicators, but not *vice versa*. Thus, interval and ratio scale measurement data can use the median as well as the mean, and ordinal scale data cannot only use the median but also the mode.

This leads us on to describe summary statistics in more detail in the next sections.

2.6 Summary statistics

Earlier, when fundamental and derived measurements were discussed, the point was made that measurements might be more meaningful if they are normalized. The value of a particular attribute may not by itself convey a lot of meaning. Students, when they receive a grade for an assignment, will normally want to know what grades their fellow students have got – not necessarily, or at least not only through any sense of competition, but because it helps them understand the meaning of their own grade. To get a better understanding of a single measurement of a particular attribute or property, we need to understand the nature of that attribute in relation to all the objects in a particular group or population. This brings us to **summary statistics**. A very direct way to begin to understand summary statistics, is by drawing up a frequency table. Frequency tables are usually drawn up as **bar-charts** with columns representing different categories or value ranges.

If the bar-chart summarizes variable measurements that are interval or ratio, then it is called a **histogram**. An example of one of these is shown in Figure 2.2.

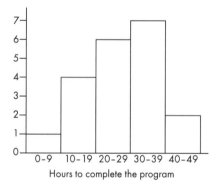

Figure 2.2 *An example of a histogram showing numbers of programmers completing a test programming task within different time spans.*

The important points about histograms are:

- all possible ranges categories are represented – no intervals are missed simply because there are no cases which have values falling in that range;

- columns are equal in width and the intervals they represent are all equal;

- column heights are in proportion to the number of cases which have values in the range represented by that column.

Where truly discrete variables are being presented then a **bar-chart** (see Figure 2.3) may be used. This is similar to a histogram except that where a particular category is missing it does not have to be shown. Because one category does not merge into another it is good practice to show the different columns as not touching. The height of histogram columns always reflect frequencies – with bar charts other types of statistic might be represented such as percentages or averages.

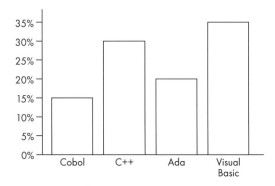

Figure 2.3 *An example of a bar-chart showing the percentage of programmers using each of four programming languages in a experiment.*

**Exercise 2.6
Drawing a histogram and calculating the average**

A group of software engineers have been e-mailed the specification for a piece of software and have been asked to estimate the number of lines of code that the software that fulfils the specification is likely to have. The results of the survey in days are as follows: 38, 43, 45, 17, 37, 35, 52, 31, 21, 47, 35, 24, 28.

  (i) Draw up a suitable histogram for this data.
  (ii) Calculate the average estimate.

If you have constructed the bar chart correctly, you will notice that the pattern is symmetrical, that is that most of the estimates are in the range 31–38 and that the estimates then trail off evenly in either direction away from these central values. The set of data conforms to a **normal distribution**. The average figure is in the middle of the most commonly occurring set of values.

**Exercise 2.7
Drawing a histogram – changing patterns**

Repeat the procedure in Exercise 2.6 which produced a histogram and an average but with the following set of estimates: 37, 37, 27, 24, 33, 32, 28, 34, 41, 36, 32, 33.

  (i) How does the bar chart produced differ from that produced in Exercise 2.6?
  (ii) What could have caused the different pattern?
  (iii) How could you modify the way that the chart has been constructed in order to accommodate this different pattern.

Different data sets that have the same mean or average may have values that are more or less tightly bunched around that average. The deviation is the amount that a particular value differs from the mean. The **standard deviation** is used as an indicator of the degree of spread or dispersion in a data set. It is rather like the average distance from the mean of values in the data set. One useful characteristic that statisticians have found is that generally speaking, in a normally distributed set of data, about 68% of values will lie within one standard deviation on each side of the mean, while about 95% will lie within two standard deviations. These characteristics mean that very powerful **parametric** forms of statistical technique can be applied to analyse the data.

The standard deviation is the square root of the sum of all the squared deviations divided by the number of instance (less 1). In Excel, the STDEV function can be used to calculate this

Construct a histogram and calculate the average for the following data set which records the amount of effort spent on each module in a set of details for a real software development project.

300, 321, 358, 370, 408, 618, 693, 723, 1506, 1639, 4680, 5747, 6921, 11936

Exercise 2.8 Histogram without a normal distribution

You can see that the real data set above does not conform to a normal distribution and that trying to find a meaningful set of equal ranges is quite difficult. In these circumstances, a useful way to portray the data is through a **box-plot.**

A box plot is shown in Figure 2.4 for the data given in Exercise 2.8. It is constructed thus. The values are examined to find the **median position** and **value**. There are fourteen values and the so the median position is (14+1)/2, that is 7.5 or halfway between the 7th and 8th positions if the data set is put into order of magnitude. The **median value** is 708 which is the average of the 7th and 8th values, 693 and 723.

The next step is to identify the bounds of the central box which represents the range where 50% of the values lie. To make things less complicated, decimals are dropped in the results of all the following calculations. The hinge position is the (median position+1)/2, in this case (7+1)/2 or 4. The **upper** and **lower hinge**

Drawing a box-plot.

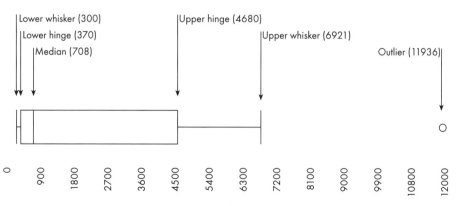

Figure 2.4 *A box-plot.*

values are therefore, in this case, the fourth highest and fourth lowest values in the data set, that is 4680 and 370.

The **hinge spread** is the upper hinge value less the lower hinge value. In the case of our data set this would be 4680−370, that is 4310. From this we can calculate the **upper** and **lower fences**. The upper fence is the upper hinge +(hinge spread×1.5). In our case this will be 4680+(4310×1.5), that is 11145.

The fence would be calculated as lower hinge − (hinge spread×1.5) which in the example comes out as 370−(4310×1.5), that is −6095. This is clearly a negative number in this case, but do not worry. We are really interested in the **adjacent values**. The **lower adjacent value** is the first inside the low outer fence, in this case 300, and the **higher adjacent value** is the first inside the high outer fence, that is 6921. The highest value in our data set, 111936, is left outside the **upper whisker** as an outlier.

Some good news is that some statistical packages, such as Minitab, will draw up a box-plot for you given a data set. Figure 2.5 shows how the box-plot in Figure 2.4 would look if it had been produced by Minitab.

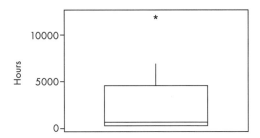

Figure 2.5   *The box-plot in Figure 2.4 as produced by Minitab.*

Exercise 2.9
Creating box plots

Draw up box-plots for the following data sets:

   (i)   the data set in Exercise 2.6
   (ii) the data set in 2.7
   (iii) 124, 108, 106, 92, 18, 38, 12, 42, 23, 35, 59, 105, 37, 41
   (iv) 17, 31, 34, 38, 21, 25, 25, 27, 28, 43, 45, 47, 52
What do the box-plots tell us about the data sets in questions?

The median was also referred to in the section on allocating ordinal ranks where there are matching values in two or more instances.

It can be seen that the average or mean is not very helpful in relation to the data set given in Exercise 2.8 because we do not seem to have any average-sized modules. A better guide to the 'central tendency' of this data set is the **median** which was used as a step in the construction of the box-plot. More formally, we can say that the use of the average or mean would be inappropriate for this data set as it does not have a normal distribution. The lack of a normal distribution also means that we cannot use parametric statistical techniques but have to fall back on **non-parametric** techniques. This rather limits our options.

Now here is some very bad news. Data sets collected as a part of a software measurement programme will almost certainly **not** be normally distributed. Bache and Bazzana (1994) in a very interesting book about real software measurement noted that they had never yet found a normally distributed data set among the many that they had examined in connection with software measurement.

2.7 Getting started: the Goal/Question/Metric (GQM) paradigm

This chapter started by emphasizing that measurement is a purposeful activity. To be effective a measurement activity in an IT environment needs to have clearly defined objectives. Where students are given the task of conducting a questionnaire survey, it is remarkable how often they start by 'brain-storming' possible questions rather than considering the reports they want to produce first and then working back to the questions that need to be asked in order to get the information needed for those reports.

A companion book to this, *The Goal/Question/Metric Method* (Solingen and Berghout 1999) is recommended.

One suggested approach is the Goal/Question/Metric (GQM) paradigm suggested by Basili and Weiss (1984) and developed in many subsequent papers. They proposed a six-stage approach to any data collection exercise.

2.7.1 Establish the goals of the study

The first step suggested in planning a data collection exercise is to identify the goals of the particular information-gathering exercise.

It is worth distinguishing between an **objective** and a **goal.** An objective is a desired outcome. In defining objectives we need to focus on *what* is required rather than *how* that outcome is to be achieved. A goal is a step on the way to achieving that outcome. In a game of soccer for example, scoring a goal by putting the ball in the back of the net is also achieving a 'goal' on the way to the objective of winning the match. Goals and objectives may be nested at several levels. Thus winning the match may be a goal on the way to the objective of winning the league competition. One way of identifying goals is by completing the sentence: 'In order to achieve objective A, the following have to be in place …' Although objectives, as we said above, should be defined in terms of what rather than how, the identification of sub-objectives or goals does involve some consideration of how the main objective is to be attained.

Some writers use 'goal' and 'objective' rather differently. Our definitions follow those suggested as long ago as 1971 by Ackoff.

This distinction between an objective and a goal is important. If we set people an objective, to be fair it must be one that is within their power to fulfil. A software house may have as a very reasonable objective the improvement of customer satisfaction. Although everyone working for the organization ought to be aware of that objective, it would, however, be unreasonable to set that as an objective for software developers. Customer satisfaction depends on many things outside the individual developer's power, including the price of the software, the degree to which the features of the application match those needed by customers and the quality of help-desk support. One element that might contribute to customer satisfaction would be the degree to which the software is reliable. The improvement of the reliability of software might be within the software developers' power and could thus reasonably be given to them as a goal. Other individuals and groups within the software house may then be given other goals, which when put together allow the organization to meet its overall objective.

A measurement programme would have one or more goals which should be contributing to some higher level objectives of the organization. A template to assist people contemplating a measurement programme has been developed by framers of the GQM approach (Basili 1995):

> **Purpose**
> *Analyse some objects <...>*
> *for the purpose of <...>*
>
> **Perspective**
> *With respect to <...>*
> *from the point of view of <...>*
>
> **Environment**
> *in the context of <...>*

Basili (1995) lists as possible reasons for measurement: characterization; evaluation; prediction; motivation; improvement.

The *objects* refer to the entities of interest to the study. We have discussed the identification of these entity types at some length already. The *purpose* describes the reason for investigating these entity types. Bush and Fenton (1990) suggest that the purpose of measurement will be either **assessment** to see how good a product, process or resource is in some way, or **prediction** – attempting to build a model that will tell us the most likely outcome of some planned activity in software development, for example how much it would cost to implement a particular set of functions.

The *with respect to* clause identifies the particular qualities, properties or theoretical constructs associated with the *objects* that the exercise is to investigate. Where individual software modules have been identified as the subject of investigation, it might be the investigation into these modules is in respect to their reliability. The importance of being aware of the viewpoint that is being adopted has already been stressed earlier in this chapter, where the different views of 'speed of problem resolution' that a customer of a help-desk and the manager of one might have was discussed.

In the case of the software house that is seeking to improve customer satisfaction and has focused on the improvement of the reliability of their software products as one component of the programme, the goal of a measurement exercise might be drafted as:

*Analyse some **components of software packages** for the purpose of **evaluation with** respect to **reliability** from the viewpoint of **users**.*

2.7.2 Develop a list of questions of interest

Basili and Weiss (1984) say that 'questions of interest form a bridge between the subjectively determined goals of the study and the quantitative measures to be used in the study.' In the case of the software house studying the reliability of the products from the viewpoint of their customers, certain questions that need to be answered can be identified. These might include:

- which modules have the most reported operational failures?

- how important were the failures to the users?

- how many actual errors caused the failures?

- how long did it take to correct the faults that were causing the failures?

- how does the perceived reliability of our products compare to those of our competitors.

In order to generate the questions of interest, those involved will need to formulate some idea of the models of behaviour involved in the processes. The term 'model' is meant here to convey the sense of a set of ideas about the chains of cause and effect that apply in the area of study. The questions above imply a model where faults in the software might cause the application to fail for a particular customer. In some cases the same fault could cause failures for more than one customer. Not all failures identified by a customer will be equally serious: some might be minor irritations while others might be catastrophic.

To some extent, the seriousness of a failure caused by a particular fault can vary from one customer to another. One aspect of the 'seriousness' of a failure is the amount of time that is needed to correct the fault that caused the failure as the longer a known fault remains, the more chance there is for other users to experience the same failure. A final question relates to the comparison of our software applications with those of other vendors. The customer's perception of the reliability of our software is possibly influenced by the perceived reliability of competitor products.

Clearly, at this point many of these ideas about the influences on the objects of interest will be speculative. Although not specifically recommended by the proponents of GQM, we would recommend a thorough exploratory study of a qualitative nature at this point.

It should be clear that the consideration of these underlying models might identify further entities of interest to the study. For example, in the discussion above, fault, failure, customer and error correction activity have all emerged as objects of interest.

2.7.3 Establish data categories

The GQM paradigm lacks some detail on how data categories are to be identified. Data categories seem to be another way of referring to the data attributes of objects of interest to us that are relevant to the goals of our study.

In the example of reliability, one piece of data that will need to be collected is the impact or seriousness of the failure. It might be possible to measure seriousness in terms of down-time or lost revenue, but it is more likely that you are going to have to fall back on some restricted ordinal measurement which will have an element of subjective judgement involved.

For each failure, you may wish to note how it was dealt with. If the failure was trivial, it might be noted as a known error and be corrected in the next planned release of the software. In other cases, there might be failures so serious that an immediate bug-fix is needed.

A key point is that the data chosen as being important must be shown to be relevant to the questions needing answers.

2.7.4 Design and test data collection form

In order to collect this information Basili and Weiss emphasize the need to design a suitable form. This could be a paper or computer input form. The design of the form should ideally involve representatives of those who will be completing the forms so that they can identify any practical problems with the proposed design.

2.7.5 Collect and validate data

A key principle that Basili and Weiss stress is that the data should be captured while the processes that generate it are actually being carried out. It should not be based on rather hazy recollections of the participants. While this is true, it appears to us to be a counsel of perfection that may have to be ignored on pragmatic grounds.

Say, for example, you are interested in failure and fault data. If you are going to use only data collected using your newly designed forms and contributed when the processes of fault reporting and correction are actually going on, you are going to wait for several months before you have enough data to analyse. On the other hand, the current fault logging and version control records might give you most of the information you need relating to the recent past, so that you can at least do some exploratory analysis.

In an ideal situation you might be able to incorporate your data collection form into some existing documentation that has to be completed. In the case of our fault data study, there is likely to be a help-desk that already has some logging system and it would be very convenient if the data collection form could be merged into this. There should be a way in which the data collected can be checked and for problems to be resolved by interviewing the people who generated the data. Basili and Weiss noted the large number of errors that were made initially before the participants became familiar with the requirements of the data collection exercise.

2.7.6 Analyse the data

This should be relatively straightforward as the questions of how the data is to be analysed and the resulting information is presented should have been determined at an early stage.

2.8 Reservations about the GQM paradigm

There have been some reservations about the GQM approach. An advantage of the approach is that the ideas of GQM can be readily conveyed to managers, but in practical application what exactly is meant by 'goal' or 'question' might not be absolutely clear. The GQM approach has however been in existence for some time and Victor Basili has taken opportunities to refine and elaborate the approach. For example the goal definition template described earlier has been a more recent clarification of one aspect of the technique.

Bache and Neil (1995) who have had considerable experience in trying to apply software measurement suggest that it is difficult to get managers to set realistic goals until the actual state of products and processes are known. Once a seemingly useful metric is identified, it may turn out very difficult to gather the corresponding data. They suggest an alternative approach Metric/Question/Goal or MQG! The initial stage is to use metrics to find out the true state of current processes. They suggest a core set of well established and well understood types of measurement:

- **failure data**, including how often the operational software products fail and the nature of those failures;

- **fault and change data**, including the nature and location of the faults and the time needed to correct them;

- **size** of the software components;

- **structural metrics** which includes the degree to which software is structured, modular and cohesive;

- **test coverage data** which shows what proportion of the code has been executed in a system;

- **time and effort measurements**.

According to Bache and Neil, once these details have been gathered, certain questions could suggest themselves. For example, it might seem that certain software components are becoming more and more expensive to modify. Questions might therefore be formulated about why this should be and what should be done about it. The answer might be that software modules are becoming more unstructured as changes are made to them over time. This could lead to the goal that the maintainability of modules should be regularly reviewed and those that would benefit from re-engineering should be identified and effort spent to put this re-engineering work in hand.

2.9 Conclusions

In this chapter we have looked at some of the factors that can affect the validity of the measurements that we might want to take. Below we summarize some of the key points.

- Measurement adopted should reflect characteristics of the entity being measured that can be perceived independently of the measurements.

- The pattern of the characteristic behaviour that can be detected in an entity can suggest the existence of some property such as 'user friendliness'. Such properties are **hypothetical constructs**, the existence of which subsequent measurements may confirm or deny.

- The attributes of interest in software measurement often belong to either **processes** in the development life-cycle, **products** that are created by those processes or the **resources** used by the processes.

- Measurements may be **fundamental** or **derived**, that is, measured directly or derived by combining two or more other measurements.

- The appropriate **scale type** must be identified for each measurement. These govern the valid comparisons and mathematical operations that can be carried out.

- The kinds of statistical operation that can be carried out will also depend on whether the set of data in question is normally distributed.

- Measurement exercises need to have clearly defined questions to be answered.

- Measurement exercises need to be based on well-understood and articulated hypothetical models of how the system under examination works.

2.10 References

Abdel-Hamid, T. K. and Madnick, S. E. (1986), 'Impact of schedule estimation on software project behaviour', *IEEE Software*: 3(4), July 70–75.

Ackoff, R. L.(1972), 'Towards a system of systems concepts' in Beishon, J. and Peters, G., *Systems Behaviour*, Harper and Row, London.

Bache, R. and Bazzana, G. (1994), *Software Product Metrics,* McGraw-Hill, Maidenhead.

Bache, R. and Neil, M. (1995), 'Introducing metrics into industry: a perspective on GQM' in Fenton, N. E., Whitty, R. and Izuka, Y. (eds), *Software Quality Assurance and Measurement: A Worldwide Perspective*, International Thomson Computer Press, London.

Basili, V. R. (1995), 'Applying the Goal/Question/Metric paradigm in the experience factory' in Fenton, N. E., Whitty, R. and Izuka, Y. (eds), *Software Quality Assurance and Measurement: A Worldwide Perspective*, International Thomson Computer Press, London.

Basili, V. R. and Musa, J. D. (1991), 'The future engineering of software: a management perspective', *IEEE Computer*: 20(4), 90–96 [Also in Kemerer 1997].

Basili, V. R. and Weiss, D. M. (1984), 'A methodology for collecting valid software engineering data', *IEEE Transactions in Software Engineering*: 10 (6), 728–738.

Boehm, B. W. (1981), *Software Engineering Economics*, Prentice-Hall, Englewood Cliffs, NJ.

Brooks, F. P. (1987), 'No silver bullet: essence and accidents of software engineering', *IEEE Computer* 24(4) 10–19 [Also in Kemerer, 1997].

Bush, M. E. and Fenton, N. E. (1990), 'Software measurement: a conceptual framework', *Journal of Systems and Software*: 12(3), 223-231.

Coolican, H (1994), *Research Methods and Statistics in Psychology*, Hodder and Stoughton, London.

Gordon, R. D. and Halstead, M. H. (1976), 'An experiment comparing Fortran programming times with the Software Physics Hypothesis', *Proceedings of AFIPS*, 935–937 [This paper is accessible in Shepperd M. (ed), *Software Engineering Metrics Volume 1: Measures And Validations*, McGraw-Hill, Maidenhead, 1993].

Henry, S. and Kafura, D. (1981), 'Software quality metrics based on interconnectivity', *Journal of Systems and Software*: 2, 121–131.

Hofstede, G. (1987), *Cultures and Organizations*, McGraw-Hill, Maidenhead.

Hughes, R. T. (1994), 'The application of software measurement to the process of information systems analysis and design', *Proceedings of the 6th European Software Cost Modelling Conference*, Ivrea, Italy, 11–13 May.

Kemerer, C. F. (1997), *Software Project Management: Readings and Cases*, Irwin, Chicago.

Kitchenham, B., Pickard, L. and Linkman, S. (1990), 'An evaluation of some design metrics', *Software Engineering Journal*: 5(1), 50–58.

Kitchenham, B., Pleeger, S. L. and Fenton, N. (1995), 'Towards a framework for software measurement validation', *IEEE Transactions on Software Engineering*: 21(12), 929–943.

Milne, A. A. (1928), *The House at Pooh Corner*, Methuen & Co, London.

Roberts, F. S. (1979), *Measurement Theory: With Applications to Decision Making, Utility, and the Social Sciences*, Addison-Wesley, Reading, MA.

Shaw, M. (1990), 'Prospects for an engineering discipline of software', *IEEE Software*: 7(11), 15–24 [Also in Kemerer 1997].

van Solingen, R. and Berghout, E. (1999), *The Goal/Question/Metric Method*, McGraw-Hill, Maidenhead.

Weinberg, G. (1971), *The Psychology of Computer Programming*, Van Nostrand Reinhold, New York.

2.11 Additional questions

1. (i) How can the consequences of the presence of the property of flexibility, that is, the ease with which a software application can be changed, be measured?

   (ii) What factors may contribute to flexibility and how can their presence be assessed?

2. In SSADM, the Structured Systems Analysis and Design Method, a Data Flow Diagram is drawn up to describe the processes in a current information processing system, the stores of data that those processes access and modify, and the flows of information between those processes. At the same time, a separate and parallel task may be conducted where a Logical Data Structure diagram is constructed of the entities of interest in the system and the relationships between those entity types. The results of the two exercises are compared and a Logicalized Data Flow Diagram is the result. For each entity on the Logical Data Structure, an Entity Life History diagram is drawn up showing the sequence of changes to the attributes of each entity that can occur over the life of an individual instance of the entity type.

   Draw up a Bush–Fenton process model portraying the processes, products and resources involved in the above activities.

3. What scale types are involved in each of the following?

   (i) Software developers are asked to rank five programming or system building tools according to the degree to which they found them useful.

   (ii) Given a specification for a change to a software component, a software developer has to rank the change as of 'high', 'low' or 'medium' difficulty.

   (iii) The number of entity types on a Logical Data Structure in SSADM.

   (iv) A book on programming languages categorizes languages as either First, Second, Third or Fourth Generation.

   (v) A software development manager notes that the number of operational failures in an application are 80% less than last year.

4. The following numbers relate to the combined number of input and output signals to and from individual modules in a real-time system: 245, 12, 8, 12, 11, 8, 57, 5, 2, 203, 6, 25, 8, 12, 12, 12.

   (i) Draw up a histogram for this data.

   (ii) Draw up a box-plot for this data.

   (iii) What are the median and average values for this set of data?

   (iv) What are the first and third quartiles in this set of data?

   (v) Is the data suitable for parametric statistical analysis?

5. A software house wishes to replace the procedural language that it uses at present with a fourth generation application-building environment. The main reason for the move is to improve development productivity. If the GQM approach was used to assess the effectiveness of the migration, what (i) goals, (ii) questions and (iii) metrics would need to be defined?

Chapter 3

How to measure software code

OBJECTIVES

When you have completed this chapter you will be able to:

☐ measure information in terms of its uncertainty

☐ explain Halstead's Software Science measurement approach and why it should be avoided

☐ apply McCabe's cyclomatic complexity measurement to assess testability

☐ apply Prather's complexity measurement to examples of structured program code

☐ use code metrics to assist in the planning of 'open box' software testing

---

3.1 Introduction

We have seen that there are some internal characteristics of software of which the users will not normally be aware, such as the way in which the code is structured. The users of the software *will* be aware of external attributes such as the range of useful features the software has or the frequency with which the software fails.

In many cases, the relationships between internal and external attributes can be traced. Generally, for instance, software that has a large number of features for the user will also have a large number of lines of software code to supply these features. In other cases, and reliability is a good example of this, the precise nature of the links between internal and external attributes are more difficult to establish.

Chapter 9, which deals with the measurement of quality, discusses this further.

3.2 The measurement of information

An early concern of computer scientists was how information was held within the computer. One of the first things we are taught in computing is that data is stored in computer memory as ones and zeros. These units are called **bits**.

Exercise 3.1 Calculating information content

What is the smallest number of bits that it would take to hold the following information?

    (a) yes or no
    (b) the years in a century
    (c) the letters of the alphabet
    the settings on a UK traffic signal (green, amber, red, red/amber)

One way of doing the exercise would be to create a table, such as Table 3.1, that shows the maximum number of different combinations of settings you can have for each number of bits.

Table 3.1   *Information capacity of bit patterns*

Note that in all cases, one of the combinations will be all zeros. The number of combinations is therefore one more than the maximum number that can be held.

Number of bits	Number of combinations
1	2
2	4
3	8
4	16
5	32
6	64
7	132

Exercise 3.2 Assessing the need for additional bits

    (a) If in addition to the 26 letters of the alphabet, you wanted codes for the digits 0 to 9, would you need additional bits?
    (b) Assume that the traffic authorities wanted to have other settings for the traffic lights, for example 'cyclists may proceed, but not other vehicles'. How many additional signals could the standard UK three-light system allow?

In the case of the traffic lights, because the physical system has three switches, the maximum number of possible combinations is 8 (2^3). Only four combinations are actually used, so we can say that there is **redundancy**.

Two children are playing a game where the first thinks of a letter of the alphabet while the other asks questions which can be answered 'yes' or 'no' and uses the answers to guess the identity of the letter. What would be the minimum number of questions needed to be sure of the answer, assuming that there is an equal probability of any letter being picked by the first child?

The answer is five if the mechanism for selecting the right letter is what software engineers call a binary search algorithm: see Figure 3.1.

A B C D E F G H I J K L M N O P Q R S T U V W X Y Z

1. Does the letter come after M?   No

A B C D E F G H I J K L M ~~N O P Q R S T U V W X Y Z~~

2. Does the letter come after G?   Yes

~~A B C D E F G~~ H I J K L M ~~N O P Q R S T U V W X Y Z~~

3. Does the letter come after J?   No

~~A B C D E F G~~ H I J ~~K L M N O P Q R S T U V W X Y Z~~

4. Does the letter come after I?   No

~~A B C D E F G~~ H I ~~J K L M N O P Q R S T U V W X Y Z~~

5. Is it H?   No

~~A B C D E F G~~ H I ~~J K L M N O P Q R S T U V W X Y Z~~
It must be I!

Figure 3.1 *An example of a binary search.*

Formally, we can say that:

$$H = \log_2 N \qquad \text{(Equation 3.1)}$$

where H is the 'amount of uncertainty' and N is the number of equally probable alternatives. This can be seen as a measure of information.

If we were guessing the next card in a pack of 52 playing cards there would be a lot more uncertainty than if we were trying to guess whether a coin was going to land as a head or a tail. We can thus talk about information in terms of the uncertainty that is involved. Using the Equation 3.1 allows us to have values of H which are not integers so that the measure can distinguish between the information holding capacity of a character that can be A–Z and another which can be A–Z, hyphen, apostrophe or space. In the case of the letters of the alphabet, the amount of uncertainty would be 4.7, which corresponds to the number of questions that had to be asked. 4.7 may seem to be a strange number of questions in the context of our guessing game, but in effect this is an average: depending on the character to be identified we could on some occasions get away with only four questions.

> These ideas were developed by two communications engineers, C. E. Shannon and W. Weaver.
>
> This is based on the assumption that each character has an equal probability of occurring. In ordinary text, some letters appear more often and this will reduce 'uncertainty'.

What are the amounts of uncertainty (H) in (a) a six-sided dice (b) a tossed coin?

Exercise 3.3 Measuring uncertainty

We can now quantify the amount of redundancy in a particular data representation. Take our traffic light example. From Table 3.2, four outcomes give:

$$H = \log_2 4 = 2$$

Table 3.2 *Logarithms to the base 2*

N	$\log_2 N$	N	$\log_2 N$	N	$\log_2 N$	N	$\log_2 N$
1	0.00	26	4.70	51	5.67	76	6.25
2	1.00	27	4.75	52	5.70	77	6.27
3	1.58	28	4.81	53	5.73	78	6.29
4	2.00	29	4.86	54	5.75	79	6.30
5	2.32	30	4.91	55	5.78	80	6.32
6	2.58	31	4.95	56	5.81	81	6.34
7	2.81	32	5.00	57	5.83	82	6.36
8	3.00	33	5.04	58	5.86	83	6.38
9	3.17	34	5.09	59	5.88	84	6.39
10	3.32	35	5.13	60	5.91	85	6.41
11	3.46	36	5.17	61	5.93	86	6.43
12	3.58	37	5.21	62	5.95	87	6.44
13	3.70	38	5.25	63	5.98	88	6.46
14	3.81	39	5.29	64	6.00	89	6.48
15	3.91	40	5.32	65	6.02	90	6.49
16	4.00	41	5.36	66	6.04	91	6.51
17	4.09	42	5.39	67	6.07	92	6.52
18	4.17	43	5.43	68	6.09	93	6.54
19	4.25	44	5.46	69	6.11	94	6.55
20	4.32	45	5.49	70	6.13	95	6.57
21	4.39	46	5.52	71	6.15	96	6.58
22	4.46	47	5.55	72	6.17	97	6.60
23	4.52	48	5.58	73	6.19	98	6.61
24	4.58	49	5.61	74	6.21	99	6.63
25	4.64	50	5.64	75	6.23	100	6.64

The three-light system is capable of holding eight combinations so that:

$$H = \log_2 8 = 3$$

Redundancy is defined as:

(maximum uncertainty) − *(actual uncertainty)*/*(maximum uncertainty)*

In our traffic light example this would be (3−2)/3 or 0.33.

(i) An ASCII character (which contains eight bits) on a database is to hold an upper or lower case alphabetic character or a numeric digit in the range 0 to 9. How much redundancy would there be?

(ii) Before the year 2000, a date format contained a two ASCII character field which held the last two digits of the year. Recalling that ASCII characters consist of eight bits, what is the highest year (starting from 1 AD) that could be held in two characters if we were not constrained by any preset format? What is the redundancy in the YY format?

Exercise 3.4 Assessing information redundancy

The measurement of information in this way has a direct relevance to questions of computer storage. It has also been used in the study of humans as information processors. Psychological experiments have shown that increases in the complexity of stimuli (the instrumentation in the cockpit of an aeroplane, for example) cause the operator reaction time to lengthen. The complexity of these stimuli can be measured in terms of information uncertainty and in fact a linear relationship between H and reaction time has been found.

Such studies of human performance influenced some aspects of computing. One example is short-term memory. Studies in the 1880s established that the average effective short-term memory of humans is 7 ± 2 'chunks' of information. This led to suggestions that you should have fewer than 10 boxes on a data flow diagram.

Early studies of short-term memory are particularly associated with Joseph Jacobs.

3.3 Programming language instructions

Computer systems are not just a means of storing information. The magic element is the ability to process the information under the control of software.

The managers of software development need to get some idea of the size of the software to be created. This, among other things, will help them to assess the 'work content' of an application and will be the basis of estimates of cost and effort. The most obvious measure of size is the number of programming language instructions. Just as a bricklayer would base the cost estimate for building a wall on the number of bricks, so a software development project planner could use **lines of code** as the building bricks for software.

3.3.1 Lines of code versus delivered source instructions

Lines of code need to be distinguished from **delivered source instructions** (DSI).

In low level languages, such as assemblers, the number of lines and the number of instructions tend to have a one-to-one relationship, except where some of the instructions are in fact data declarations. There could also be some comment lines.

We might therefore want to distinguish between:

KDSI stands for thousands of delivered source instructions.

- Comment lines of code (CLOC);

- Data declarations;

- Effective (or executable) lines of code (ELOC).

Data declarations and effective lines of code are sometimes grouped together as non-comment lines of code (NCLOC). Fenton and Pfleeger (1996) have recommended that CLOC and NCLOC are counted separately. You can then derive:

$$LOC = NCLOC + CLOC$$

They also recommend the use of the ratio CLOC/LOC which should convey an idea of the degree to which the program has been commented. With low level languages this might be important. With more modern languages it is argued that the use of meaningful variable and procedure names would make this less of an issue.

Some argue that comments can sometimes even actually obscure the meaning of the underlying code.

Some programming languages are generally more powerful than others. Assembler programming was fairly quickly replaced by higher level third generation languages (3GLs) such as Cobol for routine software development work. These had commands that could generate large amounts of executable code. Cobol, for example, has a `SEARCH ALL` command which executes a binary search and a `SORT` command ordering files into particular key sequences. Such operations would require considerable effort if they had to be coded in assembler.

Note that the yes/no questions game used earlier as an illustration is essentially a binary search.

One consequence of the more powerful nature of 3GLs was that more information had to be passed to the compiler about how these powerful commands were to be executed. This and the desire to make the code more readable led to a more free-format way of laying out the code, so that a command could be spread out over several lines: see Figure 3.2.

In Figure 3.2, it could be argued that only two programming language commands, `MOVE` and `COMPUTE` should be counted. This is not clear-cut, though, as the `MOVE` is putting zero into four different locations and in other programming languages this would have to be implemented through four different statements. Similarly, the `COMPUTE` statement could be decomposed into the separate stages of the calculation. In these circumstances, it might be decided that a count of LOC would convey a better idea of size.

```
MOVE ZERO TO WA-COUNT
               WB-COUNT
               WC-WEEKLY-PAY-TOTAL
               WD-MONTHLY-PAY-TOTAL.
     COMPUTE WEA-GROSS-PAY = (WEB-HOURLY-RATE (WEC-GRADE)) *
                             (WEC-HOURS - WED-OVERTIME) +
                             (WEB-HOURLY-RATE (WEC-GRADE)) * 1.5 *
                             WED-OVERTIME.
```

Figure 3.2 *A fragment of some Cobol code.*

Matters are made worse by the fact that individual programming styles vary. A programmer might have decided not to use `COMPUTE` but to code the calculation of gross pay using a series of statements like `MULTIPLY`, `SUBTRACT` and `ADD`. She might have wanted to do this to control rounding errors for instance. This would have an impact of the statement count.

3.3.2 The place of procedural code in software applications

Assembler and 3GLs are examples of **procedural** languages. Commands in procedural languages give the computer processor a sequence of instructions to be executed. The designer of the procedure has to work out how each step of the process is to be carried out before the code to execute that process can be written. Increasingly, **non-procedural** methods are being used to program computers. These specify what is to be achieved and then leave it to the system to generate the sequence of instructions that is needed to produce the desired result. An example of this would be a report generator, where users specify what details are to be extracted from the database, the order in which the details are to be printed and any totals and sub-totals that are required and then leave it to the system to generate the procedures needed to create the report.

Thus modern software development environments will use procedural code as only one method of recording detailed processing requirements. Graphics objects that make up the operator interface can be manipulated by clicking and dragging with a mouse. Report layouts can be specified using tables. Declarative languages such as SQL can be used to access and update databases. Figure 3.3 shows a **universal function model** based on, but different from, the one suggested by SSADM.

SSADM stands for Structured Systems Analysis and Design Method and is the method that is recommended by the UK government for IS/IT projects.

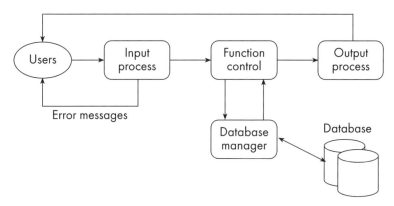

Figure 3.3 *A universal function model.*

The different components that have been identified above could be constructed using different technologies, which might or might not use procedural code, and which would need different measurement.

One approach to dealing with this is by counting 'object points' – see Chapter 6.

3.4 'Software science' – a linguistic approach to code measurement

We have noted some of the problems with counting LOC. One strategy for resolving these problems has been to seek ways of abstracting the underlying structure of the program code into a form where differences between the different languages will not matter.

One Nobel laureate scientist has said 'The only real science is physics, the rest is social work'.

One of the first attempts to do this was Halstead's (1977). He gave the name 'software science' to the subject of his studies. Earlier he had used the term 'software physics'. The proposition he put forward was that the properties of software could be studied and quantified using principles analogous to those used in the physical sciences. He proposed that the counts described in Table 3.3 for the source code of a program.

Table 3.3 *Halstead's 'Software Science' counts*

Variable	Description
n_1	The number of unique **operators**. If a READ statement were used in a program, for example, it would only be counted once, regardless of how many times it was actually used.
N_1	A count of the **uses** of operators. For example, if the READ were used three times in a program, then this would contribute 3 to the count.
n_2	The number of unique **operands**, that is the equivalent of the data declarations in languages where all variables have to be declared.
N_2	The number of times operands are referenced. These references are sometimes called **data tokens**.

In Table 3.4, we show the results of counting the variables suggested by Halstead for a small fragment of code. From these basic counts certain other measurements can be derived.

Table 3.4 *Halstead's counts used in the worked example*

Variable	Count
Unique operators (n_1)	7
Operator count (N_1)	8
Unique operands (n_2)	10
Operand count (N_2)	14

The first of these is the **vocabulary** (n) that is used. This is calculated thus:

$$n = n_1 + n_2$$

Using the example counts in Table 3.4, $n = 7 + 10 = 17$.

The next measurement that Halstead suggested was the **length**, N, of the program. This was calculated as:

$$N = N_1 + N_2$$

Using the example counts in Table 3.4, N = 8 +14 = 22.

What Halstead then did was to try and express the vocabulary used in a program in terms of the information uncertainty measurement H that has been explained earlier (Equation 3.1).

$$H = \log_2 n$$

In our example the $\log_2$ of 17 would be 4.2. We may note in passing that Halstead's proposal assumed that all operators and operands are equally likely to be used in a program.

See also Prather (1988).

A new indirect measurement, **volume** (V), was derived as:

$$V = N\log_2 n$$

In our example, this would be $22 \times 4.2 = 92.4$. This can be visualized as the minimum number of bits needed to represent the program. If you can imagine the coding task as the mental selection of the right operands and operators for each step in the algorithm and if you accept that the coder would pick each operator and operand by doing some sort of binary search, then this number might be seen as representing the number of choices made by the coder.

Halstead then went on to define an indicator of the **level of abstraction** of a program. The higher the level of abstraction, the easier the programming task ought to be. Two influences were suggested. One would be the 'powerfulness' of programming language as measured by the number of different unique operators, or instruction types, in the language. The second influence was the complexity of the algorithm measured in terms of the number of times operands (that is, variables and constants) are accessed – if the same variables are accessed a large number of times, then this is taken to indicate that the processing is likely to be complex.

Note that 'powerfulness' here is being used in a different sense to the way we used it earlier where it referred to the way that a small amount of code could carry out a large amount of processing.

This level of abstraction (L) is derived as:

$$L = (2/n_1)(n_2/N_2)$$

In our example this would be $(2/7)(10/14) = 0.20$. It was suggested by Halstead that if the same algorithm were implemented in more than one programming language, although the V and L values might vary between implementations, the product of $V \times L$ ought to be the same.

The effort (E) needed to do the coding was calculated as:

$$E = V/L$$

This was supposed to be the number of mental discriminations required to generate the code. There had been a suggestion that the average human could make about 18 of these discriminations per second and so the time in seconds to code the algorithm would be about E/18.

This brief description of the thinking behind the Software Science approach should be sufficient to indicate that the model on which it was based was highly speculative and that it was based on a very simplistic picture of the software development task. It is hardly surprising to find that the psychological model upon which it is based has been subject to criticism (see Coulter, 1983). In defence of Software Science, it can at least be said that it did suggest *some* kind of model. Software measurement theoreticians often stress the need for the identification of cause and effect to be based on some theoretical hypothesis or model that subsequent measurements can confirm or reject, but such models in reality seem to be thin on the ground. Halstead's work led to a flurry of experimental work. Much of this work was subsequently discredited. Hamer and Frewin (1982), for example, found that empirically there was a closer relationship between time to complete coding and N ('length') or V ('volume') than E. Because N is highly correlated with the number of lines of code in a program, what the model was probably really showing was that effort was related to the number of lines of code written. As will be seen, this is a key test of the effectiveness of any measurement that is designed to assess the 'complexity' of programs: is it a better predictor of development effort or the number of errors than a simple count of the lines of code in the program?

Despite the discrediting of Software Science, some code analysis software tools still produce reports of the Halstead metric. One suspects that having developed the feature in the analyser, there is a reluctance to discard it. Some research papers still emerge that use Software Science. Most recently this has been in relation to object oriented software where Michelle Cartwright (1998) has noted several of these papers. Our advice is: steer clear of this 'measurement'.

3.5   Cyclomatic complexity

3.5.1 Flowgraph analysis

The view of programming that lay behind Software Science was focused on coding to the exclusion of other elements in the development task such as analysis, design and testing. The structure of the software was not considered. A software module can be more difficult to comprehend because it tests more conditions and sub-conditions embodying complicated and nested rules of decision-making. Thomas McCabe (1976) attempted to take account of this by devising a measurement based on the number of decisions and branches in a software component. The more branches a software component has the more test cases are needed to test it. It therefore seems reasonable to hypothesize that the decision density will have a bearing on the ease of testing and consequently maintaining the software component.

In order to apply this count, the software component has to be portrayed as a **flowgraph** containing a number of **nodes** which represent either **predicates which** express the conditions (by means of *if...else* for example) or **processes**. In this context a process is one or more operations that are always carried out in sequence. A predicate is easily identified on a flowgraph as a node with at least two branches coming out of it. Nodes are connected by **edges** or **arcs** which show how control can be passed from one node to another.

For example, the Pascal program fragment in Figure 3.4 can be converted to the flowgraph in Figure 3.5.

```
var
    i,squared : integer;
begin
    writeln ('squares of 1 to 99');
    for i:= 1 to 99 do
    begin
        squared := i * i;
        writeln (squared)
    end;
    writeln ('end of table')
end;
```

Figure 3.4 *Pascal fragment to produce list of squares.*

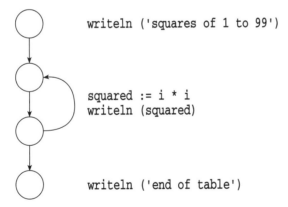

```
                    writeln ('squares of 1 to 99')



                    squared := i * i
                    writeln (squared)



                    writeln ('end of table')
```

Figure 3.5 *Flowgraph of Pascal fragment in 3.4.*

Draw up a flowgraph for the following Pascal fragment:
```
var
    count, fizz, buzz : integer;
begin
    writeln ('fizz buzz generator');
    for count := 1 to 100 do
    begin
```

Exercise 3.5 Drawing a flowgraph

```
            fizz := count - ((count/3) * 3);
            buzz : = count - ((count/5) * 5);
            if fizz = 0 then writeln ('fizz');
            if buzz = 0 then writeln ('buzz');
            if (fizz <> 0) and (buzz <> 0) then
            writeln (count)
        end;
end;
```

Some software developers might be uneasy at the use of flowgraphs because they look like flowcharts and many software engineering authorities frown on these as leading to such poor practices as the unwarranted use of 'gotos'. Interestingly, there is empirical evidence that the use of flowcharts, if properly structured, can lead to more easily understood documentation than the use of pseudocode (Scanlan, 1989), but that is not the argument at this point. In the present context, flowgraphs are generated to characterize the structure of the code after it has been implemented, *not* as a design tool to create the structure. As an analysis tool, it has to be able to cope with the code may or may not be properly structured.

3.5.2 McCabe cyclomatic complexity metric

McCabe cyclomatic complexity (v) is counted as:

$$number\ of\ edges - number\ of\ nodes + 1$$

Intuitively this is the equivalent of the number of decision points in the program. Formally, the cyclomatic complexity v of a graph g can be expressed as:

$$v(g) = e - n + 1$$

where e is the number of edges and n the number of nodes. In the case of Figure 3.5, e is 4, n is 4, so that the cyclomatic complexity is $4 - 4 + 1 = 1$.

Exercise 3.6 Cyclomatic complexity

What would be the cyclomatic complexity of the program fragment shown in Exercise 3.5?

The use of sub-routines or called procedures has an effect on cyclomatic complexity. In the program fragment in Figure 3.4 where the squares of the integers from 1 to 99 are calculated, we might decide to code the calculation of the square as a separate procedure to the main iteration – see Figure 3.6.

Figure 3.7 illustrates how the fragment of code in Figure 3.6 could be translated into two flowgraphs. If the cyclomatic complexity is calculated for each procedure

```
var
    i : integer;
begin
    writeln ('squares of 1 to 99');
    for i: = 1 to 99 do
        squared (i);
        writeln ('end of table')
    end;

procedure squared (i : integer);
var
    squared : integer;
begin
    squared := i * i;
    writeln (squared)
end
```

Figure 3.6 *Pascal fragment with a called procedure.*

and the results are summed then it will be seen that the result will be different from that calculated for the unified procedure. Applying graph theory, McCabe suggested a modified method to deal with software which is divided into modules or procedures:

$$v(s) = e - n + 2p$$

where *v(s)* is the cyclomatic complexity of the whole program and *p* is the number of procedures in the program and *e* and *n* are as in the previous calculations.

McCabe suggested that modules should not have a cyclomatic complexity above 10 unless there were special circumstances. He made no mention of the 7 ± 2 short term memory phenomenon but his recommendation is consistent with an awareness of it.

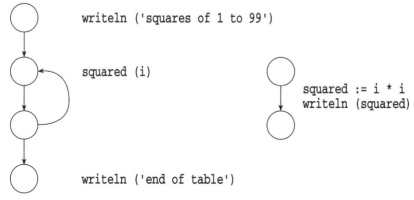

Figure 3.7 *Flowgraphs for the Pascal fragments in Figure 3.6.*

McCabe was conscious of the requirements of structured programming. Readers may recall that one of the tenets of this approach is that all software code can be represented in combinations of straight **sequences** of statements, **selections** (involving *if...then...else*, for example) and **iterations** (such as *repeat...until*). McCabe pointed out that another way of looking at this is to say that a program is unstructured if it contains branches into or out of the middle of iterated sequences. It would also be unstructured if it has branches into or out of sequences of statements that are already conditional on a decision (for example, through an *if* statement). The examination of the flowgraph can reveal where this is the case.

Most importantly, cyclomatic complexity can assist the planning of testing. The number of paths tested by a set of test data can be compared with the cyclomatic complexity. If the number of paths tested is less than the cyclomatic complexity then this *could* indicate that more test cases are needed. On the other hand if the test cases reflect accurately the inputs that can be expected, it may show that the structure of the code is unduly complicated.

Martin Shepperd (1988) has summarized the criticisms that have been levelled at the McCabe measurement. Some of the criticisms seem to be those of detail. For example, cyclomatic complexity counting gives the same rating to *if...then...else...endif* and *if...then...endif*. It has been suggested that McCabe counts *if* statements but not the *else*, but this is not strictly true: effectively an *else* path is always counted for every *if*. As McCabe's primary concern was with testability his approach seems reasonable. With the *if...then...endif*, there is an implied null *else* action. A good tester would create test cases to make sure that no action was taken if the condition specified by the *if* statement was not true.

McCabe has also been criticized for not explicitly defining a model, but his papers seem to me to argue clearly the link between amount of testing required and decision density so that such a model could easily be derived.

A more practical argument is illustrated by the two flowgraphs in Figure 3.8.

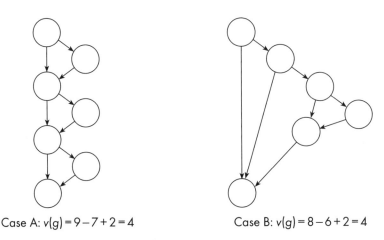

Case A: $v(g) = 9 - 7 + 2 = 4$ Case B: $v(g) = 8 - 6 + 2 = 4$

Figure 3.8 *Effect of nesting on cyclomatic complexity.*

Although both fragments have the same cyclomatic complexity, most developers would regard Case B as the more complicated because of nesting. As will be seen, proposals have been made to remedy this perceived failing.

3.5.3 The Prather metric

Prather (1984) suggested an approach to assessing complexity that takes account of nesting. The basic Prather approach assumes that the software component is written in a structured manner using only sequences, selections and iterations. Unlike in the McCabe approach, simple procedural statements in the program each contribute to the count.

Where there is an *if*, then the statements that would be executed in the 'true' and 'false' branches are counted, and the number of statements which is greatest is then doubled and added to an overall count. In the case of iterations, the number of statements in the repeated code is doubled and added to the overall count. Of course, the statements in the branches of an *if...else* or in the repeated code in a *do...while...* could themselves have selections and iterations.

To illustrate how the Prather metric works we will take a procedure – see Figure 3.9 – which rearranges an array of numbers so that the highest value in the array is in the first cell. The Prather metric counts the three statements in lines 7, 8 and 9 and doubles this to get 6. To get a count for the number of statements in the repeat loop, 1 is added to the 6 to take account of line 11, so that the count is now 7. The count for the iteration is doubled to make 14 and then another 1 is added to take account of line 4. The final Prather metric value is 15.

```
procedure maxAtTop (var a : array [1..n] of integer; n : integer);    1
var i, j, temp : integer;                                             2
begin                                                                 3
    i :=n;                                         1×1=1              4
    repeat                                                            5
        if a [i] > a [i-1] then begin                                 6
            temp := a [i-1];                                          7
            a [i-1] := a [i];              3×2=6    7×2=14            8
            a [i] :=temp                                              9
        end;                                                         10
        i := i-1                           1×1=1                     11
    until i =1                                                       12
end                                                                  13
```

Figure 3.9 *Pascal code to place highest value in the first cell of an array.*

Calculate the Prather metric for the fragment of code in Figure 3.10.

Exercise 3.7 The Prather metric

While the Prather metric has the merit of taking into account the number of statements and the nesting in a software component, it seems to us to be rather remote from the idea of testability with which McCabe was concerned.

```
procedure maxmin (var entry : array [1..last] of integer;
                       last : integer);
var max, min, range, x : integer;
begin
    max := 0;
    min :=9999;
    x := 1;
    repeat
        if entry [x] > max then max := entry [x];
        if entry [x] < min then min := entry [x];
        x := x+1
    until x > last
    range := max - min;
    if range = 0 then
        writeln 'all entries are the same'
    else begin
        writeln ('maximum ',max);
        writeln ('minimum ', min)
    end
end;
```

Figure 3.10 *Code to find the minimum and maximum values in an array.*

It is noteworthy that the QUALMS tool discussed in the next sub-section does not attempt to derive a Prather metric for unstructured code.

Prather's approach in general assumes a structured program is being analysed. He does describe ways of extending the approach to take into account instances of the unstructured goto. This involves measuring in some way the complexity of the code between the source and the destination of the goto. The interested reader is directed to Prather's paper for details, but it is enough to comment at this point that Prather himself concedes that the method is problematic.

An interesting aspect is that Prather discusses the need for a measurement that will 'penalize' developers who use unstructured elements in their code. However, measurements do not necessarily reflect good practice. For example, Evangelist (1982) reported that only two out of the 26 rules of good programming style suggested by Kernighan and Plauger (1978) would invariably lead to a decrease in cyclomatic complexity.

Unfortunately complexity measurements tend to be highly correlated with lines of code. This does not mean that the measurement is invalid as some imply, but that it is not useful, as in general decision density would seem to be evenly spread throughout most software components. Such measurements can still be useful in identifying software components that have abnormally high decision densities and might therefore require additional testing. Our own experience with this measure (Hughes *et al.* 1999) is that it is indeed correlated with software size, however measured. In predicting fault counts, although size seems to be the main driver, taking account of cyclomatic complexity as well can add marginally to the power of a prediction model. This would appear to be in line with the findings of Troster at IBM, as reported in Kan (1995).

3.5.4 Code complexity analysers

A potential problem with code complexity metrics is the time-consuming task of analysing software components in order to glean the measurement details. An effective solution can be to develop or acquire a software tool such as QUALMS (Bache and Leelasena, 1992) or Prometrix which will scan the code and automatically report the measurement data. An advantage of this approach is that data collection will be objectively and consistently executed.

An obstacle for the developers of such tools is that each programming language has its own way of expressing control and structure. To avoid having to create a completely new version of the tool each time a new programming language needs to be dealt with, one technique is to have a series of 'front end' analysers, each of which is designed to deal with a particular programming language. Each front end converts the code to a common format which can represent the original software in the form of a sequence of **primes**, basic logical building blocks.

A tool like QUALMS, for example, analyses these sequences of primes and produces a range of software measurement information. Some of these reports might be by-products created while deriving other measurements. As QUALMS needs to identify particular types of prime, there are features which allow these to be distinguished and counted. This information can then be used to report on whether the software is structured (that is, has only the primes allowed by structured programming principles) and on the number of nodes in the largest prime found.

Recalling that the original motivation for measuring cyclomatic complexity was to assess testability, some of the most interesting measurements produced by QUALMS relate to test coverage which is dealt with in the next section.

3.5.5 Test coverage

Testing can be categorized as either **open box** or **closed box**. As the names imply, in the case of open box testing, the test designers know the code structure and can plan the tests accordingly. In the case of closed box testing the test designers are only aware of the specification of what the software should output given specified inputs and have no idea of the internal workings of the software. Here, we are concerned with open box testing.

Open box testing is sometimes called glass box testing.

Code analysers such as QUALMS can assist the planning of testing by reporting such predictive measurements as:

- The minimum number of test cases needed to execute all the **statements** in a software component;

- The minimum number of test cases needed to execute every **branch** in the software component (this differs from statement coverage because some branches – the 'false' branch where you have an *if* without an *else* for instance – will not have any associated statements);

- The number of **simple paths** in the software component. A path in this context is a sequence of branches or edges from the start to the end of the software component. This count only includes simple paths that do not involve the same edge being traversed more than once;

- **Visit-each-loop** testing count. This is a count of the number of test cases that will execute all the simple paths and will also, for every loop, execute the branch (if any) which by-passes the loop and the branch that executes the loop at least once.

A dynamic analyser might for example be used to indicate which software components are most heavily used when execution performance needs to speeded up.

Tests can then be monitored to see what paths are actually executed. For this a **dynamic** analyser could be employed which records and reports the actual paths executed in the software under test. A dynamic analyser is a software tool that analyses the behaviour of a software component when it is executed with a set of data. The technology involved is often an extension of that used to implement symbolic debuggers. **Dynamic analysis** can be contrasted with the **static analysis** of tools like QUALMS which only examine code.

Comparing the number of paths actually executed with the number executed by the static analysis can allow a **test effectiveness ratio** to be calculated:

$$\textit{Test effectiveness ratio} = (\textit{number of objects executed}) / (\textit{total number of objects})$$

where *number of objects* can refer to one of the counts we listed above, such as that for statements. In the case of the test effectiveness for branches, for example, the number of objects would be the number of branches that are traversed in tests as opposed to the total number of branches that have been identified during the static analysis.

Exercise 3.8 Test effectiveness

A set of data to test the *maxmin* procedure in Figure 3.10 consists of an array *entry* containing 1, 2 and 3 in the first three cells and the variable *last* containing 3. What would be the test effectiveness ratio of this test data in respect of statements and branches? In the context of this exercise assume that a statement is a command in the programming language which manipulates a variable (which means *ifs, repeat …until*s and so on, are excluded).

3.5.6 Using cyclomatic complexity to predict size

The high correlation between cyclomatic complexity and size (measured in LOC, for example) can be exploited in some environments. The **Jackson structured programming** technique (Jackson 1975) is based on the Dijkstra (1976) principle that software code should be built up solely of sequences, selections and iterations. However, Jackson went further and argued that the internal structures of software should be mapped as far as possible from the structures of the inputs and outputs processed by the software: in other words that the design should be **data-driven**. Jackson demonstrated that these inputs and outputs could themselves be analysed into sequences, selections and iterations.

For example, a procedure is to read a feeder file of employee payroll details. This file has been structured so that there is a section of the file for each department in the organization. The start of a sequence of records for a department is signalled by the presence of a departmental title record. Following the departmental title is a record for each employee in that department. The details held for a weekly paid employee are different in some respects from those for a monthly paid employee. The structure of this input file can be portrayed using the Jackson notation as shown in Figure 3.11. The asterisk in a box indicates that it is iterated, while a little circle indicates an alternative.

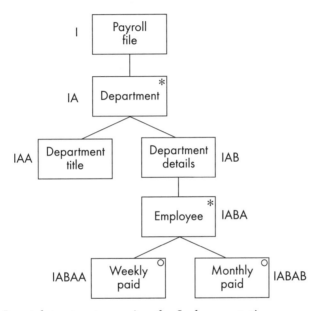

Figure 3.11 *Input data structure using the Jackson notation.*

Let us assume that a report is to be produced which has one line per department giving the name of the department and two counts: one for the number of weekly paid employees and the other for the monthly paid employees in that department. A Jackson structure can be drawn up for this too – see Figure 3.12.

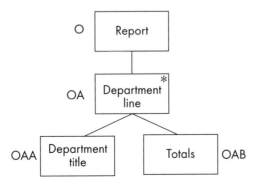

Figure 3.12 *Output structure using Jackson notation.*

A first-cut program structure can be created by merging the two data structures. The starting point is the identification of matching elements in the input and output structures. For example, IA and OA would both occur once for each department. IAA and OAA both refer to the title of the department. Thus it is likely that the same software component would be dealing with both IA and OA while another one would be dealing with IAA and OAA together. We can use these links to create a combined structure – see Figure 3.13. Note that in the combined structure the three pairs of boxes, I/O, IA/OA and IAA/OAA have all been merged.

What is interesting from a measurement and prediction point of view is that cyclomatic complexity measures can be taken of the input and output structures and the first-cut design. Taking account of the widely recognized relationship between cyclomatic complexity and size and hence development effort, a useful prediction model can be constructed.

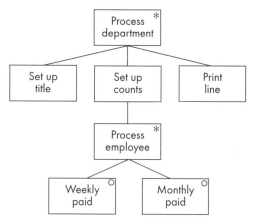

Figure 3.13 *First-cut program structure.*

3.6   Conclusions

This chapter has explored some of the attempts that have been made to quantify the internal characteristics of software. We would pick out the following important points.

- Halstead's Software Science measurements have been discredited on both empirical and theoretical grounds. However, it should be noted that the use of delivered source instructions and the number of unique operand uses (or data tokens) can by themselves be useful measurements.

- Cyclomatic complexity can be a useful measurement in the planning and assessment of testing. Outside this application area, its usefulness may be limited because of its close relationship with LOC.

- The practical use of many of the code based metrics requires the adoption of software tools to carry out the analysis. Because these tools work on programming language source code statements, they have to be language-dependent to a great extent.

3.7 References

Bache, R. and Leelasena, L. (1992), *QUALMS – A Tool For Control Flow Analysis*, Centre for Systems and Software Engineering, South Bank University, London SE1 0AA.

Cartwright, M. (1998), *An Empirical Investigation Into Metrics For Object-oriented Systems*, PhD. thesis, Bournemouth University.

Coulter, N. S. (1983), 'Software science and cognitive psychology', *IEEE Transactions on Software Engineering*: 9(2), 166–171.

Dijkstra, E. W. (1976), *A Discipline Of Programming*, Prentice-Hall, Englewood Cliffs, NJ.

Evangelist, W. M. (1982), 'Software, complexity metric sensitivity to program structuring rules', *Journal of Systems and Software*: 3, 231–43.

Fenton, N. E. and Pfleeger, S. L. (1996), *Software Metrics: A Rigorous and Practical Approach*, International Thomson Press, London.

Halstead, M. H. (1977), *Elements of Software Science*, Elsevier North-Holland, New York.

Hamer, P. G. and Frewin, G. D. (1982), 'M. H. Halstead's software science: a critical examination', *Proceedings of the 6th International Conference on Software Engineering*, 197–206 (reprinted in Shepperd, 1993).

Hughes, R. T., Young-Martos, F. and Cunliffe, A. (1999), 'The prediction of fault counts and fault density', *Project Control For Software Quality: Proceedings of ESCOM-SCOPE 99*, Shaker Publishing, Mastricht.

Jackson, M. (1975), *Principles of program design*, Academic Press, London.

Kan, S. H. (1995), *Metrics and Models in Software Quality Engineering*, Addison-Wesley, Reading, MA.

Kernighan, B. W. and Plauger, P. (1978), *The Elements of Programming Style*, McGraw-Hill, New York.

McCabe, T. J. (1976), 'A complexity measure', *IEEE Transactions on Software Engineering*: 20(4), 308–320 (reprinted in Shepperd, 1993).

Prather, R. E. (1984), 'An axiomatic theory of software complexity metrics', *Computer Journal*: 27(4), 340–347.

Prather, R. E. (1988), 'Comparison and extension of theories of Zipf and Halstead', *Computer Journal*: 31(3), 248–252.

Scanlan, D. A. (1989), 'Structural flowcharts outperform pseudocode: an experimental comparison', *IEEE Software*: September, 28–36.

Shen, V., Yu, T., Thebaut, S. and Paulsen, L. (1985), 'Identifying error-prone software: an empirical study', *IEEE Transactions on Software Engineering*: 11(4), 317–324.

Shepperd, M. J. (1988), 'A critique of cyclomatic complexity as a software metric', *Software Engineering Journal*: 3(2), 1–8.

Shepperd, M. J. (1993), *Software Engineering Metrics, Volume 1: Measures and Validations*, McGraw-Hill, Maidenhead.

3.8   Additional questions

1. A display consists of an array of 8 × 5 lights. By switching on certain of the lights, the numbers 0 to 5 can be represented in lights. Figure 3.14, for example is shown a representation of the number '2'.

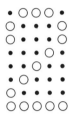

Figure 3.14 *An 8 × 5 light display.*

(i)   How much data redundancy would there be in the display?
(ii) Are there any advantages in having so much redundancy?

2. The following entries appear in a Cobol Data Division:

```
05 wa-count      pic 9(5) comp.

... ...
05 wb-result     pic $$$,$$9.99CR blank when zero.
```

In the Procedure Division, there are two statements in different places:

```
add 1 to wa-count

... ...
compute wb-result = wa-count * 0.70
```

(i)   If you are unfamiliar with Cobol, find out what the two Procedure Division statements do at run-time.
(ii) Describe how the processing involved in the add and the compute would be coded in a language like C++.
(iii) Discuss how this affects the way that counts of lines of program code should collected and compared.

3. Halstead based some of his ideas on assumptions about how the quickly someone could code an algorithm that had already been specified in detail. Devise a practical experiment to establish how long it would take the average programmer to produce code given a very detailed specification in pseudocode format. Assume that this would involve volunteers carrying out a test that would take up about an hour of their time. What variable factors would you have to take into account?

4. Below is some pseudocode for an algorithm that merges two sequential files, FileA and FileB which are both sorted into ascending order on the keys FileKeyA and FileKeyB respectively. The merged file that is created is MergedFile.

```
Open input FileA, FileB; output MergedFile;
Read FileA
IF end of FileA
THEN FileKeyA:= high-value
ENDIF;
Read FileB
IF end of FileB
THEN FileKeyB:= high-value
ENDIF;
WHILE FileKeyA <> high-value and FileKeyB <> high-value
DO
    IF FileKeyA < FileKeyB
    THEN write FileRecordA to MergedFile
        Read FileA
        IF end of FileA
        THEN FileKeyA:= high-value
        ENDIF;
    ELSE write FileRecordB to MergedFile
        Read FileB
        IF end of FileB
        THEN FileKeyB:= high-value
        ENDIF;
END-DO
Close FileA, FileB, MergedFile
```

(a) Draw up a flowgraph for the pseudocode above;
(b) Calculate the McCabe cyclomatic complexity;
(c) Calculate the Prather complexity metric;
(d) Whenever a record is read, if an end of file is detected, the particular file key is set to high values. Lines of code could be reduced by making this a called procedure. How would this change of design affect the McCabe cyclomatic complexity?

5. When testing an implementation of the algorithm described in Additional Question 4, what would be:

(i) the statement coverage,
(ii) the branch coverage

of

(a) a test set where both FileA and FileB were empty, and
(b) a test set where FileA had three records with key values of 1, 2 and 3 and FileB had three records with key values of 4, 5 and 6?

Chapter 4

How to measure software structure

OBJECTIVES

When you have completed this chapter you will be able to:

☐ recognize cases where software has a good modular structure

☐ measure the degree of cohesion in a software module

☐ measure the fan-in to and fan-out from a software module

☐ measure the degree to which software modules in a program are clustered

☐ explain and apply information flow complexity measures

4.1 Introduction

A disadvantage of many of the measurements we looked at in Chapter 3 is that because they relate to code they can only be properly taken once software has been written. Prior to that they have to be estimated. Attention has therefore turned towards measurement that relates to the quality of the design or the overall architecture of the software. At first such measurement was mainly applied to the **modularity** of software – the best way to structure and link software components so that they could be easily understood and, if need arose, modified. Latterly, the ideas behind modularity have been further developed and to some extent merged with ideas from data analysis to form the **object oriented** approach to the analysis and design of computer-based systems. While this chapter looks at the measurement of various aspects of modularity, the next examines the measurement of object oriented software.

Software engineering thinkers have been keen to identify the characteristics of good modular and good object oriented software. One way of clarifying ideas is by trying to formulate measurements of the attributes that are thought to be desirable. A danger, however, if you express your ideas quantitatively is that you open yourself to criticism of, for example, gaps in counting rules, the lack of experimental validation or your lack of a detailed theoretical model. However, you might have been simply trying to express some idea (which might be mistaken, but must be judged on its merits before being discounted), and that simply to dismiss it as 'meaningless' is to risk rejecting it prematurely.

4.2   Evaluating software engineering techniques

Where the rigoristic approach is certainly deployed usefully is in validating the claims that software engineering techniques do really lead to practical improvements, whether in more efficient software development or in better quality software. In the context of this chapter, the techniques in question would be various modularization and object oriented development techniques. Fenton and Pfleeger (1995) have commented on the claims of those advocating the use of formal methods. These require the specification of the software to be defined using a mathematical notation so that an algorithm that implements that specification can then be proved to be correct, just as at school we might have learnt to prove the correctness of Pythagoras' theorem. Fenton and Pfleeger have pointed out that there is very little empirical evidence that in practice the approach has been effective. This is not to say that the approach might not be of benefit, just that it has not been proved conclusively that in practice it is. Indeed, even with structured methods where we would expect virtually universal agreement among serious software engineers about the merits of the approach, there is in fact little statistically based evidence to show that, for instance, structured techniques lead to less errors in delivered code, or to code that is less time-consuming to modify.

Iris Vessey and Ron Weber have discussed (1984) the reasons for the difficulties in verifying the effectiveness of structured techniques. The first problem is the relative lack of models linking the internal structural attributes with the external qualities of the software, apart from some references to the 5 ± 2 short term memory limitation. It is not clear, for instance, exactly why, over a period of time, one structure should allow particular errors that have occurred operationally to be found more easily than another structure. Another problem is that software construction typically involves several phases – for example, requirements gathering, analysis, external design, internal design, coding, debugging, acceptance testing – each involving many types of task. Each of these tasks is likely to be influenced by different factors. Furthermore, the situation is complicated by the differences between new developments and different types of subsequent modification.

Exercise 4.1 Elements of the testing activity

List the different types of activity that would be undertaken by someone carrying out system testing designed to check that a software application meets the requirements set out in a user requirements document.

A typical argument, for example, is that structured techniques save on the overall development time, because less time has to be spent on debugging the software. It can, however, also be argued that structured design requires more time at the coding stage, but that this will be compensated for at the testing stage because less time will be needed for rework. To test these claims we would initially have to record the effort for these two phases: this, in itself, may be quite difficult. The timings will however be affected by many other influences as well – for example the quality of the specifications or the thoroughness of the testing that is conducted. Because of these problems, evaluation tends to be at a higher level where systems or projects as a whole are considered. This means that the low-level distinctions between different types of development task and their effect on specific characteristics of the final product tend to be ignored. It also means that the results, because they may be affected by all sorts of extraneous influences, are likely to be inconclusive.

Despite these difficulties, the need remains for the proponents of techniques such as the object oriented approach, if they are to deserve serious attention as 'engineers', to demonstrate that the techniques are genuinely useful.

In this chapter we are first going to look at the ideas behind modularity and then at the attempts to convert these ideas into measurable concepts.

4.3   The principles of modularity

The concept of modularity stems in part from the idea of **abstraction**. Quite early in the evolution of software development, it became evident that the software being commissioned was getting larger and larger, while the mental capacity of human developers remained the same. Thus it was becoming impossible for an individual programmer to comprehend the complications of many computer systems. The problem was well expressed in the title of a work by Tony Hoare, an early doyen of software engineering in the United Kingdom, *Software engineering: science or sorcery?*, which conjures up the picture of the sorcerer's apprentice summoning up powers that he is unable to control.

The proposed answer to this problem was to divide and conquer. A problem could be broken down into components that, if reasonably self-contained, would be more susceptible to solution. If needed, these components could be further sub-divided into smaller and therefore more manageable components, and so on.

For example, in statistics, a measurement of 'skew' in a set of numbers is the Pearson skew measure which is calculated as:

$$Skew = (mean - mode)/(standard\ deviation) \qquad \text{(Equation 4.1)}$$

If required to create code to calculate this measure, we could break the problem into a number of sub-problems as shown in Figure 4.1. The phrases, such as *calculate mean,* describe procedures that need to be carried out. The names in brackets describe the data upon which these procedures will operate. Where the

If the skew is zero, this reflects a normal distribution in the set of numbers. A negative number indicates a negative skew and a positive one a positive skew.

name is underlined then this means that the procedure may create or change the value. For example, *calculate mean* will read the **input parameter** *set_of_numbers*, calculate its mean and place the result in the **output parameter** *mean*.

```
calculate mean (set_of_numbers, mean);
calculate mode (set_of_numbers, mode);
calculate standard_deviation (set_of_numbers, standard_deviation);
calculate skew (mean, mode, standard_deviation, skew).
```

Figure 4.1 *Give skew: component procedures*

Exercise 4.2 Possible disadvantages of a design

What are the possible disadvantages of the design implied by the initial division into the four sub-problems shown in Figure 4.1?

The discussion of Exercise 4.2 should illustrate that there may be several different designs that can solve a particular problem. One solution might be better than another in one way, but inferior in some other. We can see, for example, that the clarity of what each function does could be at the expense of execution efficiency. One way that measurement can assist is in evaluating the respective qualities of each of several design options.

We can also see from the discussion of Exercise 4.2 that the abstraction approach that breaks down a problem into more easily handled sub-problems clearly raises questions about how elements of the designed solution are to be clustered together. We call these functional clusters **modules**.

While Alexander's book has had a great influence, many of the ideas had already been current for some time. Herbert Simon (1962), for example, had argued that systems that survive are often organized as hierarchies of loosely coupled sub-systems with internal **cohesion**.

The architectural thinker Christopher Alexander is often identified as a major influence on the ideas of software modularization through his book *Notes on the Synthesis of Form* (1964) which described how robust design solutions could be more readily arrived at by grouping requirements into relatively independent clusters. Through this clustering process, a solution to one part of the design problem could be achieved which was unlikely to have a negative impact on the other parts. Having isolated each cluster of closely related design factors, each cluster could be tackled in turn. He likened this process to those puzzles where there is a sealed transparent container with little beads which you have to get into certain holes by shaking. The secret is not to shake the container randomly, hoping that the beads will drop into the holes all in one go, but to try and deal with one bead at a time. Alexander suggested that the way that the problem could best be divided into component parts was by having an arrangement that reduced **coupling**, the connections between components to a minimum.

4.4 Modes of coupling between modules

In software, the concept of modularization and coupling and cohesion as attributes of modularity are particularly associated with Yourdon and Constantine (Yourdon

1975, Yourdon and Constantine 1979). In a software environment, modules may be coupled in a number of different ways including the following:

- **Shared data.** Modules may be considered to be coupled if they access the same data. This could be by means of **global variables** that all the modules in a program can access or via a shared database.

- **Control.** One or more of the parameters passed from one module to another are indicators or 'flags', which direct the internal processing in the called module. One module, for example, might call another to output a record to a serial file. An indicator might then be passed to the called module which communicates the fact that there are no more records to be output and that the serial file can now be closed.

- **Stamp coupling.** A complete data structure is passed. In the example in Figure 4.1 *set_of_numbers* would probably be an array. The called modules would need to be designed with a particular format in mind – for example, the number of elements in the array in Figure 4.1 is not explicitly stated in the module call and so this would have to be fixed for both the calling and the called module.

- **Data coupling.** A simple data element is passed.

It has been suggested that the list of types of coupling above is in decreasing order of tightness of coupling. For example, it would be argued that two developers of modules linked by control coupling would need to know more about the internal workings of each other's modules than two whose modules were linked by simple data coupling.

The weaker the coupling between modules the better for a number of reasons which include the following:

- work on different modules can more easily be allocated to different developers;

- when changes are required they are more likely to be confined to just one module;

- the modules created are more likely to be reusable.

The complementary quality to loose coupling is the tight internal cohesion of the modules in question. **Tight cohesion** refers to the unity of purpose of the elements within a module. Yourdon and Constantine suggested that there were seven types of cohesion. These are listed below in what was felt to be their ascending order of 'strength'.

1. **Coincidental cohesion.** Elements in modules seem to be grouped together in a way that does not seem to conform to any discernible rules.

2. **Logical cohesion.** Elements in the module carry out similar types of task. For example, you might have a module which is called to print reports. Different

elements within the module print different reports, but the reports are unrelated.

3. **Temporal cohesion.** Processes that happen to be carried out at the same time are grouped together. An example is a termination module which carries out all the various tasks that need to be executed when an application has completed its processing.

4. **Procedural cohesion.** The elements in the module have to be carried out in a predetermined order and the module controls that sequence of execution.

5. **Communication cohesion.** The components in the module operate on the same externally obtained data. A module could, for example, deal with all accesses to a certain external database.

6. **Sequential cohesion.** Results from one element in the module are used as input to another element in the module.

7. **Functional cohesion.** All the elements in a module relate to a single process.

Exercise 4.3 Types of module cohesion

(a) To what extent does the organization of the module *give skew* shown in Figure 4.1 display the following types of cohesion:

(i)   procedural cohesion,
(ii) communication cohesion,
(iii) sequential cohesion,
(iv) functional cohesion?

(b) How would the types of cohesion mentioned in (a) above be affected in the following circumstances:

(i)   the *mean* that results from the procedure *calculate mean* is used by the procedure *calculate standard deviation.*
(ii) the overall module that calls these procedures has an indicator which governs whether the mean, mode, standard deviation or skew is calculated and output.

It will be noted that, paradoxically, a module that has a high internal cohesion – which is regarded as a good thing – could well have a high coupling of the components within it – which is regarded as a bad thing!

4.5   Program slicing

Backward slices that start at the end of the software component are called **end-slices**.

The measurement of cohesion has been tackled in the technique of **program slicing**. A program slice relates to a variable and to a particular point in a program. The program slice consists of those statements that are executed up to the nominated point in the program and which in some way have affected the value of the variable. Another way of seeing a program slice is as the executable statements up to this point in the program with all the statements that do not affect the variable deleted. Strictly speaking, this is a **backward slice.** A **forward slice** is where all the statements the results of which will be affected by the current value of the nominated variable are identified.

Figure 4.2 shows how a backward slice could be constructed out of the Pascal fragment that has already been shown in Figure 3.10. The slice relates to the variable *max* at the end-point of the procedure.

```
procedure maxmin (var entry : array [1..last] of integer;
                        last : integer);
var max, min, x : integer;
begin
    max := 0;
    min :=9999;
    x := 1;
    repeat
        if entry [x] > max then
            max := entry [x];
        if entry [x] < min then
            min := entry [x];
        x := x+1
    until x > last;
    if min = max then
        writeln 'all entries are the same'
    else begin
    writeln ('maximum ',max);
    writeln ('minimum ', min)
    end
end;
```

Figure 4.2 *Example of a backward program slice in respect of the variable max at the end-point of the procedure.*

Bieman and Ott (1994) have suggested a measurement of the cohesion of software components based on program slicing concepts. They postulate that the more overlap there is between the program slices for different variables, the more the processing in the component is interwoven and cohesive.

Bieman and Ott have developed a technique based on **data slice profiles**. A data slice is a list of the **data tokens used** by a program slice. A data token is a reference to a data element which can either be a variable or a constant. In the program slice in Figure 4.2, the data slice in respect of *max* would be:

$$max_1,0_1,x_1,1_1,entry_1,x_2,max_2,max_3,entry_2,x_3,x_6,x_7,1_2,x_8,last_1$$

The subscript (which, for example, distinguishes *max₁* and *max₂*) simply allows us to identify different uses of the same variable.

Another data slice could be produced for *min*:

$$min_1,9999_1,x_1,1_1,entry_3,x_4,min_2,min_3,entry_4,x_5,x_6,x_7,1_2,x_8,last_1$$

Yet another data slice could be produced for *range*:

$$max_1,0_1,min_1,9999_1,x_1,1_1,entry_1,x_2,max_2,max_3,entry_2,x_3,entry_3,x_4,min_2,min_3,$$
$$entry_4,x_5,x_6,x_7,1_2,x_8,last_1$$

From these data slices, a data slice profile can be constructed – see Table 4.1. Where a data token is used by more than one slice, Bieman and Ott call this a **glue** token. If a token is used by all the slices then this is called a **super glue** token. In the example in Table 4.1, all tokens are glue, but only the last five are super glue.

Table 4.1   *Data slices for the Pascal fragment in Figure 4.2*

Slice	min	max	range	Slice	min	max	range
max_1	×		×	$entry_3$		×	×
0_1	×		×	x_4		×	×
min_1		×	×	min_2		×	×
9999_1		×	×	min_3		×	×
x_1	×	×	×	$entry_4$		×	×
1_1	×	×	×	x_5		×	×
$entry_1$	×		×	x_6	×	×	×
x_2	×		×	x_7	×	×	×
max_2	×		×	1_2	×	×	×
max_3	×		×	x_8	×	×	×
$entry_2$	×		×	$last_1$	×	×	×
x_3	×		×				

The **weak functional cohesion** (wfc) metric is the ratio of the glue tokens to all the tokens in the program. In our example, all tokens are glue tokens so wfc = 1.0.

Strong functional cohesion metric (sfc) is the ratio of super glue tokens to the total number of tokens. In our example this would be 5/23 or 0.213.

The most sensitive measurement of adhesiveness is calculated by summing the number of tokens that influence an output variable. In our example, the counts to be summed would be 15 for *max*, 15 for *min* and 23 for *range*, a total of 53 accesses. The maximum possible value would be the count of all the data tokens (that is 23) times the number of data slices (3) which in our example gives 69. The **adhesiveness** is therefore 53/69 = 0.77.

Bieman and Ott are at pains to explain that they would consider these measures to be good ordinal metrics which could be used, for example, to say that one module is more cohesive than another. It cannot be used as a ratio scale metric to say, for instance, that one module is twice as cohesive than another.

4.6 Graph impurity

An early attempt at measuring the relationships between modules was that of Yin and Winchester (1978). They regarded a good modular structure as one which was strictly hierarchical with no cases where the same module was called from more than one place in the program.

A structure where each module is called only once is called a **pure tree structure**. Figure 4.3 is an example representation of a pure tree structure.

Figure 4.4 illustrates an impure tree graph where module ZA is called from more than one place.

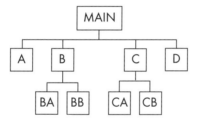

Figure 4.3 *An example of a pure tree structure.*

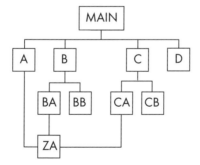

Figure 4.4 *An example of an impure tree graph.*

The number of times that a particular module is called by other modules is called its **fan-in**. In the case of a pure tree the fan-in for all modules is 1 (except for the top module where it is zero).

The **graph impurity metric** (c) is derived as:

$$c = e - n + 1 \qquad \text{(Equation 4.2)}$$

where e is the number of module calls and n is the number of modules. Attentive readers will note the similarity with the McCabe cyclomatic complexity measurement that was discussed in the last chapter. In the case of Figure 4.3, this would be $8-9+1=0$. The zero score indicates that this is a pure tree. In Figure 4.4, the score would be $11-10+1=2$ and this indicates that the hierarchy is impure.

Exercise 4.4 Graph impurity metric

Calculate the graph impurity metric for the two structures shown below:

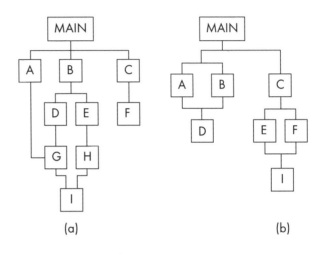

(a)   (b)

4.7 Logical ripple effect

A major motivation for the effective modularization of software is to improve its **flexibility**, the ease with which it can be changed. We hope that by having loosely coupled and tightly cohesive modules, any required changes will be restricted to one locality. One way of assessing this was suggested by Yau and his colleagues (1978) and involves examining the impact a change in one part of the software would have on other parts.

In Section 4.5, the idea of backward slicing was explored. It will be recalled that this is one of the techniques that a software developer uses to locate the source of an error. A fault will have made itself apparent at some point in the execution of the program, say at the moment when an application aborts because of an out of range value in a variable. Software maintenance staff would trace back all the manipulations in the code that have affected that variable up to the point where the fault became apparent through the abnormal termination. When, on the other hand, software maintainers want to modify the way that a variable is set at some point, they will typically perform the equivalent of **forward slicing** to discover the later processes in the code that might be affected by the change. Yau *et al.* call this **logical ripple effect analysis**. This might be done not only when implementing a necessary change, but also when evaluating the cost of a change or when weighing the safety or ease of execution of different ways of carrying out a change. A key difference between the kind of approach suggested here and that in Section 4.5 is that there the attention was centred on the internal module code, whereas here inter-module communication is taken into account.

The work of Yau and his colleagues suggested that when assessing the impact of a change, the 'complexity' of modules needs to be taken into account, but no definition of complexity was specified. As we will continue to see the question of what is meant by the term 'complexity' continues to be vexed. The suggestion of Yau *et al.* was that the effort to implement a change would depend on:

- the proportion of code to be altered in the module where the new value for the variable is to be set;

- the complexity of that module;

- the effort needed to understand the structure and code in each module that could be affected by the ripple effect;

- the effort required to design and apply any consequential changes in the modules affected by the ripple effect.

While this model helps to characterize the maintenance process and suggests how the work involved in a change to a software product can be analysed and assessed, the model is incomplete. As noted, it skirts around the key issue of how complexity is to be measured. It also puts off the question of what productivity rates can be applied to derive actual developer effort.

Another problem is that, in so far as this can be called a 'measurement' rather than a 'prediction', it would be an attribute not just of an entity *module* but also of a particular *change* to a module. Clearly, it would be possible to use the assessment technique to judge the ease of implementing sample changes in a number of different design options to see which option appears to be the most flexible. However, it can easily be imagined that certain modular structures might make one type of change easy to deal with, but another more problematic.

4.8 Cluster analysis

Hutchens and Basili (1985) suggested a measurement that did attempt the assessment of the attributes of a particular module structure.

They focused on the interfaces between modules and categorized different types of **data bindings**. A data binding is where a variable is set in one module and is then used in some way in another. A data binding is described by the notation (p,x,q) where p and q are procedures and x is a variable that is passed between them. For example, the module *CheckInput* calls another module *CheckDate* to check the format of the date. *CheckInput* passes the date to *CheckDate* and this is expressed as (*CheckInput, Date, CheckDate*). *CheckDate* may then pass back *ErrorIndicator* and this would be expressed as (*CheckDate, Indicator, CheckInput*).

Hutchens and Basili categorized four types of data binding.

- **Potential data bindings.** This is where there is the possibility that the called module might use an item of data that is passed to it but we do not know for sure whether this is the case. For example, a module might simply pass on a variable with which it has been presented to some other module.

- **Used data bindings.** Both the calling module and the called module use the variable that is passed between them. 'Use' means that either the module changes the value of the variable or that it accesses the value of the variable in some way but does not change it. In the latter case, the value might be used to calculate the value of some other variable. It could be that both modules use the variable without changing it: the key thing is that they have in common the fact that they both use the variable.

- **Actual data bindings.** Here one module has modified the value of the variable and another module references it. The variable may be passed from the modifying module to the referencing module via other modules. We are not sure, however, that data is genuinely passed between the two modules however.

- **Control flow data bindings.** This is where the data-modifying module passes control to the data-using module, so that a value does definitely seem to have been passed between the two modules.

Exercise 4.5 Data bindings

(a) In the ripple effect analysis of Yau and his colleagues, what types of data bindings are of interest?

(b) Figure 4.5 shows some pseudocode that represents an attempt to structure an algorithm to calculate the difference in days between two dates. The approach might not be the best one, but this is what we have been presented with. The *DateDifference* module calls *CheckDate* to check the format of the two dates with which it has been presented. If the dates are in the correct format then a module with the name *DateToDays* is called which converts the date with which it has been presented into the number of days since 1 January 1900. This is done for both dates and then the difference between the two dates in days is derived by subtracting one from the other. *DateToDays* works by calling another module *DayNumber* which when given a date converts it to a day number in the year, so that, for instance, 3 February would become Day 34. A FOR loop is then executed which calculates and accumulates the number of days in each year since 1900 up to the current year. This requires a module *AddDaysInYear* to be called which calculates the number of days in the year with which it has been presented and adds this number to the running total of days.

   (i) Which modules would be affected by the ripple effect if the format of the dates passed to date difference was changed from MMDDYYYY format to DDMMYYYY? What could be done, in this case, to reduce the extent of the ripple effect?

(ii) Calculate the Yin and Winchester graph impurity metric for this module structure. Is it a pure tree?

(iii) Identify the actual and control data bindings.

```
Procedure DateDifference (Date1, Date2, DifferenceInDays, ErrorInidicator);
BEGIN
    CheckDate (Date1, ErrorIndicator);
    IF ErrorIndicator = 'error'
        THEN ErrorIndicator:= 'date1 error';
    ELSE BEGIN CheckDate (Date2, ErrorIndicator)
        IF ErrorIndicator = 'error'
            THEN ErrorIndicator := 'date2 error';
        ELSE IF Date2 < Date1
            THEN ErrorIndicator = 'date1 after date2'
            ELSE DateToDays (Date1,Days1);
                DateToDays (Date2, Days2);
                DifferenceInDays := (Days2-Days1);
            END
        END
    END
END


Procedure DateToDays (Date, Days);
BEGIN
    DayNumber (Date, Days);
    FOR Year := 1900 to (year in Date -1) do
        AddDaysInYear (Year, Days);
    END
END
```
Note paramater variables that are underlined can be modified by the called module.

Figure 4.5 *DateDifference procedure.*

The next question that Hutchens and Basili had to address with this approach was how the various modules involved are clustered. Are there groups of modules where there is intense communication between the modules but little contact with modules outside the group? A large number of algorithms that analyse patterns of clustering in different contexts have been devised. Indeed, Alexander's (1964) book on architectural design contains a description of one. Hutchens and Basili favoured a method called **hierarchical clustering**.

Let us explain what this means by an example. Figure 4.6 represents the module organization of a piece of software. Each box represents a module. The numbers on the lines between the boxes are the numbers of data bindings between each pair of connected modules. Each number includes data flows in either direction.

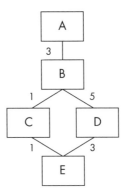

Figure 4.6 *A module structure.*

From this we can draw up a matrix showing the number of data bindings
between each module (Table 4.2). It can be seen that module D has a large number
of bindings with B and E and *vice versa*. We could use these numbers to analyse
the clustering of modules, but it has been argued that a large number of data
bindings might not be that significant if one of the modules has many bindings
with lots of other modules. This reminds me of how, at school, one's best friend
was somehow not really your best friend if he or she was every one else's best
friend as well!

Table 4.2 *Data bindings between modules in Figure 4.7*

	A	B	C	D	E	Totals
A	0	3	0	0	0	3
B	3	0	1	5	0	9
C	0	1	0	0	1	2
D	0	5	0	0	5	10
E	0	0	1	5	0	6
Totals	3	9	2	10	6	30

To get around this problem, Hutchens and Basili suggested that the dissimilarity
between modules x and y could be assessed by first calculating the number of data
bindings that both x and y have:

$$\text{sum } (x \text{ bindings}) + \text{sum } (y \text{ bindings}) - (\text{bindings of } x \text{ and } y \text{ together})$$

In Table 4.2, for example, if we take modules B and D we can get the x bindings
by looking at the column total for B (9) and the row total for D (10). If we were to
add these together we would double-count the 5 at the intersection of the B column
and the D row and so this needs to be subtracted.

The 5 at the intersection of B and D represents the number of connections between the two modules. We want now to measure the 'connectedness' of the two modules with the outside world. We do this by subtracting the number of connections between B and D from the count of all the connections between B or D and other modules.

To find the number of data bindings of x and y with other modules, where x and y are not *both* involved, we have:

sum (x bindings) + sum (y bindings) − (2 × bindings of x and y together)

We can now measure the degree of dissimilarity of x and y:

(sum of bindings of x and y with other modules)/(sum of bindings of x and y)

In the cases of modules B and D, this would be:

$$((9+10) - (2 \times 5))/9 + 10 - 5 = 9/14 = 0.64$$

We can repeat this calculation for each pair of modules and get the results shown in Table 4.3. This suggests, for example, that modules D and E ought to be regarded as more tightly coupled than B and D, because B's relationship with D is diluted not only by its relationship with C but also with A.

If D and E are regarded as one cluster, a new data bindings table can be drawn up – see Table 4.4 – and the process of calculating dissimilarities between modules and thus identifying those that are clustered can continue.

Table 4.3 *Degrees of dissimilarity between modules in Figure 4.7*

	A	B	C	D	E
A	1	0.66	1	1	1
B	0.66	1	0.9	0.9	1
C	1	0.9	1	1	0.85
D	1	0.64	1	1	0.54
E	1	1	0.86	0.86	1

Table 4.4 *Data bindings between modules in Figure 4.7 after combining modules D and E*

	A	B	C	D/E	
A	0	3	0	0	3
B	3	0	1	5	9
C	0	1	0	1	2
D/E	0	5	1	0	6
	3	9	2	6	20

'Dendrogram' simply means a diagram with branches like a tree.

The findings of these calculations can be put into a form of diagram called a **dendrogram** by Hutchens and Basili. In Figure 4.8 there is an example of one derived from the structure in Figure 4.6.

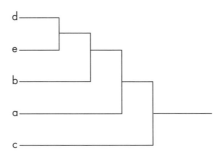

Figure 4.7 *Dendrogram of the module structure in Figure 4.7.*

Hutchens and Basili suggested that such dendrograms could be used to identify particular types of module organization. They likened dendrograms to star clusters. **Planetary systems** are where modules seem to be clustered into low-level sub-systems which are then clustered into higher level groups and so on. A **black hole** is where one particular cluster seems to be predominant and other modules are clustered around it. In our small example, module D seems to have this characteristic. A final type of arrangement that is identified is the **gas cloud** where no obvious clusters of modules emerge from the analysis. Hutchens and Basili suggest that this may be an indication of poor design, but why this should necessarily be the case is not explained.

One drawback of the techniques of clustering analysis is that different clustering algorithms produce different results. The method we have described does not take into account the direction of data flows or whether one module is calling or being called by the other module in the pair. As Hutchens and Basili themselves point out, re-use can distort the apparent pattern of clustering. Where there are modules carrying out utility functions, like the date checking module we encountered earlier, the fact that different modules call that utility does not indicate that those calling modules are logically connected even though the clustering algorithm could suggest that this is so.

As can be imagined, clustering algorithms tend to be quite complicated and require iterations of the calculations for each level of the hierarchy analysed. This really demands automated analysis using a software tool. As noted before, this can be problematic as different versions of the tools will be required for different programming language environments.

Given these problems, the question arises of how much really useful information is provided by cluster analysis. It seems that an understanding of certain aspects of module organization can be generated, given the existence of a suitable tool to produce the information. However, little can be gleaned from the analysis about the real merits or otherwise of the organization without further examination.

4.9 Information flow complexity metrics

Sallie Henry and Dennis Kafura (1984) adopted a different approach which did result in a measurement that allowed different designs to be put into some order of merit. Part of their work was based on an analysis of the code in the UNIX operating system in relation to its change history. They identified the information flows between modules in the system. Some of these flows were **direct local flows** between modules, as when one module calls another and passes one or more parameters. Module *DateDifference* calls module *CheckDate* passing *Date1* as a parameter in Figure 4.6 for example. Other information flows could be **indirect local flows** where one module calls another and passes a variable to it which it has obtained from another module but which it has not modified in the process. For instance, in Figure 4.5, module *DatetoDays* passes the variable *Days* which has been set initially by the module *DayNumber* to module *AddDaysInYear*. Hence there is an indirect flow between modules *AddDaysInYear* and *DayNumber*. Finally there are global flows where one module creates or modifies a variable in some global data store, such as a database, which another module then accesses.

As noted earlier, the **fan-in** of a module is the number of local flows that are received by that module. **Fan-out is** the number of local flows that are initiated by the module in question.

'Fan-in' was referred to in the discussion of the Yin-Winchester metric.

In Figure 4.5, what are the fan-out and fan-in for each procedure/module?

Exercise 4.6 Fan-in and fan-out

Note that a module can have data flows from a calling module or via a value returned to it when it calls another module. Identifying indirect flows can be a problem unless the internal workings of the modules in question are known. We have already pointed out that in the *DateDifference* example there is an indirect information flow between *AddDaysInYear* and *DateDifference* via the *Date1/Date* variable. The fact that variable *Date1* is not modified by *DateToDays* can only be established by examining the code in this intermediate module.

To calculate the **information flow complexity**, Kafura and Henry specified the following model:

$$\text{Flow complexity} = (\text{lines of code}) \times (\text{fan-in} \times \text{fan-out})^2$$

The results of applying this to the module in our example can be seen in Table 4.5. The lines of code figures are one that have been estimated.

The results for each component can then be summed to get an overall figure for the whole program. The intrusion of lines of code into the model seems to be mixing two different measurements and also detracts from the advantage of the information flow complexity measurement that it can be calculated, at least provisionally, from design documents.

Darryl Ince and Martin Shepperd (1989) have found other problems with this metric. While on the face of it the Henry–Kafura metric seems relatively straight-

Using lines of code might make for a better *model* for predicting other attributes of the software, but that is not the same as a *measurement*.

Table 4.5 *Information flow complexity measurements*

Modules	Fan-in	Fan-out	Lines of code	IF complexity
DateDifference	6	6	35	45360
Checkdate	2	2	49	784
DateToDays	3	5	30	6750
DayNumber	1	1	30	30
AddDaysInYear	2	1	32	128

forward, closer examination finds some ambiguities. Echoing an earlier observation of Barbara Kitchenham (1988) they had difficulties, as we have had, in tracing indirect information flows. They therefore suggested that this element be dropped. They also suggested that values passed by a global variable should be treated in just the same way as those passed by means of parameters. The original Henry–Kafura metric seemed to penalize reuse: if a utility routine such as a date-checking module were called from several places in a program structure, then the counts of the parameters in each individual call were accumulated. Ince and Shepperd recommended that while each parameter call should be counted individually as part of fan-out, for the called module they should be counted just once. The use of lines of code in the calculation of the measurement was also dropped. For Ince and Shepperd, the important fact was that data was passed between two modules, the actual number of variables passed was immaterial. Ince and Shepperd's work had looked at several variations of the information flow metric and their recommended model was a variant that they had labelled as IF4.

Ince and Shepperd then needed to have some way of testing out the predictive power of IF4. It is worth looking at how they did this as it illustrates nicely the practical problems of empirical validation. The first validation exercise was using student group projects. Ince and Shepperd obtained a 0.80 correlation between IF4 measurements and effort which contrasted with 0.43 for the original Henry–Kafura metric. There are some grounds for caution with this finding. 'Effort' was not the total effort used for development, but was measured as on-line connect time. Hence, the time used for desk design, for example, was excluded. Almost universally, a strong positive correlation would be expected between lines of code and development effort, but in this case the negative correlation of -0.21 seemed to imply that more code required less effort. It is possible to make up explanations to rationalize this away. Perhaps better design, which might have needed more effort, would have led to more reuse and thus less code. However, better design would also presumably lead to looser coupling between modules and fewer information flows, but a high positive correlation was found between effort and IF4.

The purpose of these comments is not to undermine this validation, but to illustrate how even with relatively simple development environments, the interactions between different aspects of the development process can be quite complicated. Our own experience with attempting to predict development effort is that effort prediction for smaller projects can be more difficult in some ways than for larger projects because there are many unpredictable factors associated with project start-up. Once a substantial project is under way, the pattern of the true productivity influences, related to task size, can emerge.

The use of student projects attracts criticism on the not unreasonable grounds that they are not real projects. However, getting hold of real practitioners who are gripped by the demands of real development is difficult, while researchers who happen to be based in a university have easy access to student guinea pigs. Student projects do allow initial trials to be carried out and are valuable where the link between the measurement and the thing being measured is tightly coupled: tests of the meaningfulness of variable names might be a good example of this. Where the experiment is concerned with more complex developmental issues, then the relevance of student simulation looms large as a question.

Subsequently (Shepperd, 1990), another validation exercise was carried out in an industrial setting. Four software engineers were asked to rate the maintainability of 89 modules in a real-time control system using a four point scale. The raters were only in complete agreement in 10% of the cases, but generally the researcher felt subjectively that there was a good enough correspondence between the judgements of the four engineers. The scores of the engineers were summed for each module. A Spearman rank correlation of 0.70 was found between the summed subjective scores for each module and the IF4 measurement. However, a correlation of 0.70 might indicate a relationship, but it does not encourage a strong belief in IF4 as a *measurement* rather than a *predictor*. Having said that, the general approach of comparing the subjective judgements of different engineering professionals to establish whether the candidate attribute is one about which there is general agreement among practitioners seems an excellent one. The comparison of the subjective judgements with the results of using a putative measurement seems to go to the root of the issue of the validity of software measurements. We would certainly urge that the approach was extended to other candidate measurements.

It was noted in Chapter 2 that adding together ordinal measurements is normally not recommended.

Our own view is that the IF4 measurement has much merit. Even so, the multiplication of the numbers of input and output flows in both the original Henry–Kafura metric and the later Shepperd–Ince variation has been criticized by Barbara Kitchenham et al. (1995) as confusing two different attributes, fan-in and fan-out. We do not necessarily see this as a problem as it would seem to us that information flow complexity is an indicator of the potential *internal* complexity of a module. For example, given three inputs and four outputs to a module, the potential number of links between inputs and outputs would be $3 \times 4 = 12$. This represents only potential links because in reality not all possible links between inputs and outputs will exist. One way of reducing this potential complexity is through decomposition which eliminates some of the potential links – see Figure 4.8.

Ince and Hekmatour (1988) developed a tool to assist software design based on this principle. They noted that as a design is decomposed into smaller components,

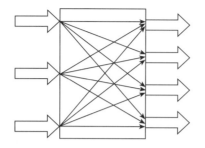   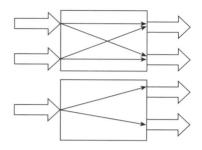

3 x 4 = 12 potential input-output links   2 x 2 + 2 x 1 = 6 potential input-output links

Figure 4.8   *The effect of decomposition on potential input–output links.*

a point is reached where further decomposition does not result in any reduction in complexity. An obvious application of this would be in the decomposition of top level data flow diagrams.

4.10 Conclusions

This chapter has explored the ways in which the qualities in particular arrangements of components within a software program can be assessed using various types of measurement.

It will have been seen that in some cases – and the graph impurity is one example – the relevant measurement is relatively easy to derive, but it is difficult to use that information to draw useful conclusions.

We have seen that various measurements can be taken to assess the cohesiveness and coupling of modules. We have once again seen how measurement can be hampered by the lack of counting rules that can be applied objectively and accurately in all circumstances.

In Chapter 5 we will see how many of the ideas concerning the measurement of modularity have been further developed to deal with object oriented systems and their development.

4.11 References

Alexander, C. (1964), *Notes on The Synthesis of Form*, Harvard University Press, Cambridge, MA.

Bieman, J. M. and Ott, L. M. (1994), 'Measuring function cohesion', *IEEE Transactions on Software Engineering*: 20(8), 644–657.

Fenton, N. E. and Pfleeger, S. L. (1995), *Software metrics: a rigorous and practical approach*, International Thomson Computer Press, London.

Henry, S. and Kafura, D. (1984), 'The evaluation of software systems' structure using quantitative software metrics', *Software Practice and Experience*: 14(6), 561–73. This can be found in Shepperd (1993).

Hutchens, D. H. and Basili, V. R. (1985), 'System structure analysis: clustering with data bindings', *IEEE Transactions in Software Engineering*: 11(8), 749–757. This can be found in Shepperd (1993).

Ince, D. and Hekmatpour, S. (1988), 'An approach to automated software design based on product metrics', *Software Engineering Journal*: 32(2), 53–56.

Ince, D. and Shepperd, M. (1989), 'An empirical and theoretical analysis of an information flow based design metric', *Procs. European Software Engineering Conference,* 86–99 This can be found in Shepperd (1993).

Kitchenham, B. A. (1988), 'An evaluation of software structure metrics', *Procs. COMPSAC, 88,* Chicago.

Kitchenham, B. A., Pfleeger, S. L. and Fenton, N. (1996), 'Towards a framework for software measurement validation', *IEEE Transactions in Software Engineering*: 22(1), 68–86.

Shepperd, M. (1990), 'Early life-cycle metrics and software quality models', *Information and Software Technology*: 32(4), 311–316.

Shepperd, M. (ed) (1993), *Software Engineering Metrics Volume 1: Measures and Validations*, McGraw-Hill, Maidenhead.

Simon, H. (1962), 'The architecture of complexity' in *Proc. Amer. Phil*: 106, 467–482, December.

Vessey, I. and Weber, R. (1984), 'Research on structured programming: an empiricist's evaluation', *IEEE Transactions in Software Engineering*: 10(4), 397–407.

Yau, S. S., Collofello, J. S. and McGregor, T. M. (1978), 'Ripple effect analysis of software maintenance', *Procs. COMPSAC 78,* 60–65. This can be found in Shepperd (1993).

Yin, B. H. and Winchester, J. W. (1978), 'The establishment and use of measures to evaluate the quality of designs', *Procs. of ACM Software Quality Workshop*, 45–52.

Yourdon, E. (1975), *Techniques of program structure and design*, Prentice-Hall, Englewood Cliffs.

Yourdon, E. and Constantine, L. (1979), *Structured design*, Prentice-Hall, Englewood Cliffs, NJ.

4.12 Additional questions

1. Identify the type of cohesiveness that is exhibited by each of the three procedures that are represented in pseudocode below.

   (a) ConvertTemp(<u>celsius</u>, fahrenheit, indicator)

```
IF indicator = 'celsius'
THEN celsius:= (fahrenheit - 32) / 9 * 5;
ELSE
    IF indicator = 'fahrenheit'
    THEN fahrenheit:= (celsius * 5 / 9) + 32;
```

```
        ELSE
            Display('invalid indicator');
        ENDIF
    ENDIF
```

(b)   `ErrorMessage(errorInd)`

```
CASE errorInd OF
0: display 'input not numeric';
1: display 'input not alphabetic';
2: display 'input blank';
3: display 'invalid date'
ENDCASE
```

(c)   `ConvertCurrency(FromCurType,ToCurType,FromAmount, ToAmount)`

```
ObtainRateTable(Rates);
ChooseRate(ConversionRate,Rates,FromCurType,ToCurType);
ToAmount:=FromAmount * ConversionRate;
```

2. Assuming that each called module is self-contained and does not call any other module, what would be the Yin-Winchester graph impurity measurement for the *Give skew* algorithm in Figure 4.1.

   A software developer is asked to modify the software that implements the algorithm in Figure 4.1 in the following ways:

   (i)   depending on the value of a parameter that is passed to the module, either the mean, mode, standard deviation or skew is calculated;
   (ii) a new sub-module is introduced *Calculate median* which can be executed if the input parameter indicates that there is a request to do this;
   (iii) the *Calculate skew* sub-module will now call *Calculate mean*, *Calculate mode*, and *Calculate standard deviation* directly to carry out intermediate calculations;
   (iv) both *Calculate mode* and *Calculate median* will call a module *Sort numbers* which puts a set of numbers into ascending order.

   Draw up a module structure diagram that reflects these changes and calculate the Yin-Winchester graph impurity metric for the new structure.

3. The diagram in Figure 4.9 represents that module structure of a piece of software. The number by each of the lines represents the count of the parameters that pass in either direction between the two modules concerned.

   • Calculate the degrees of dissimilarity between the modules using the Hutchens–Basili method.

   • Which pair of modules is most closely bound together according to this measurement?

4. Calculate the IF4 metric for the revised module structure created in Additional Question 2. Try modifying the structure to make it more efficient, flexible or understandable. Calculate the IF4 metric for the revised structure and compare it to the old one.

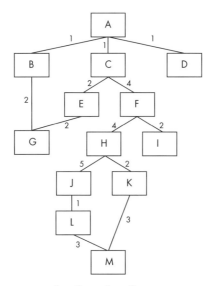

Figure 4.9 *Module structure for Question 3.*

5. Figure 4.10 shows the module structure for a program which accepts the name of an author from the operator. It then accesses a table of author details and if it cannot find the name of the author on that file, issues an error message. Otherwise, it accesses a table of book titles and for each title it counts the number of copies. Calculate the IF4 for the structure.

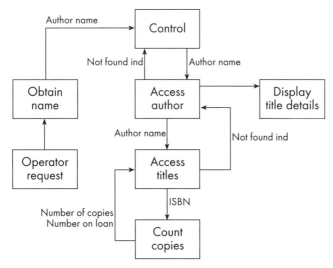

Figure 4.10 *Diagram for Question 5.*

6. Explain how a measurement like IF4 could be incorporated into a CASE tool which was used to record Data Flow Diagrams. Could IF4 be further simplified for this purpose?

7. It would be very convenient if a software tool could be created which automatically calculated IF4. Outline the features of such a tool.

Chapter 5

How to measure object-oriented software

OBJECTIVES

When you have completed this chapter you will be able to:

☐ identify the key characteristics of the object-oriented approach;

☐ show awareness of the factors that affect the transition to a new technology;

☐ measure some of the important attributes of classes in object-oriented systems using the Chidamber–Kemerer suite of metrics;

☐ identify some supplementary metrics that may be useful in the assessment of object-oriented systems.

5.1 Introduction

In this chapter we will explain how many of the ideas associated with a modular approach to software development have been developed into the object-oriented (OO) approach. What is meant by OO will be briefly reviewed. The developing role of OO is an example of the adoption of a new technology and the general implications of such shifts will be touched upon. The degree to which this shift in development methods has meant that new types of software measurement are required will be explored. There has been what amounts practically to an explosion in proposed metrics for OO. We will concentrate on a suite of metrics that have been proposed by Chidamber and Kemerer (1991) as they have probably been the most widely tested and discussed of these new metrics. Although this set of metrics was very carefully thought out it is inevitable that others should find room for improvements to it. Some of these suggestions will be examined. Finally, some examples of the practical application of OO metrics will be described.

It will be seen later in this chapter that regarding OO as simply a development of structured methods has its dangers.

5.2 What is OO?

In one way, object orientation can be seen as a development of the practice in structured systems analysis and design methods of structuring the data that a computer application needs to access and manipulate by organizing it so that it models the corresponding objects in the 'real world'. These entities may be physical entities, such as a person or a car, or more conceptual objects, such as a bank account.

This well-established idea has been combined with a principle, more oriented towards software engineering, that you can categorize an item of data by the types of operation that can be executed upon it. An obvious example is that you cannot do arithmetic on a person's name. A common type of programming error is the use of inappropriate operations on a particular type of variable. It has been realized that these errors can be eliminated by devising mechanisms, such as **abstract data types**, that bind the permitted operations closely to the data and that allow the data to be accessed or manipulated only by means of these permitted operations.

Similar considerations can be applied to entities. The attributes of an entity will have a constrained range of changes that may be validly applied to them. To be valid, these changes might have to have certain preconditions – for example, *marital status* can only be set to 'divorced' if it was previously 'married'. Additionally there may be rules enforcing consistency so that, for instance, *age* has to be consistent with *date of birth*. It therefore makes sense to bind in the permitted operations, or **methods**, with the entity itself to make an **object**. Strictly speaking, an object is a specific instance of a **class**, so that for example 'Jane Austen' might be an object belonging to the class *person,* and it is with the class that the methods are associated.

The major concepts associated with the OO paradigm include the following.

- **Abstraction** – the identification of the common characteristics of a group of objects in order to form a class with the shared characteristics.

- **Encapsulation** – a development of the idea of **information hiding**. An object is only accessible through a predetermined interface. Thus the precise way in which variables are structured and the detail of the mechanisms by which they are actually manipulated can be concealed from the user of that object. As long as the behaviour of the interface is unchanged, the underlying mechanisms can be changed at will.

- **Inheritance** – a class can be part of a larger class. For example, *car* may belong to a higher level **superclass**, *vehicle*. A class can also be divided into subclasses so that the *person* class could have the subclasses *employee* and *customer. Person* may have certain attributes such as *name*, *address*, *date of birth* and methods to access and manipulate them. The class *employee* would inherit these attributes and their methods, but would also include other ones such as *salary grade* and *pay to date* along with their methods. The class *customer* could equally inherit the attributes and methods of *person* but could incorporate other attributes such as *credit rating* and *amount outstanding*. One motivation for the use of inheritance is the hope that it might lead to economic savings through the increased code reuse that the ability to inherit methods might bring.

- **Polymorphism** – a method belonging to a class would be executed when a request to carry out a particular service is made to an object belonging to that class. Polymorphism allows the same type of request to be made to different classes and for each class to deal with that request in its own way. In the example shown in Figure 5.1 which represents a fragment of an application for a library system, *display details* would have a different result if the library holding was *printed material,* such as a book, as opposed to *recorded material* such as an audio tape of a musical performance. This is because, in this case, the two subclasses have different attributes.

The advocates of OO would see it not merely as a technical development from structured methods but also as being radically different in its management philosophy. Proponents of OO advocate the **incremental construction** of software so that the application is partitioned into clusters of classes each of which can be made to work in turn.

Rather than the strict sequential development broken down into clearly demarcated phases that is characterized by the waterfall model, rapid iterations between analysis, design and coding are envisaged. This is said to erode, to some extent, the traditional divisions between analyst, designer and code developer.

OO can be seen as a natural companion to other alternative approaches to the waterfall model such as the use of **rapid application development** (RAD) and **time-boxing**. RAD attempts to remove the delays to system development caused by obstacles to fast communication and negotiation between system developers and the users of a system (or at least their representatives). RAD employs intensive workshops where development and user staff get together to thrash out the requirements for the proposed application in a highly concentrated and interactive process. Time-boxing is a complementary technique where the amount of functionality to be delivered to the customers for an application is constrained by a fixed delivery date – if certain features cannot be developed in time they have to be left to the next increment. This highly dynamic environment needs careful and intelligent management and control and appropriate measurement can be seen as playing an important role in this.

As has been noted already, another distinctive feature of the OO approach is the emphasis on the economic savings that should accrue from increased use of existing components. **Reuse**, however, is not without cost as effort has to be put into creating generally usable components and into the construction and maintenance of libraries of reusable components. Measurement has an important role to play here, particularly in ensuring that the effort that is put into reuse is justified.

5.3   The adoption of OO as a new technology

When a new development technique emerges in information technology (IT), its proponents will usually declare that it represents a revolutionary new step that sweeps away outmoded and inefficient ways of doing things. It is typical that others will comment that the ideas have already been around for decades, or can be seen as a natural progression from previously existing ideas. Robert Fichman and Chris Kemerer in 1993 published a paper reviewing the factors that have been identified as affecting the adoption of new techniques and in particular examining how these factors might affect the uptake of OO.

One of their sources was Everett Rogers (1983) who had reviewed hundreds of examples of the diffusion of new techniques and products and who had identified five attributes of a product that could influence its uptake:

Relative advantage. This is the extent to which the innovation is technically superior to the thing that it supersedes.

Compatibility. This is the extent to which the new technique fits into the new environment, including the skills and work practices of potential adopters.

Complexity. This is the degree to which the new technique is difficult to understand and use.

Trialability. Can the new technique be realistically trialled without excessive cost? Can the new technique be introduced in increments and still yield improvements and benefits?

Observability. Can the impact of the new techniques be easily observed and communicated to others?

What is noteworthy is that all these factors could be the subject of measurement activities. In order to assess the effectiveness of a new technology we would like to do the following.

- Identify the improvements or benefits that the new technology is said to bring and devise ways of measuring those benefits – for example, the technology might be said to improve productivity. Some way of measuring the current productivity would then need to be found in order to establish a **baseline**.

- Introduce the new technology on a trial basis and measure its outcomes, for example its effect on productivity.

- Assess the actual costs of the new technology.

- Compare the actual costs with the improvements the new technology has brought compared to the baseline situation.

The results of such an assessment will not be wholly conclusive. First, productivity is likely to be decreased on the first use of a technique because of the existence of **learning curves**. There might, however, be an opposite tendency: the **Hawthorne effect** where because development staff feel they are 'special' as they are pioneering a new technique they might be more motivated and productive than would be the case once the new way of working has settled in.

However, adoption of a new technique does not depend solely on its innate qualities. There are external considerations that we will explore very briefly to illustrate that conventional measurement techniques with their focus on what happens within the software process do have limitations in their usefulness to managers. Basically, a manager contemplating a new technology will have to consider certain **environmental factors**.

1. **Prior technology drag.** The old technology may still have advantages that outweigh the benefits of the new one because of the large number of users and developers with expertise in that technology. This would mean that it is easier (and probably cheaper) to recruit staff with experience in the old technology.

2. **Irreversibility of investment.** Does the new technology require large investments in structural changes? If the answer is yes, then adoption is risky. The new technique may be better, but there is a risk that an organization might be stranded if no other organization adopts the technology.

3. **Sponsorship.** Is there a recognized authority which exists to define the technology, set standards and promote the exchange of information on the new technology? In the case of OO for example a problem for potential adopters is that there are several different methodologies from which to choose.

4. **Expectations.** Is there a generally held expectation that the technology is going to become pervasive?

New technologies are thus inevitably accompanied by 'hype'. Some of this will come from entrepreneurs hoping to profit from the sales of goods and services related to the new technology. Much of it, however, will come from the adopters of the new technology who, while they wish to hold a competitive edge as early adopters, do not want to become stranded in a technological cul-de-sac.

Within the general tidal movement in the adoption of a new technology there will be local eddies and whirls. There will be some individual successes and some disasters. Improvements might be difficult to measure at first because often there is an initial drop in productivity, noted above, when a new technique is adopted while practitioners learn to use the methods effectively and efficiently. Realistic measurement may be able to guide managers in the successful adoption of new technologies such as OO. Many of the measurement techniques that are relevant here relate to the general monitoring and control of process improvements and are dealt with in a later chapter.

A journal article by Chris Kemerer (1992) has a useful discussion about how the learning curve for a new technology might be measured.

5.4 Some preliminary difficulties with OO metrics

Some difficulties that we are going to encounter with attempting measurement in an OO environment include the following.

1. There is no one authoritative and precise definition of what object orientation actually is. If OO techniques are seen as a set of desirable practices then there can be disagreement over what these practices actually are.

2. Following on the first point, it might not be clear whether a software product is genuinely object-oriented. For example, just because a program is written in

C++ does not mean necessarily that it has all the characteristics regarded as desirable in object-oriented code.

3. Different OO development methods have different procedures and products.

4. Different programming languages and tools have different features that support different aspects of OO.

This will mean that it is difficult to develop a single set of measurement types that will be equally applicable across the whole range of OO development methods and products.

5.5   Can conventional metrics be used with OO applications?

One researcher into OO metrics has stated that the idea that 'traditional metrics' could be applied successfully to object-oriented software is intuitively implausible. However, it seems to us that there is some plausibility in the application of 'traditional metrics' to OO applications. In the end, all software code ends up as machine instructions regardless of the way that it has been constructed and all applications, however built, should allow the users of the final product to execute transactions. At these levels at least, the highest and the lowest, existing metrics would seem to remain valid and even useful as they would allow software constructed in OO and non-OO ways to be compared.

The main reason why conventional measurements might not be directly applicable is that the main entity of interest is now a **class** rather than a **module**. Many of the OO measurements that have been proposed such as those of Chidamber and Kemerer (1991, 1994) are thus concerned with classes.

5.6   Categorizing OO metrics

Looking at the work done on the development of OO metrics, it is easy to become overwhelmed by the sheer volume of measurements that have been suggested. In this chapter we are not going to attempt to describe the full range of possible measurements. Fernando Abreu and Rogério Carapuça (1994) have produced a useful taxonomy of OO metrics which can help us to place some order on the mass of candidate measurements available. We will then examine a suite of six metrics proposed by Chidamber and Kemerer as it has been the most influential set of measurements in this area to date. This will be followed by a very brief discussion of some of the other measurements that have been suggested. We will conclude the chapter by looking at some examples of the practical application of these measurements.

It is claimed that TAPROOT stands for 'TAxonomy PRecis for Object-oriented meTrics'!

Abreu and Carapuça have devised what they have named the TAPROOT framework for categorizing OO metrics which has two axes: **granularity** and **category**. Granularity refers to the level at which measurements are taken; there are three of these identified: **system**, **class** and **method**. Category refers to the particular high level properties of the product or process that the metric is trying to capture. Table 5.1.shows the categories suggested by Abreu and Carapuça and the identifiers they use to label different groups of metrics. One drawback of this taxonomy is that while some of the categories relate to products – for example, complexity – others, such as productivity, relate to processes.

Table 5.1 *TAPROOT classification framework*

	Method	Class	System
Design	MD	CD	SD
Size	MS	CS	SS
Complexity	MC	CC	SC
Reuse	MR	CR	SR
Productivity	MP	CP	SP
Quality	MQ	CQ	SQ

How would you categorize the following metrics according to the TAPROOT framework?

Exercise 5.1 Classifying metrics

(i)   the number of lines that constitute an application;
(ii) number of methods inherited by a class;
(iii) average number of methods per class in a system.

The examples that they give of possible measurement types are a mixture of existing measurement types that have been developed for conventional systems and specialized OO measurements. For example, for size the metrics in Table 5.2 are suggested.

Table 5.2 *TAPROOT classification of size measurements*

Method type	Examples
SS System size	Number of classes Number of methods Number of attributes
CS Class size	Number of methods Number of attributes Size of class interface – number of different types of message that may be sent to a class
MS Method size	Number of executable statements Number of operators and operands Number of attributes used

Exercise 5.2 and the explanation of OO metrics that follows will use the example shown in Figure 5.1. Note that in that diagram, each of the boxes represents a class. Where there is an arrowed line between boxes, this indicates that there is an inheritance relationship between the two classes. It can be seen, for example, that *loan item* (items that can be lent to borrowers) and *copy item* (items of which copies can be given to library users but not the original) are both subclasses of the superclass *holding*. It should be noted that in a fuller and more realistic object model there would also be relationships that do not involve inheritance. For example, the users of the system when issuing of a loan would need to carry out a transaction that would associate a borrower with a loan.

In this fragment of an object model, all subclasses are descended for the class *holding*. Every holding has the attributes *acquisition number*, *title*, *acquisition date* and *removal date* (the last of which will be initially null). The methods which can manipulate the values of these attributes are *acquire holding* which creates a new object in the class of *holding*, *amend title* and *remove holding*, which sets the removal date. Holdings can be categorized into two subclasses, *loan item* and *copy item*: loan items may be actually lent to borrowers while copy items always remain in the library though copies of it can be made. In the case of copy items, the *number of copies* attribute has to be updated so that the requisite fees can be paid to the owners of the intellectual property rights involved. Loan items are, at present, either books (class *printed material*) or audio recordings (class *recorded material*) while copy items are either *sheet music* or *journal articles*. In the case of printed material items may be loaned out on *long loans, short loans* or *desk loans* depending on the demand for the item. In this scenario some necessary details are clearly missing. We have purposely kept things simple to assist clarity.

Exercise 5.2 OO system size measurements   Work out the system size measurements, as suggested by Abreu and Carapuça, for the fragment of an object model shown in Figure 5.1.

5.7   Chidamber–Kemerer OO metrics suite

The first major attempt at suggesting measurements applicable to OO was that of Chidamber and Kemerer (1991). They suggested six metrics.

5.7.1 Weighted methods per class (WMC)

This can be simply a count of the methods in each class if it can be assumed that each method is of similar complexity. Alternatively, a measurement such as a line of code count or cyclomatic complexity can be extracted for each method and used as a weighting so that account can be taken of the relative 'complexity' or size of each method. It should be noted that only the methods defined for the class in question and not those that are inherited are counted. In the example in Figure 5.1, *holding* has four methods, *loan item* has two methods and *copy item* has three

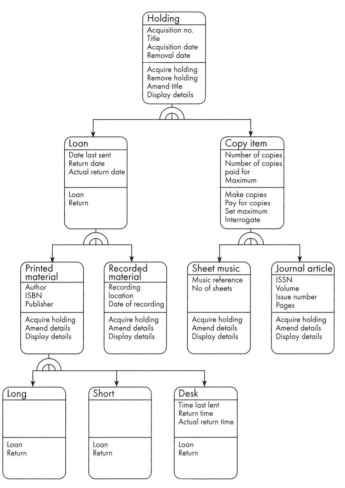

Figure 5.1 *An object model of a fragment of a system for a library.*

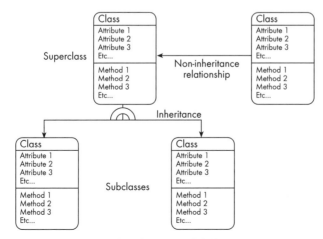

Figure 5.2 *Notation used for the object model diagram.*

methods. If no account is to be taken of the relative complexity of each method, then these numbers will be the WMC for these methods.

Exercise 5.3 Weighted methods per class
What are the WMC values for the remaining classes? Assume that each method counts as 1.

We have already noted that a subclass will inherit the methods from the higher level classes in its inheritance tree – these inherited methods are not counted for the subclass. It can also be seen that there are methods with the same name, *display details* for example, that are associated with a number of distinct classes. These are examples of polymorphism. The methods execute analogous but different procedures, so that *display details* will cause different details to be displayed in the case of the class *sheet music* and the class *journal article*. Because each of these is a different process, they are each counted individually. Other methods with the same name appear in different classes in the same inheritance tree. For example, the classes *long loan* and *short loan* both have *loan* as a method. Here the methods in *long loan* and *short loan* override the original definition of the method in the *loan item* class and as new procedures are counted as methods in their own right. Lorenz and Kidd (1994) recognize these different sets of circumstances and suggest that the WMC metric be supplemented by a count of the number of methods overridden by a class (NORM) and the number of methods added by a class (NAM).

If lines of code were used to gauge complexity in the calculation of WMC then the WMC of a class would be the number of lines of code used to implement the class. It is therefore clear that WMC is strongly related to the idea of class size.

5.7.2 Depth of inheritance tree (DIT)

DIT relates to a specific class and is the number of levels of superclass from which it can inherit methods. If it inherits methods from more than one class at the same level – that is, is subject to **multiple inheritance** – the number of classes in the longest branch is used.

In the example in Figure 5.1, DIT for the class *sheet music* would be 2 and for *long loan* would be 3.

Exercise 5.4 Depth of inheritance
What would be the DIT for each of the remaining classes in Figure 5.1?

The potential usefulness of this was demonstrated by Michelle Cartwright (1998) who analysed C++ software that had been written for a telecommunications application. It was found that the highest defect densities found were for classes at the lowest level of their respective inheritance trees and which would therefore have higher DIT values. This echoed an earlier experience recorded by Letjer *et al.* (1992).

5.7.3 Number of children (NOC)

This is the number of immediate subclasses that belong to a specific class in the class hierarchy. In Figure 5.1, in the case of the class *loan item* it is 2 – *printed material* and *recorded material* – while in the case of the class *printed material* it is 3 – *long loan*, *short loan* and *desk loan*.

What are the NOC values for the remaining classes in Figure 5.1?

Exercise 5.5 Number of children

Chidamber and Kemerer suggest that the NOC values will be significant because classes with large numbers of children could indicate:

- considerable reuse – as inheritance is a form of reuse;
- possible misuse of subclasses;
- a requirement for additional testing.

5.7.4 Coupling between objects (CBO)

Chidamber and Kemerer define CBO as the count of the number of other classes to which a class is coupled. Coupling occurs where one class manipulates the values of an attribute of another class or uses the same methods as another class. One way in which coupling will occur is when a class inherits methods from a super-class to which it belongs. For example, in Figure 5.1, the class *loan item* will inherit four methods from the class *holding*: these are *acquire holding*, *amend title*, *remove holding* and *display details*. Another way in which coupling can occur is where a method belonging to one class passes a message to another class requesting a service. In Figure 5.3 we show a situation where the class *loan item* is called by the class *borrower* after the class borrower had checked that the *borrower reference* attribute is valid and that the borrower will not exceed the number of books that he or she is permitted to borrow. The class *borrower* also passes *borrower type* as a parameter to the class *loan item* as this may affect the duration of short or long loans. If the loan transaction is successful, then a message will be passed back requesting that the attribute *number of loans* of the class *borrower type* be incremented. It is the second message, from *loan item* to *borrower* that counts for CBO purposes for *loan item*. The first message would add to the CBO count for *borrower*.

Note that it is the number of classes that is counted, not the number of methods.

Wei Li and Sallie Henry (1993) proposed that CBO could be subdivided into three separate elements. One was **coupling through inheritance**. Li and Henry suggested that this had already been adequately captured by the DIT and NOC counts. The second type of coupling was **coupling through message passing**. They recommended the counting of the number of send statements defined by a class. This count was named by Li and Henry **message-passing coupling** (MPC). In the fragment of an object model in Figure 5.3, the MPC for both *borrower* and *loan item* would be 1. The final type of coupling identified by Li and Henry was **coupling through abstract data types**. In some OO environments, one class can

We have already come across Sallie Henry in the last chapter when discussing information flow metrics.

call another through an abstract data type (ADT). Li and Henry cater for this by counting the number of ADTs defined in a class (DAC).

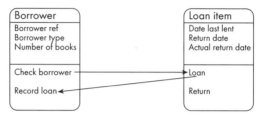

Figure 5.3   *An example of message passing.*

This discussion echoes that in the last chapter concerning 'planetary systems', 'black holes' and 'gas clouds' (Hutchens and Basili, 1985).

According to Chidamber and Kemerer, the taking of CBO counts could be a useful check as large counts might indicate that maintenance will be difficult because a change in one area is more likely to have a ripple effect. High levels of coupling are also likely to make reuse of classes more difficult and to require more testing. Brian Henderson-Sellers (1996) quotes sources that suggest that a single class with a large CBO along with other classes with zero CBO counts indicates that the organization of the software follows structured design precepts rather than being genuinely object-oriented. On the other hand, a substantial number of classes with large CBO values might indicate that classes have been defined at too fine a level of granularity.

5.7.5 Response for a class (RFC)

This is a count of the number of methods that could be executed in response to a message received by an object of the class in question.

This can be calculated as:

(number of local methods) +
(number of methods called by the local methods)

In the example shown in Figure 5.1, the class *sheet music* has three methods of its own, *acquire holding*, *amend details* and *display details*. Class *sheet music* inherits four methods from the superclass *copy item – make copies*, *pay for copies*, *set maximum* and *interrogate*. It does not use the *acquire holding* or *display details* method belonging to the class *holding* because the local methods with these names overwrite them, but it can use *remove holding* and *amend title*. This makes nine methods in all. As in the case of CBO, methods can be invoked not just through inheritance, as in this case, but also through message passing and through the direct invocation of one method by another. When one method causes another method to be executed, this may have a ripple effect causing the executed method to invoke further methods. As we have seen in the last chapter, attempting to follow all possible execution paths through a group of software components is very time-consuming and would be difficult to automate, so, for these practical reasons, these consequential methods calls are ignored.

Calculate the response for a class (RFC) for all the remaining classes in the fragment of the object model shown in Figure 5.1 plus the additional detail shown in Figure 5.3.

Exercise 5.6 Response for a class

5.7.6 Lack of cohesion of methods (LCOM)

The idea of cohesiveness has already been discussed in Chapter 4. You might recall that high cohesion in software is often associated with the intensive use of the same variables by the components concerned. These 'components' in the case of the research of Bieman and Ott (1994) were lines of code. Chidamber and Kemerer suggest a measurement **lack of cohesion in methods** (LCOM). Each method that belongs to a class is considered in relation to every other method in that class. If there are no cases where the pair of methods access the same attributes, then the pair of methods is regarded as **dissimilar**. If there is even just one attribute that they both use, then the pair is regarded as **similar**. The count of pairs that are similar is subtracted from the count of dissimilar pairs to give LCOM for the class.

This can be illustrated by the situation shown in Table 5.3.

Table 5.3 *Attributes accessed by methods m1, m2 and m3*

	Methods		
Attributes	*m1*	*m2*	*m3*
a1	×	—	—
a2	—	×	—
a3	—	×	—
a4	—	×	×
a5	—	—	×

An '×' in a cell indicates that a method (such as *m1*) accesses a particular attribute (such as *a1*). Using a table such as this the similarities and dissimilarities between pairs of methods can be identified and recorded in the way shown in Table 5.4. Subtracting the count of similarities from dissimilarities gives us an LCOM of 1. Under the Chidamber and Kemerer method negative results are set to 0.

Table 5.4 *Similarity/dissimilarity table*

	m1	*m2*	*m3*
m1	—	dissimilar	dissimilar
m2	—	—	similar
m3	—	—	—

Exercise 5.7 Lack of cohesion of methods

What would be the LCOM for the methods and the attributes that they use which are shown in Table 5.5?

Table 5.5   *Method/attribute cross-reference table for Exercise 5.7*

	Methods			
Attributes	*m1*	*m2*	*m3*	*m4*
a1	×	—	—	—
a2	—	×	—	—
a3	—	×	—	—
a4	—	×	×	—
a5	—	—	—	×
a6	—	—	×	—

Some problems have been found with the way that LCOM has been defined.

- Because negative values are all adjusted to zero, an LCOM of zero may be associated with different classes which in fact have different levels of cohesion in terms of the gap between similar and dissimilar pairs of methods.

- A low score may be caused by the class having a large number of methods many of which are dissimilar, or a small method where most methods are similar.

Brian Henderson-Sellers (1996) has suggested that a fractional measure would be more informative. Following the example of Bieman and Ott (1994), the number of dissimilar pairs divided by the total number of pairs would seem to be a more useful, ordinal, number. It seems probable that Chidamber and Kemerer were reluctant to take this seemingly obvious step as ordinal measurements are less useful as they cannot easily be used in prediction models.

5.8   Some other OO metrics

Other suites of OO metrics have been proposed such as those of Tegarden and Sheetz (1992), which has 32 suggested possible measurements, and those of Lorenz and Kidd (1994) which has 31 items. We will focus on the developments where people have taken the basic Chidamber and Kemerer metrics and have suggested additional measurements to meet particular needs or to resolve particular problems. An example of this has already been described in the work of Li and Henry (1993).

The metrics in the Chidamber and Kemerer suite all measure **class** attributes. According to Kolewe (1993), these measurements should be supplemented by **system** level measurements such as the following:

- number of class hierarchies;

- number of class clusters;

- association complexity.

Association complexity requires the drawing up of a **directed acyclic graph** (DAG) of the classes and the relationships between classes. A DAG is a diagram where each class is portrayed as a node and each relationship between nodes is drawn as a line between the two nodes. Once the DAG has been drawn up, the association complexity is calculated using the familiar formula:

DAGs were used when deriving the McCabe cyclomatic complexity metric in Chapter 3

$$association\ complexity = a - c + 2p \qquad \text{(Equation 5.1)}$$

Where:

a = number of associations in the class diagram;
c = number of classes in the class diagram;
p = the number of disconnected parts.

A pair of classes is said to have an association where one of the classes uses the methods of the other. In Figure 5.1, there are nine direct associations and ten classes, so that the association complexity is $9 - 10 + 1 = 0$. This seems to be similar in principle to the Yin and Winchester (1978) graph impurity metric that was discussed in Chapter 4.

Although the Chidamber and Kemerer metrics deal with some important aspects of the construction of OO applications, it has been argued that other important issues have been missed. For example, a good OO design ought to have a high degree of information hiding, both of attributes and methods. Also, while both DIT and NOC take account of the hierarchical structure in the object model, no account is taken of the actual volumes of methods and attributes inherited.

Abreu and Goulao (1995) have created an alternative suite of OO metrics that capture some aspects of OO applications that the Chidamber and Kemerer suite does not. The MOOD metrics as they have named them apply at system level, by totalling the measures derived for each class.

Abreu and Goulao have suggested that information hiding can be measured through the **method hiding factor** (MHF) which for a class is calculated as:

$$MHF = hidden\ methods/(hidden\ methods + visible\ methods)$$
$$\text{(Equation 5.2)}$$

A similar measurement (AHF) can be derived for **attribute hiding**.

Abreu and Goulao propose a **method inheritance factor** (MIF) which attempts to capture the degree to which methods are inherited. This is calculated as:

$$MIF = number\ of\ methods\ inherited/number\ of\ all\ methods\ available$$
(Equation 5.3)

As in the case of the method hiding factor, the number of inherited methods and new methods is derived for each class individually and are then summed for the whole system. Once again, an analogous measurement exists for attributes, the **attribute inheritance factor** (AHF).

The degree of polymorphism is assessed by a **polymorphism factor** (PF). At class level this counts the number of methods which override methods that have already been defined at a higher level in the inheritance tree. In Figure 5.1, for instance, the class *copy item* does not overwrite any of the methods it inherits, while the class *sheet music* overwrites two methods (*acquire holding* and *display details*). At class level the number of new methods defined is also counted. This count is amplified according to the number of children the class has. For example, in the fragment of the object model shown in Figure 5.1, the class *copy item* has four new methods that have not been defined at a higher level, *make copy, pay for copies*, *set maximum* and *interrogate*. These four methods will be passed down to two subclasses, *journal article* and *sheet music*. This is accounted for by multiplying the number of new methods by the number of descendents of the class in question. An overall indicator of the degree of polymorphism in the system is then worked out as:

$$PF = (number\ of\ overriding\ methods\ in\ all\ classes)/$$
$$sum\ of((new\ methods\ in\ class) \times$$
$$(number\ of\ descendents\ of\ the\ class))\ for\ all\ classes \quad \text{(Equation 5.3)}$$

Exercise 5.8 Calculating the method inheritance and polymorphism factors

Calculate (a) the method inheritance factor and (b) the polymorphism factor (PF) for the object model portrayed in Figure 5.1.

In the next section we want to move away from consideration of the detail of the individual OO metrics that have been proposed and to consider some of the actual uses to which these metrics have been put. Two points need to be emphasized before we move on. First, a complete and precise definition is lacking for almost every metric that has been proposed. On paper a particular measurement might appear straightforward, but almost immediately you try to apply it in practice questions will arise. As we will see in the case of function points, one response could be to set up some kind of authority on the counting practices which could issue detailed guidelines. While this might assist consistency, it does introduce a level of bureaucracy which can make difficult the modification of the method of measurement to meet new circumstances. Secondly, actually doing the counting will be time-consuming and prone to error and inconsistency unless there are tools available to automate this process.

5.9 Practical applications of OO metrics

The question remains: has the measurement of OO applications actually told us anything useful?

One of the first practical exercises that the proposer of a new metric should undertake is to try applying the measurement to some real applications. This helps to check the practical feasibility of the measurement approach and identifies potential anomalies that may require elaboration or modification of the counting rules. As a by-product, it will also start to reveal typical values for the metric and might also show any correlations between associated metrics. A particular metric may be **valid** but not **worthwhile** collecting because some other metric already captures all the variation between objects being measured. To use an example outside the realm of software, you might find the weight of a person is so closely related to their height and waist measurements that if you already have these, it is superfluous to collect weight as well.

Chidamber and Kemerer carried out such a measurement exercise on two different applications, one written in C++ and the other written in Smalltalk. We show in Table 5.6 a summary of the statistics that they collected as this gives an idea of some typical values for each of their metrics.

While the original figures come from Chidamber and Kemerer (1994) they were put into this particular form by Henderson-Sellers (1996).

Table 5.6 *Summary of Chidamber and Kemerer (1994) metric results*

	Site A (C++)		Site B (Smalltalk)	
	Median	Range	Median	Range
WMC	5	0–106	10	0–346
DIT	1	0–8	3	0–10
NOC	0	0–42	0	0–50
CBO	0	0–84	9	0–234
RFC	6	0–120	29	3–422
LCOM	0	0–200	2	0–17

Table 5.6 shows that designers at both sites seemed cautious about having structures with high DIT and NOC. The Smalltalk site had a higher median DIT and it was suggested that this might be because Smalltalk has a library of reusable classes that are part of the language. Another difference that might be attributable to differences in languages is that between the RFC figures, the median value of which is 29 for the Smalltalk site and 6 for the C++ site. This is probably because

in Smalltalk, the system developer is forced to implement communication between classes using message passing while in C++, a less 'pure' OOP language, other ways are available.

Clearly, we should be cautious about drawing too many conclusions about the reasons for the differences between the two sites as there may be many other reasons other than the languages used. However, we can at least use these results to formulate possible hypotheses that can be validated in further investigations.

A differing initial approach to using measurement in an OO environment is to attempt to monitor what differences the use of a new development approach has on conventional measurements such as size defined in lines of code. Does OO reduce or increase the number of lines of code in an application? Does it increase or decrease decision density, as measured by the McCabe cyclomatic complexity metric for instance?

Tegarden, Sheetz and Monarchi (1992) implemented the same application, a small accounts package, in four different ways:

- no polymorphism, no inheritance;

- polymorphism, no inheritance;

- no polymorphism, inheritance;

- polymorphism, inheritance

Some of their results are shown in Table 5.7. While polymorphism seems to have some influence on reducing the amount of code, inheritance has a much bigger impact. It can be speculated that the decrease in the lines of code is at least partly due to increased reuse through the deployment of inheritance. What is also interesting is that inheritance in this case has increased the number of classes while decreasing the average number of methods per class.

Table 5.7   *Metrics for four different implementation of the same application*

Polymorphism	no	yes	no	yes
Inheritance	no	no	yes	yes
Count or metric				
classes	7	7	12	12
members/class	7	7	2	2
methods	42	42	30	30
operators	955	735	541	521
operands	453	259	254	245
cyclomatic complexity	95	71	57	55
Executable SLOC	202	181	126	124

Table 5.8 *Comparison of metrics for data-driven and responsibility driven implementations*

	WMC	DIT	NOC	CBO	RFC	LCOM
data driven	130	21	19	42	293	64
responsibility driven	71	19	13	20	127	44

Sharble and Cohen (1993), who have both worked for Boeing, carried a comparable investigation to that of Tegarden and colleagues except that in this case they produced an application – a brewery control system – using two different OO design approaches: a **data-driven** OO approach and **a responsibility-driven** approach. To appreciate fully the differences between the two approaches, the reader should read Sharble and Cohen's article or descriptions of the methodologies concerned such as that of Shlaer and Mellor (1988) for the data-driven approach or Wirfs-Brock and his co-workers (1990) for the responsibility-driven approach. At the risk of over-simplification, the data-driven approach has grown out of the structured system analysis way of analysing and designing systems. This identifies the data entities and the relationships between those entities, the processes that manipulate the data, and the models that describe the sequences of changes to which the attributes of entities can be subjected. The responsibility-driven approach is in some ways a 'purer' and more directly object-oriented approach. It seems to address the question of how objects can model the dynamics of the system at an earlier stage. Table 5.6 compares the metrics for the two implementations. It can be seen that the responsibility-driven approach produced a system that was much less complex. Sharble and Cohen observed that most noticeably the responsibility-driven design showed more cohesion and less coupling. Once again some caution needs to be exercised in weighing the results of the study. If subsequent studies by other investigators in other environments produce similar results then a pattern could be confirmed as emerging. The results of this investigation do however seem to confirm the comments made by some OO proponents that OO design requires the application of a different mindset from that used in more structured analysis and design environments.

The most convincing evidence of the usefulness of these metrics would be if they could predict reliably the project and product outcomes that are of prime managerial concern. These are the things that have major cost implications such as the effort required to design and implement applications and subsequently to maintain them.

Wei Li and Sallie Henry (1993) started to move in this direction by not only collecting OO type metrics but also the size of individual classes in lines of code and the number of lines of code that were changed in their subsequent maintenance histories. We need to be a little cautious here. It will be recalled from our earlier discussion of measurement principles that a metric and the entity/attribute that it reflects should be clearly and unambiguously associated.

The work of Adams (1984) at IBM was among the first to shed light on this aspect.

Changes to software are not all internally generated. Many changes will be consequences of alterations in the environment. Even actual system failures and the amount of consequential correction work may be influenced not just by the density of errors in the software component but also by the volume of use to which individual software components are subjected. Bearing in mind these provisos, it can be seen that Wei Li and Sallie Henry still found that OO metrics could be used to predict maintenance effort. Some questions have been raised about the statistical techniques that were used, but a huge plus in this work is that the complete data sets derived in the case studies have been published so that others can do their own analyses using their own preferred methods.

Cartwright (1998) collected various figures for an application written in C++ and designed using the Shlaer and Mellor method. The implementation showed low DIT and NOC values indicating that inheritance was used very sparingly – the largest value for DIT was 2 and for NOC was 4. Even with these shallow inheritance structures higher defect rates were found in classes at the bottom of class hierarchies. Interestingly, the researcher was unable to collect other Chidamber and Kemerer metrics, apart from DIT and NOC, because the design and construction method did not produce documentation from which the figures could be calculated.

Spearman rank correlation was used – the reasons for this choice will be explored in a later chapter.

Other metrics could, however, be extracted from the Case tool used such as the number of events and the number of states per class. The number of defects in a class was the most highly correlated with the number of events (a correlation of 0.84) while the number of lines of code was most highly correlated with the number of states (0.97). Events, states, lines of code and defects were all highly correlated with each other – this is not surprising as big things in general tend to have more of everything than small ones. It is revealing that events and states are measures which could just as well be derived for conventional applications that have been written using structured approaches. This seems to confirm the perception of the Shlaer and Mellor method as being very data driven and thus quite akin to the structured approach.

All these examples, we believe, illustrate how empirical investigations based on measurement can help our understanding of the factors that affect software and software development.

5.10 Conclusions

Among the conclusions that could be drawn from this chapter are the following.

- Many of the measurements that can be applied to conventional systems can also be applied to OO applications. Indeed, these measurements may be useful as they let us compare the characteristics of different types of software construction.

- Specialized OO metrics may, however, be required because the main unit of interest is the class rather than the module and because the focus is on different issues e.g. the effects of inheritance.

- Major obstacles to be overcome in applying the newer OO metrics include obtaining clear guidelines on the detail of the counting procedures and acquiring suitable tools to assist automation.

- Empirical investigations using OO metrics have produced useful insights into the nature of OO development and products.

5.11 References

Abreu, F. B and Carapuça, R. (1994), 'Candidate metrics for object-oriented software within a taxonomy framework', *J. Systems Software*: 26, 87–96.

Abreu, F. B. and Goulao, M. (1995), 'Toward the design quality evaluation of object-oriented software systems', *Proceedings of 5th International Conference On Software Quality*, Austin, Texas.

Adams, E. (1984), 'Optimizing preventive service of software products', *IBM Research Journal*: 28(1), 2–14.

Bieman, J. H. and Ott, L. M. (1994), 'Measuring functional cohesion' *IEEE Transactions in Software Engineering*: 20(8), 644–657.

Cartwright, M. H. (1998), 'An empirical view of inheritance', *Information and Software Technology*.

Chidamber, S. R. and Kemerer, C. F. (1991), 'Towards a metrics suite for object oriented design', *Proceedings of 6th ACM Conference on Object Oriented Programming, Systems, Languages and Applications (OOPSLA)*, Phoenix, Arizona, 197–211.

Chidamber, S. R. and Kemerer, C. F. (1994), 'A metrics suite for object oriented design', *IEEE Transactions in Software Engineering*: 20(6), 476–493.

Fichman, R. and Kemerer, C. F. (1993), 'Adoption of software engineering process innovations', *Sloan Management Review*: 34, 7-22 (This has been reprinted in Kemerer 1997).

Henderson-Sellers, B. (1996), *Object-oriented Metrics: Measures of Complexity*, Prentice Hall, New Jersey.

Hutchens, D. H. and Basili, V. R. (1985), 'System structure analysis: clustering with data bindings', *IEEE Transactions in Software Engineering*: 11(8), 749–757.

Kemerer, C. F. (1992), 'How the learning curve affects CASE tool adoption', *IEEE Software*: 9(5), 23-28 (This has been reprinted in Kemerer 1997).

Kemerer, C. F. (1997), *Software Project Management: Readings and Cases*, Irwin, Chicago.

Kolewe, R. (1993), 'Metrics in object-oriented design and programming', *Software Development*: October, 53–62.

Letjer, M., Meyers, S. and Reiss, P. R. (1992), 'Support for maintaining object-oriented programs', *IEEE Transactions in Software Engineering*: 18(12), 1045–1052.

Li, W. and Henry, S. (1993), 'Object-oriented metrics that predict maintainability', *J. Systems Software*: 23, 111–122.

Lorenz M. and Kidd, J. (1994), *Object Oriented Software Metrics*, Prentice-Hall, New Jersey.

Rogers, E. M. (1983), *Diffusion of Innovations*, Free Press, New York.

Schlaer, S. and Mellor, S. (1988), *Object Oriented Systems Analysis: Modelling The World in Data*, Yourdon Press, Englewood Cliffs.

Sharble, R. C. and Cohen, S. S. (1993), 'The object-oriented brewery: a comparison of two object-oriented methods', *ACM Sigsoft Software Engineering Notes*: 18(2), 60–73.

Tegarden, D. P. and Sheetz, S. D. (1992), 'Object oriented system complexity: an integrated model of structure and perceptions', *Proceedings of ACM Conference on Object Oriented Programming, Systems, Languages and Applications (OOPSLA)*, Washington DC. (The measurement suite is summarized in Henderson-Sellers 1996).

Tegarden, D. P., Sheetz, S. D. and Monarchi, D. E. (1992), 'Effectiveness of traditional software metrics for object-oriented systems', *Proceedings of Hawaii International Conference on Systems Science (HICSS)*, San Diego, IEEE, 359–368.

Wirfs-Brock, R., Wilkerson, B. and Weiner, L. (1990), *Designing Object-Oriented Software,* Prentice-Hall.

Yin, B. H. and Winchester, J. W. (1978), 'The establishment and use of measures to evaluate the quality of software designs', *Proceedings of the ACM Software Quality Assurance Workshop*: 3, 45–52.

5.12 Additional questions

1. How would you categorize the following measurements according to the TAPROOT framework?

   (a) number of operational errors found in each method;
   (b) the average lines of code a day delivered during an OO software development project;
   (c) the Chidamber–Kemerer coupling between objects (CBO) metric;
   (d) the Abreu–Goulao method inheritance Factor (MIF).

2. Given the skeleton object model in Figure 5.4, calculate for each class:

   (a) weighted methods per class (WMC);
   (b) depth of inheritance (DIT);
   (c) number of children (NOC);
   (d) coupling between objects (CBO);
   (e) response for a class (RFC).

3. m_1 to m_6 are the methods used by a class and a_1 to a_4 are the attributes of the class. The matrix in Figure 5.9 shows which methods use which attributes. Calculate the Chidamber–Kemerer lack of cohesion of methods (LCOM) metric.

4. Calculate the Kolewe association complexity that might be derived from the skeleton object model shown in Figure 5.4.

5. Given the profile for an object model shown in Table 5.10, what would be the Abreu-Goulao polymorphism factor?

Table 5.9 *Matrix for Question 3*

	a_1	a_2	a_3	a_4
m_1	×			×
m_2	×		×	
m_3		×	×	
m_4				×
m_5				×
m_6		×		

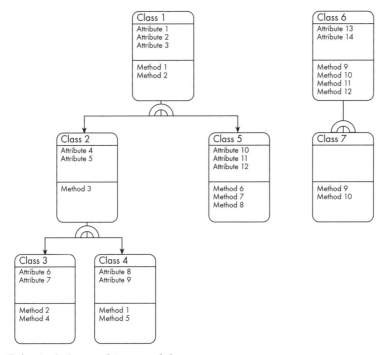

Figure 5.4 *A skeleton object model.*

Table 5.10 *Profile for Question 5*

class	inherited methods	over-written methods	new methods	children
a	0	0	4	2
b	4	2	3	0
c	4	0	4	2
d	8	2	1	0
e	8	2	2	0

Chapter 6

How to measure software size

OBJECTIVES

When you have completed this chapter you will be able to:

☐ understand the difficulties with measuring software size

☐ assess the size of a software application by counting the occurrences of various types of feature

☐ count Albrecht function points

☐ understand how the International Function Point User Group (IFPUG) has developed the principles of Albrecht function points

☐ count Symons Mark II function points

☐ understand the difficulties that have been found with function points

☐ apply the ideas of function point counting to real time systems

☐ understand how the ideas of function point counting have been extended to object-oriented systems development environments

---

6.1 Introduction

In the preceding chapters the features considered have been internal to software components and the users of the software would not have been directly aware of them.

In this and the following chapters, we will look at some externally apparent attributes starting with **size**. Size might be considered a relatively easy measurement to take, but, as will be seen, is difficult because of the intangible nature of software. Despite this difficulty, size involves important issues, in particular because of the relationship that is generally perceived between size and costs.

One general line of attack on the problem of assessing the size of software applications has been to classify different types of externally observable features and then to count the occurrences of each type of feature. The features could, for example, be the inputs and outputs from a software component. **Function point** counting is the most prominent of these approaches. It will be seen that there are many variations on this theme, each counting different types of feature. There is also variation in the way different types of count are combined to get an approximate indicator of overall size. For example, one software component has a large number of inputs but few outputs while the other has a small number of inputs but many outputs – how can we obtain a combined size measurement for them both?

Exercise 6.1 Examples of different types of program

Give an example of the sort of software program that would have:
    (a)   a large number of inputs, but few outputs;
    (b)   few inputs but a large number of outputs;
    (c)   a large number of both inputs and outputs.

The problem is how to combine the counts of inputs and outputs. We could simply add them together. However, it would be argued that inputs and outputs are two very different things and that adding them together would not give a meaningful measurement.

Exercise 6.2 Effort needed to implement inputs and outputs

In general terms, what in your opinion is more likely to require more work to implement: a software component which has six different input types and only one output type, or a component which has one input and six outputs? Assume that both components access the same number of record types on the same database.

One way of combining different types of count is to give them different weightings depending on their relevant importance, but as will be seen this is not without controversy.

There might also be differences in the methods of counting features because different types of software application have different types of feature that are important. Function points, for example, have been developed primarily for information systems applications and different counting methods might well be needed in other application areas such as systems software or real-time applications.

6.2 Difficulties in measuring the size of software

6.2.1 Why measure software size?

In this section we are going to explore further why the measurement of software size presents difficulties. To understand these difficulties we need to consider why people would want to measure the size of software in the first place.

As already noted, being able to assess software size is one of the keys to forecasting the amount of effort needed to develop a software component.

The other key to estimating software effort is being able to estimate development productivity. Simplistically, given performance information about development tasks that have already been completed, it is possible to derive a productivity rate by applying Equation 6.1:

$$productivity = size/effort \qquad \text{(Equation 6.1)}$$

For example, *size* might be measured in 'source lines of code' (SLOC) and *effort* in 'staff-days'. In these circumstances *productivity* would be expressed as 'lines of code per day'.

Given a new software development task, we might know what the size of the end-product is going to be in SLOC. Using the productivity rate we have already derived we can apply the calculation shown in Equation 6.2 and obtain an estimate for the effort needed to develop the new component.

$$effort = size/productivity \qquad \text{(Equation 6.2)}$$

Realistically 'size' and 'effort' totals would be accumulated from a range of past software development tasks. In the next chapter we will look at a more sophisticated method of using past project data.

The size in SLOC and the development effort in staff-days is shown for four software components that have already been completed.

Exercise 6.3 Estimating effort for a new software component

Module	SLOC	Staff-days
A	1200	48
B	750	29
C	2000	86
D	1450	60

A new component is to be written which has an estimated 900 SLOC.

(i) Produce an estimate of the effort needed to develop this component, based on the performance data given.
(ii) What sorts of factors are *not* taken into account in the method we have used so far?

We have calculated the productivity rate in order to estimate the effort for new software tasks, but we could equally use the productivity rate, as calculated by Equation 6.2 to compare the productivity of different projects, development environments, or even individuals. This is an example of using the division of an attribute value by size in order to **normalize** it, that is, to put measurements from different sources into a format which allows them to be compared. Size can be used to normalize other types of measurement. For example, you would normally expect that a software component that is larger will also have more errors, simply on account of its size. To compare the error proneness of the two components, we ought to compare **error densities** which could be calculated according to Equation 6.3.

$$error\ density = (number\ of\ errors)/size \qquad \text{(Equation 6.3)}$$

Exercise 6.4 Calculating error densities

54 errors were found in module A during system testing. It had 1200 SLOC. Module B had 33 errors found during system testing and had 900 SLOC. Which module had the highest fault density?

See Chapter 3. Park (1992) contains standards for measuring SLOC.

We have already come across some of the problems with SLOC. Apart from the difficulty of ensuring the application of consistent counting rules – which in our opinion has now been largely addressed through the establishment of recognized standards – two major problems remain. First, there is the question of the differences in programming languages and secondly there is the need for details of the actual software code to be available. Using SLOC to generate an estimate of development effort requires an *estimate* of the number of SLOC, because the actual figure for SLOC will not be known until the software has been written, which is rather late for estimating purposes!

As we have seen, the answer might lie in using counts of externally visible features. Advantages of this are that the existence of these features can be ascertained at the design (or even requirements) stage of development and that these requirements are understood not just by the developers of code, but by systems analysts and even users.

6.2.2 Combining counts of different types of feature

What people have tried to do is to combine counts of different types of feature to produce some overall number that is a size indicator. In most cases, different weightings are applied to the different types of count before they are added together in order to take account of their relative importance. The questions present themselves of where these weightings come from and how the particular values used can be justified. Usually they are justified on the grounds of the relative difficulty of implementing the particular type of feature. What we have here is not really a *measurement,* but a *model* which attempts to predict the relative difficulty of developing a particular set of requirements. It could therefore be argued that the output from this functionality model ought to be in some unit of effort. However, such a model only takes into account the size of the task to be done and not the variations that there can be in the productivity of the staff and other resources. What is needed is a second, productivity, model which takes the task-size derived from the functionality model and applies productivity drivers to create the final effort estimate.

The COCOMO model, which will be looked at in the next chapter, produces a 'nominal effort' figure which is purely related to task size and which is then modified to take into account productivity factors.

The reader needs to be warned that while seeing 'measurement' approaches such as function points as really effort models may seem to be common sense, many users of function points will strenuously maintain that they are *measurements*.

6.2.3 Taking account of complexity

The size of the task involved in developing software depends not just on the size in terms of the number of features to be incorporated, but also the **complexity** of the processing to be done. It will be recalled from earlier chapters, that there have been arguments over what is meant by complexity. We are going to follow the dictionary definition where the description 'complex' is seen as '*comprehending various parts connected together*'. Thus size refers to having a large number of components, while complexity is concerned with the degree to which these components are joined together. Size and complexity are not independent of each other. As a system grows in terms of the number of components it has, the number of possible relationships between those components grows exponentially – see Equation 6.4.

This definition is from the Shorter Oxford English Dictionary

$$(number\ of\ possible\ relationships) = ((number\ of\ components)^2 - (number\ of\ components))/2$$

(Equation 6.4)

It will also be recalled from Chapters 4 and 5 that techniques such as modularization and object-orientation are ways of partitioning software structures so that the possibilities of interactions between the various components are reduced. This type of complexity clearly has a bearing on task effort. Some have treated complexity as an element of size, while others have argued that size is a component of complexity. Yet others have tried to treat complexity and size as two completely separate attributes which can be assessed independently of each other. In the discussion of specific techniques we will need to be aware of the tactics that have been used to deal with this.

6.2.4 Taking account of reuse

The remaining problem that will be noted here is that of **code reuse**. We would like to have a measurement of software size with which both the supplier and customer of the software product are happy. Say, for example, that a customer goes to a software supplier with a set of requirements which they have estimated will require 200 staff-days of effort to produce. The supplier happens to have an existing software product which can be modified with 20 staff days' of effort to meet the customer's requirement. For how many days of effort should the supplier in fairness charge the customer? Assuming that the new software is worth at least the equivalent of 200 staff days of effort to the customer, the supplier could happily charge the money equivalent of that effort and make a handsome profit. Rightly or wrongly, the customer organization, if they subsequently found out the true cost to the supplier, would probably feel disgruntled. Ideally, what we would like is to have a measurement that reflects both the content of that product to the customer and the development cost to the supplier. However, the existence of reuse makes this problematic.

6.3   Albrecht function points

The technique of function point analysis was originally described by Allan Albrecht (1979) and later developed by Allan Albrecht and John Gaffney (1983) and was the result of work done at IBM on the measurement of systems development productivity. To measure productivity, Albrecht needed some measurement of size, but the existing practice of using SLOC clearly had problems when you were comparing the productivity rates obtained from projects using different programming languages.

Exercise 6.5 Comparing productivity using SLOC

The same program specification is implemented by two different software developers, one using Assembler and the other using a high level language. The final software products look identical to the user. The Assembler programmer took 50 days and wrote a program containing 2000 SLOC while the high level language programmer took 32 days and wrote a program containing 800 SLOC. Which of the two code developers was the more productive?

What was needed was some way of assessing product size in terms of the functionality delivered to the users. An approach was suggested where, for the system in question, counts of the different types of transaction and also of the files accessed were collected. Descriptions of the different types of **user function types** as Albrecht and Gaffney termed them are given below.

- **External input types** (EI) are input transactions which update internal computer files.

- **External output types** (EO) are transactions where data is output to the user. Typically these would be printed reports as screen displays would tend to come under external inquiry types, which are described below.

Later uses of this approach renamed these Internal logical files (ILFs).

- **Logical internal file types** are the standing files used by the system. The term 'file' does not sit easily with modern information systems. It refers to a group of data that is usually accessed together. It may be made up of one or more **record types**. For example, a bank account file might be made up of a record type CUSTOMERACCOUNT plus a second which is repeated for transaction moving money into or out of the account – CASHMOVEMENT.

Albrecht also indicated that outgoing external interface files should be double counted as logical internal file types as well.

- **External interface file types** (EIF) allow for output and input that can pass to and from other computer applications. An example of this would be the transmission of bank credits from a payroll system to the Bankers' Automated Clearing Scheme (BACS). Files shared between applications would also be counted here. We will see that later developments of FPs have restricted the definition to those data stores are used by the current application but that have been created by other some other application.

- **External inquiry types** (EQ) – note the US spelling of inquiry – are transactions initiated by the user which provide information but do not update the internal files. The user inputs some information that directs the system to the details required.

You have to identify each instance of each user function type in the projected system. You then have to classify each component as having either high, average or low complexity. The count of each user function type in each complexity band is multiplied by a specified weight (see Table 6.1) to get a number of function points (FPs) which are summed to obtain an overall FP count which indicates the **information processing size**.

'Complexity' here seems to refer to size, but note the disproportionately larger weights given to components rated as of higher complexity.

Table 6.1 *Albrecht complexity multipliers*

External user type	Multiplier		
	Average	High	Low
External input type	3	4	6
External output type	4	5	7
Logical internal file type	7	10	15
External interface file type	5	7	10
External inquiry type	3	4	6

A payroll application accesses details of each employee such as name and address and grade from a database of personnel records that belongs to a separate personnel records system. The structure and scope of the data is rated as being of average complexity. Financial details of salary payments actually made and tax deducted are held in a separate data store that is wholly maintained by the payroll application – this file is also perceived as being of average complexity. Once salary payments have been calculated, a file of accounting details is passed to a separate project accounting system and a file of electronic bank credit transfers is created for processing by the Bankers Automated Clearing System. Both these files are assessed as being simple in complexity. Two simple tables are also maintained and accessed by the system: a tax code table which holds details of the amount of tax that is deductible in different circumstances and the salaries table that gives the salary for each staff grade within the organization.

For the purposes of this exercise, we will assume that there are four main software components in the application. One component calculates the pay each month for each employee and updates the payroll main file with the new pay details. This process is regarded as complex. A second component which is of average complexity produces payslips using details recorded on the payroll main

Exercise 6.6 Calculating Albrecht FPs

file while a third, simple, component is used to update the details in the tax code and salary tables as required. The final process generates a summary of the payments made to each employee and the tax and other deductions made in the previous tax year. This report is rated as being of average complexity.

What would be the Albrecht FP count for the application as described above?

The FP count described so far is sometimes known as the **unadjusted FP** count (UFP). This did not capture all the value that was delivered to the users. There could be additional, technical, requirements that would give the users additional value and which would also require additional expenditure by the suppliers of the application. It is important to note that these technical attributes relate solely to the system delivered to the users and *not* to the technical environment in which the application is developed. Hence the use of application tools would not be relevant.

Technical complexity adjustments are also sometimes referred to as 'processing complexity adjustments' (PCA) or 'Value Adjustment Factors' (VAF).

To cater for these additional possible requirements the concept of **technical complexity adjustments** (TCA) was introduced. Each of the fourteen general application characteristics listed below is rated for the degree to which they are absent or present in a particular application. A scale of 0 to 5 is used, where 0 indicates that it has no influence at all, while 3 indicates average influence and 5 indicates a strong influence throughout the application. The characteristics that are assessed are:

- data communications;
- distributed functions;
- performance requirements;
- heavy hardware configuration usage;
- high transaction rate;
- on-line data entry;
- end-user efficiency;
- on-line update;
- complex processing;
- reusability requirements;
- ease of installation;
- operational ease (for technical staff as opposed to end users);
- multiple sites;
- ease of modification.

The fourteen scores are summed to create a **degree of influence** (DI) which has a maximum value of $14 \times 5 = 70$. The TCA factor is then derived according to Equation 6.5.

$$technical\ complexity\ adjustment = 0.65 + (0.01 \times DI) \qquad \text{(Equation 6.5)}.$$

The resulting TCA must be in the range 0.65 to 1.35. The information processing size in UFPs is then multiplied by the TCA to get **adjusted function points**.

Let us assume that there is an application that has been counted as having 800 FPs. Most of the technical complexity factors have been rated as of average influence. However, the application is a personal desk-top application where data communications, distributed functions, high transaction rate and operations ease of use are not at all relevant. On the other hand ease of use by the end-user is of paramount importance. We would therefore rate the technical complexity factors as shown in Table 6.2.

Table 6.2 *Rating technical complexity*

Factor	Rating
Data communications	0
Distributed functions	0
Performance requirements	3
Heavy hardware configuration usage	3
High transaction rate	0
On-line data entry	3
End-user efficiency	5
On-line update	3
Complex processing	3
Reusability requirements	3
Ease of installation	3
Operational ease (for technical staff as opposed to end users)	0
Multiple sites	3
Ease of modification	3

The DI is therefore 32 and the TCA is $0.65+0.32 = 0.97$. The adjusted FPs ought therefore to be $800\times0.97 = 776$ FPs.

We will be discussing the difficulties that people have found with FPs in a later section, but we will note here that many have found the calculation of TCA the least convincing feature of the FP approach.

As was noted earlier, the original motivation for function points was as a tool to assist in the measurement of productivity. Behrens (1983), for example, used FPs to compare the productivity of development environments which used on-line editing and debugging and those where amendments and testing had to be done by batch processing. Bearing in mind the relationship we have already explored between size, productivity and effort, it was only a short step to use FPs as a size driver in effort estimation. Because of the initial lack of extensive historical project data that included FP counts, the approach as first was to use FPs to generate a SLOC count which could then be used to generate a estimate of development effort using existing SLOC-based performance data. To assist this, Capers Jones (1986) produced tables of FP to SLOC conversion factors for various programming languages. For example, for Cobol the conversion factor was 106 SLOC per FP, for Assembler 320 SLOC per FP and for Prolog 64 SLOC per FP.

6.4   IFPUG development of the function point count

The huge interest that has been taken in the method of assessing the size of software functionality proposed by Albrecht clearly shows that the need for effective software size assessment is widely experienced. An International FP Users' Group (IFPUG) was set up in the mid-1980s, which despite its name, is based in the USA. A common theme that has emerged from our examination of software metrics has been how the practical application of a measurement invariably shows up a need for the clarification of counting rules. It can be seen, for example, that the original Albrecht approach required each instance of a feature to be categorized as being of 'low', 'average' or 'high' complexity. However, the way in which the classification was made was left largely to subjective judgement and this could lead to inconsistencies in the way FPs were counted.

IFPUG has gone a long way to clarifying FP counting rules. The brief guidelines in the original description of the approach by Albrecht have been expanded into a hefty volume that is several centimetres thick (IFPUG 1999). IFPUG have now promulgated rules on how the complexity of a feature is to be judged. For example, in the case of logical internal files and external interface files, the boundaries shown in Table 6.3 are used to decide the complexity level.

Table 6.3   *IFPUG file type complexity*

Number of record types	Number of data types		
	<20	20–50	>50
1	low	low	average
2 to 5	low	average	high
>5	average	high	high

It is assumed that a date is one item and not three (day/month/year) and that name and address is effectively one item.

The way that the table is used is best shown through an example. A logical internal file might contain data about employees. These employee details might be organized into two separate record types. One would be the main EMPLOYEE details, namely payroll reference, name and address, date of birth and date of joining the company. The second would contain details for each POSITION in the company that the employee has filled namely the position reference, job title, start and end dates, and salary grade. The number of record types for that file would therefore be 2 and the number of data types would be 9. According to Table 6.3, this file type would be rated as 'low'. This would mean that according to Table 6.1, the FP count would be 7 for this file.

Tables 6.4 and 6.5 are used to scope external inputs and external outputs. Each external inquiry has to be counted both as if it were an external input and an external output and whichever score is higher is used.

Table 6.4   *IFPUG external input complexity*

Number of file types accessed	Number of data types referenced		
	<5	5–15	>15
0 or 1	low	low	average
2	low	average	high
>2	average	high	high

Table 6.5   *IFPUG external output complexity*

Number of file types	Number of data types output		
	<6	6–19	>19
0 or 1	low	low	average
2 or 3	low	average	high
>3	average	high	high

An output report is produced by scanning all the EMPLOYEE records in a personnel database, plus all the POSITION records belonging to each employee. There is a POSITION record for each position or job that an employee has had within the organization. Note that EMPLOYEE and POSITION records are regarded as logically belonging to the same data store or file. The report will show the payroll reference, name and address, date of birth and date of joining the organization for each employee of the organization. In addition, for each employee, the following details of each position he or she has held within the organization will be displayed: position reference number, start date, end date (if relevant), and the salary grade. For the position currently held, the salary grade will be looked up in a SALARY table and the corresponding annual salary will be extracted and displayed.

What would be the FP count for this transaction?

Exercise 6.7 FP count for an External Output

6.5   Function points Mark II

Function points have been subjected to much criticism. Some of the more general criticisms will be considered in Section 6.6. In this section we want to look at some specific criticisms made by Charles Symons (1988) which led to the proposal for a revised method which was called **Mark II function points**. This was later described in more detail in a book (Symons 1991).

Symons drew attention to the range of values that the weightings for user function types could be assigned – see Table 6.1. For external inputs, for example, the highest weighting (6) was only twice that of the lowest (3). This implied that the biggest and most complex transaction was only twice the size of the smallest – which suggested that the largest possible update module only needed twice the development effort of the most trivial. Symons went on to question the validity of these weightings in more general terms. According to Albrecht and Gaffney they had been '*determined by debate and trial*' but the figures appeared to be based on subjective judgement. Some more objective method of establishing the weightings would appear to be desirable. Symons also pointed out that function point counts varied depending upon the way that system boundaries were drawn. In particular, because files and records generated function points in their own right, separate systems which duplicated data generated larger FP counts than a more inclusive system which used an integrated data base.

Symons suggested that files and records should not be considered directly in functional size measurement but only indirectly through the transactions that accessed them. He also suggested that the distinction between the three types of transaction – inputs, outputs and inquiries – was artificial and suggested a method which treated all transactions in a uniform way.

As with Albrecht, in Mark II function points the information processing size is initially measured in unadjusted function points (UFPs) to which a technical complexity adjustment can then be applied (TCA). The assumption here is that an information system comprises transactions which have the basic structure shown in Figure 6.1.

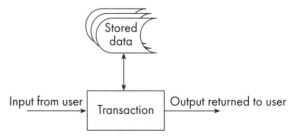

Figure 6.1   *Model of a transaction.*

For each transaction the UFPs are calculated:

$$W_i \times \text{(number of input data element types)}$$
$$+ W_e \times \text{(number of entity types referenced)}$$
$$+ W_o \times \text{(number of output data element types)}$$

Here, W_i, W_e, and W_o are weightings that may be derived by asking developers what proportion of effort has been spent in previous projects developing those parts of the software that deal with processing inputs, accessing and modifying stored data and processing outputs. From this it should be possible to work out the average hours of work generated by instances of each type of element.

The averages are then normalized into ratios, or weightings, which add up to 2.5. If this way of getting hold of the weightings seems too time-consuming then some industry averages are available which are currently (that is, in 2000) 0.58 for W_i, 1.66 for W_e and 0.26 for W_o.

> The only reason why 2.5 was adopted here was to produce FP counts similar to the Albrecht equivalents.

To take an example, a transaction in a personnel system which records when a member of staff moves to a new job within the organization accesses two entity types – EMPLOYEE and POSITION.

The data elements that are input are:

- payroll reference;

- date of commencement;

- position reference number;

- salary grade.

If an EMPLOYEE record is not found for the payroll reference then an error message is issued. If the payroll reference is found then a new POSITION record is created.

The name of the employee found on the EMPLOYEE record is displayed to confirm that the correct record had been accessed. The error message constitutes the only other output data element for which the transaction has to cater.

The unadjusted function points, using the industry average weightings, for this transaction would therefore be:

$$(0.58 \times 4) + (1.66 \times 2) + (0.26 \times 2) = 6.16$$

Calculate the number of unadjusted Mark II function points for the transaction described in Exercise 6.7, using the industry average weightings.

Exercise 6.8 Mark II FP calculation

The FP count for an individual transaction is a very crude indicator of the size of its functionality, but Symons claimed that the total FPs for a complete application would be a good size indicator for comparing with other applications.

Mark II FPs follow the Albrecht method in recognizing that one system delivering the same functionality as another may be more difficult to implement (but also more valuable to the users) because of additional technical requirements. For example, the incorporation of additional security measures would increase the amount of effort to deliver the system. The original Albrecht FP method identified 14 technical complexity adjustment factors – Mark II FPs identify five more factors:

- interfaces to other applications;

- special security features;

- direct access for third parties;

- user training features;

- documentation requirements.

Symons suggested that many of the original technical factors that presented problems in the late 1970s were now run of the mill. For instance, the on-line updating of records was standard practice. In view of this it was suggested that the 'industry average coefficient' by which the degree of influence (DI) is multiplied by reduced from 0.01 to 0.005.

Exercise 6.9 Mark II calculation of TCA

In Section 6.4 there was an example in Table 6.2 of applying TCA to an unadjusted FP count of 800 FPs using the fourteen technical complexity factors. Recalculate adjusted FP count using the Mark II method. Assume that the requirements for interfaces with other systems and for third party access are non-existent and that the other new, Mark II, factors are all average except for the need for user training features which is all-pervasive.

Mark II function points were originally devised as part of an exercise carried out in the late 1980s by Nolan, Norton and Company, a wing of KPMG Management Consulting, for the Central Computer and Telecommunications Agency (CCTA). The CCTA was responsible for the general policy on IT matters in UK government departments. It has been instrumental in the development of the SSADM (Structured Systems Analysis and Design Method) and PRINCE 2, the project management standard. The CCTA adopted Mark II FPs, probably because it seemed to fit well with SSADM. As a consequence Mark II FPs are widely used in the United Kingdom, but elsewhere the original Albrecht method as further developed by IFPUG has been dominant. In the United Kingdom, the UK Software Metrics Association (UKSMA) is the design authority for Mark II FPs, but it is significant that UKSMA attempts to represent and service the needs of both Mark II and IFPUG FP users.

6.6   Some difficulties that have been found with function points

6.6.1 Function points: the great debate

The reader needs to be warned that function points have been the subject of much heated debate. To some extent this has been a dispute between practitioners seeking a practical way to assess software size and academics, who point out the theoretical defects in the methods adopted. Groups like IFPUG have spent considerable effort developing detailed counting rules. The use of function points can be seen as being very similar to the use of standard accounting procedures to assess the financial standing of organizations. To be effective the procedures need to be consistent and, if possible, universally used and trusted. Even though the procedures might have some shortcomings, at least all know where they stand. To a large extent the adoption of standards is influenced by the factors we noted in the last chapter with regard to the adoption of innovation. It is in the long-term interest of adopters of new methods that other members of their community eventually adopt the new methods. In addition there is the direct financial stake of consultants and trainers who have developed services to support FP counting. Hence there is a vested interest in maintaining the momentum in favour of the wide-spread adoption of FPs, and hostility to what can be perceived as threats to the acceptance of FPs. Defensiveness on one side can cause defensiveness on the other. Academics perceive that commercial interests are being put before scientific validity. Unfortunately, this means that a cool, rational, debate on ways of improving functional size measurement could be impeded.

Some of the criticisms that have been made and difficulties found will now be discussed. We will concentrate initially on the IFPUG flavour of FPs.

6.6.2 Function points and measurement theory

In Chapter 2, we noted that measurements can be classified as belonging to different scalar types, for each of which only certain mathematical operations are valid. The validity of FPs has been questioned on these grounds (Abran and Robillard, 1994). For example, the mapping of counts of record and data types to the 'high', 'medium' and 'low' categories in Table 6.3 transforms absolute measurements into ordinal ones and thus reduces the range of arithmetic operations that can be performed. A 'high' rating is greater than an 'average' one but the proportion by which this is the case is lost. A numeric score is allocated to the rating – see Table 6.1 – and these scores are then aggregated. Referring back to Chapter 2, we can see that ordinal scales are now being treated, incorrectly, as ratio scales. An example of the kind of result that can occur can be seen in Tables 6.6 and 6.7.

Table 6.6   *Logical internal file types for Project X*

File	Record types	Data types	Rating	FP count
a	2	20	average	10
b	2	20	average	10
c	1	3	low	7
Totals	5	43		27

As can be seen Project Y has a higher number of both record types and data types than Project X but has a lower FP count.

Table 6.7 *Logical internal file types for Project Y*

File	Record types	Data types	Rating	FP count
a	4	19	low	7
b	4	19	low	7
c	6	19	average	10
Totals	14	57		24

It might be that in practice errors in one direction tend to be compensated for by errors in the other. Abran and Robillard (1996) subsequently carried out trials that found that in practice the various components of FPs, and FPs themselves, were good indicators of effort.

6.6.3 Inter-rater consistency

The coefficient of variation for a second case study was a little better at 33.8%.

This refers to the degree to which different people counting FPs for the same system will come up with the same result. Low and Jeffery (1990) conducted a test where 22 analysts were asked to count function points for two different applications. In one case, the counts ranged from 26 to 159. The mean FP count derived was 57.7 with a standard deviation of 26.3. A convenient way of expressing the degree of spread is by the **coefficient of variation** which is calculated as (standard deviation/ mean x 100) and was in this case 45.5. It needs to be noted that this was using the original Albrecht guidelines and as we have seen IFPUG has since gone a long way in tightening up the counting rules. This study is worth mentioning, however, as it found that many of the discrepancies came not from the FP counting process but from differences in the way that the analysts had interpreted the specification.

Kemerer used the *median* percentage difference because there was a 'rogue' case with an abnormally high difference between raters which might have distorted the mean difference figure.

Kemerer (1993) conducted a test where there were 27 different applications and 27 pairs of FP counters. The median percentage difference between the pairs of counts was about 12%. In this experiment, later and fuller, IFPUG guidelines on counting FPs were used. Thus it appears that the problems of inter-rater consistency can be addressed through tighter counting rules and more consistent training so that it could become an issue of minor importance.

Exercise 6.10 Evaluating inter-rater consistency

(a) In order to test the consistency of FP counting in an organization, six applications were selected and were each FP counted by two different raters. The results are shown in Table 6.8. Calculate the mean percentage variation between raters. Note that the percentage difference is calculated as absolute *(rater a estimate − rater b estimate)*/*rater a estimate* × 100.

(b) Would be the answer to the above if the percentage difference was calculated as absolute *(rater b estimate − rater a estimate)*/*rater b estimate* × 100?

(c) As an alternative test, nine different analysts FP counted the same application with these results: 450, 455, 397, 425, 433, 315, 315, 452, 388. What was the coefficient of variation?

Table 6.8 *FP counts for Exercise 6.10.*

system	rater a	rater b
a	120	135
b	352	333
c	190	202
d	300	394
e	260	255
f	600	612

Low and Jeffery also collected *estimates* of SLOC as well as FP counts and found that the FP counts were more accurate. They concluded that FPs rather than SLOC should be assessed at the early stages of a project, a view later supported by Barbara Kitchenham (1995). Of course there remains a risk that the specification could change and thus invalidate the initial FP count (Jeffery and Stathis 1993).

Note that these were *estimates* and not actual SLOC.

6.6.4 Consistency with size indicators

The effectiveness of function points has also been evaluated by examining the degree to which FP counts relate to SLOC or development effort. One statistical test is to calculate the **correlation** between FPs and SLOC or effort. The result of a correlation test is a **coefficient** which can take a value from −1.00 to +1.00. A correlation coefficient of 1.00 indicates that the two sets of values are completely in step with each other. A high value in the FP count is matched with a high value in SLOC and a low value in the FP count with a low value in SLOC. Furthermore, where one FP value is twice another, the matching SLOC counts are in the same proportions. A correlation coefficient of 0 on the other hand indicates that there is no relationship at all between the two sets of variables. A coefficient of −1.00 would indicate that there is a perfect negative relationship between the two sets of variables so that a high value in one variable is matched by a low value in the other, or vice versa. Intermediate coefficient values indicate different degrees of correlation.

A good way to get an intuitive idea of the correlation is to plot the two variables as x and y coordinates on a graph.

Microsoft Excel has a CORREL function for calculating the correlation coefficient.

Albrecht and Gaffney (1983) found a correlation of 0.93 between FP counts and effort in a data set of 24 projects. However, it has been pointed out that in this data set there were three very big projects, and if these results were removed, the correlation would be much reduced. This does not detract from the fact that more recent studies by, for example, Barbara Kitchenham (1992, 1995) and Alain Abran and Pierre Robillard (1996) have also shown strong correlations between FPs and development effort. These later studies are convincing because the researchers involved have been people who have expressed some scepticism about the theoretical basis of FPs. However, the precise relationship between FPs and effort varies from one environment to another, and FP-based effort prediction models can give poor results if they are not calibrated for the local environment (Kemerer 1987).

The effort estimate generated by a model should, at the least, be compared with that produced by expert opinion. A model that appears to be poor might still be better than just guessing!

As we will see in the next chapter, measuring the predictive power of a single effort estimation method is not very useful. The result of such an exercise is only useful if there is something with which to compare it. The predictive power of estimation models based on FPs might be compared with those using SLOC. If this is done, it must be remembered that SLOC-based prediction models, when used for real estimating, will be using an *estimate* of SLOC, not the figure for actual SLOC in the final application which, of course, is not yet known. Clearly the original SLOC estimate ought to be used for a fair comparison (Kemerer 1987).

6.6.5 Relationship between the input elements

When more than one element is combined to get an overall measurement, it is desirable that each of those elements is independent of the others. In practice, this means that each contributory element should have a very low or null correlation with the others. If two or more elements are highly correlated, then this suggests that one of the elements is not required and can be discarded. **Multicollinearity** is the name given to the existence of a correlation between two or more of the inputs to a prediction model. Some researchers (Kitchenham and Kansala 1993, Jeffery and Stathis 1993) have found that there are correlations between the various components of the function point count. As a result, Jeffery and Stathis (1993) have suggested that the count of logical internal files by itself would be a better predictor of effort.

Multicollinearity is not simply a technical problem for statisticians. When two size drivers vary in size together, it is difficult to judge the degree of influence each one has independently. It also suggests that one size driver might influence the other or that a third factor influences both. For instance, the reason why the number of data items input to a system is correlated with the number of output data items might be that both are related to the number of data item types stored on the database. This would indicate that the underlying theoretical model – in other words, the basic picture of the system in question – might need to be re-examined.

However, our view is that the truth of a model must not be made the victim of statistical convenience. In general big things have a tendency to be bigger than small things in a whole range of respects. For example, a correlation between the height and weight might be expected in a human population. However, we are all aware of individual exceptions – of tall, skinny people or fat, short people. Moving back to the world on information systems, one would agree that in general systems with a large number of inputs have a large number of outputs, but exceptions to this rule can easily be envisaged.

6.6.6 Mark II function points

The theoretical basis of Mark II function points has also been the subject of criticism. The different weightings for input and output data items have been attacked ·on the grounds that as they are measured in the same unit ('data elements') they ought to have the same weightings (Kitchenham *et al.* 1995). This objection seems to be rather arbitrary to us – the same paper argues that the module calls that make up fan-in and fan-out in the Henry–Kafura measurement (Henry and Kafura 1981), described in Chapter 4, should be treated as different measurements, even though they are measured in the same unit. Furthermore, the objection seems to be removed if the units are named 'input data elements' and 'output data elements'.

The main objection to Mark II FPs, which as we have already indicated we find incontrovertible, is that the method really presents an effort model, rather than a size measurement. Indeed, to us it increasingly seems to be the case that there can be no true measurement of 'software size' – 'size' implies a physical bulk that software does not possess. As the term is commonly used, software size seems to equate with difficulty (which is reflected in effort) in constructing the software. Kitchenham *et al.* (1995) go on to suggest that as the output from the FP model is really a value for effort, it is not possible to talk about productivity in terms of 'FPs per day' as that would be simply dividing effort expressed in one unit by effort expressed in another unit. However, the core Mark II function point model does not take account of productivity. In effect it produces the equivalent of an index value that represents the standard amount of effort to produce a piece of software, but the actual effort figure will vary because of differences in productivity. Productivity expressed in 'FPs per day' is therefore the equivalent of a ratio of a 'standard' effort to the actual.

With regard to inter-rater consistency, the UK Software Metrics Association have published the results of a study (Rule 1998) which gave an overall coefficient of variation of 22.5 and for expert counters of 12.8. This would seem to compare well with the corresponding results for the IFPUG flavour of FPs.

There have been a very few published studies examining the relationship between Mark II FPs and SLOC and effort. An early and influential study was one conducted at the Inland Revenue organization in the United Kingdom and found a 0.89 correlation between Mark II FPs and effort compared to a 0.94 correlation for SLOC and effort. These figures are not quite so impressive when it is realized that the data set included only three new development projects! Based on a data set of five enhancement projects a correlation of 0.70 was found in this case between FPs and effort (Betteridge *et al.* 1990).

Apparently the measurement of land area 'acre' was originally based on the amount of land that could be ploughed in one day, but was then standardized to a specific physical area. Talking about acres ploughed per day seems to be quite valid.

6.6.7 Technical complexity adjustment

The technical complexity adjustment has been seen as the weakest aspect of both the IFPUG and Mark II flavours of FPs despite some stout defenders (for example, Dreger 1989). It has been found that taking into account technical complexity can in fact make the Albrecht method a poorer predictor (Kemerer 1987). Many FP counters therefore either do not use the TCA or use an adjustment close to 1.00 which in effect is no adjustment at all (Heemstra and Kusters 1991, Kemerer and Porter 1992).

It has also been argued that the TCA does not seem to take effective account of the actual abnormal costs that can be experienced (Betteridge 1992). These might be user requirements that would not be apparent from a purely logical model of a proposed system but which might typically account for around 20% of the final system size (Verner *et al.* 1989). Grant Rule (1993) suggested a modified version of the TCA based on the identification and quantification of 'non-functional' requirements such as usability and adaptability to cope with this.

Some of the technical complexity factors seem to overlap: for example, performance requirements, heavy configuration use and a high transaction rate all relate to physical performance (Symons 1988). **Principal component analysis** (PCA) is a sophisticated statistical technique that analyses data sets. It groups together variables that tend to vary together and associates them with **principal components**, conceptual factors that capture the common variation of the variables. For each variable associated with a principal component, the degree to which it contributes to that component is assessed. The technique identifies the grouping of variables, but it is up to the investigator to work out to what underlying characteristic the cluster of variables really relates. Barbara Kitchenham (1992) has reported on an analysis which used PCA on a set of FP data. Six principal components were identified which accounted for 85.5% of the variation in the data. This might suggest that the original fourteen Albrecht factors could be reduced to six.

In general, the technical complexity adjustments are only useful where the same development environment is producing systems that have radically different characteristics. Most development environments, however, will tend to produce applications which have broadly the same characteristics.

6.7   Extending the function point approach to real-time systems

6.7.1 Overview of this section

The FP counting approach that has been described so far has been concerned with data processing and information systems. Initially there was some caution about applying the principles to other types of system as it was felt that these could implement large and complex algorithms that would not necessarily be apparent from the inputs and outputs of the software. This might well be the case with software that was being used to carry out scientific calculations. However with most real-time control systems the principle of identifying and counting key features of the software that would be apparent at specification stage seemed to be just as applicable as with information systems. In this section we will look at some of the attempts that have been made to extend the FP approach to real-time systems. This includes the **feature point** approach of Capers Jones and the **3D Function Points** described by Scott A. Whitmire. These two real-time FP methods have the Albrecht/IFPUG method as their foundation. In contrast, the FPs for Highly Constrained Systems (FP-HCS) method, which has its roots in the Symons/Mark II method will also be briefly examined. We will conclude this section by looking at what appears to be the most determined attack on this problem, **full function points**, which uses the IFPUG method but adds on consideration of additional types of feature in order to extend its range.

6.7.2 Feature points

This approach (Jones 1987) adapts the IFPUG method by adding a new user function type called **algorithm** which takes account of internal processing. Feature points use a single weighting for each type of feature rather than the three (for 'simple', 'average' and 'complex') that the conventional IFPUG method allows for – see Table 6.9.

Table 6.9 *Feature point weights*

Function types	Weight
Logical internal files	7
External interface files	7
External inputs	4
External outputs	5
External inquiries	4
Algorithms	3

At conferences Capers Jones, the originator of feature points, has said that they had been devised to reassure real-time computing practitioners who felt uneasy about using an FP method with origins in an information systems environment. It was his opinion, however, the mainstream Albrecht/IFPUG method was quite adequate in real-time environments.

Capers Jones is very much involved in the accumulation of a repository of project data based on FP counts, and has carried out extensive analyses using FPs to compare development productivity across a wide range of environments. The success of such an enterprise depends on there being one standard method of FP counting.

IFPUG have produced 'Case Study 4' which aims to show how conventional FP counts can be derived for a control system.

6.7.3 3D function points

A description of this approach, developed at the Boeing Company can be found in Whitmire (1992). It is based on the perception that there are three categories of software application.

- **Data strong systems**, typically business information systems where the data structure is a key determinant of difficulty.

- **Function strong systems**, typically scientific and engineering applications where the difficulty lies in the nature of the processing that is executed.

- **Control strong systems**, typically real time control systems where a key influence on difficulty is the number and sequence of different system states for which the application has to cater.

These represent the three dimensions of 3D function points. The originators of 3D FPs felt that the conventional IFPUG FP approach could adequately reflect the size of data strong applications. In the case of function strong applications, the **transformations** or functions that transform inputs into outputs have to be identified. For each of these transformations, the processing **steps** have to be counted along with the semantic statements or predicates which test conditions and control the steps that will actually be executed in a particular situation. Table 6.10 is then used to decide whether the transformation is of low, average or high 'complexity'.

Table 6.10 *Complexity table for transformations*

	1 to 5 semantic statements	6 to 10 semantic statements	>10 semantic statements
1 to 10 steps	low	low	average
11 to 20 steps	low	average	high
>20 steps	average	high	high

It will be recalled from Chapter 5 that a close correlation was found by Cartwright between 'states' and lines of code.

In the case of control strong applications, the control dimension is measured by counting the number of **system states** and the number of valid paths or **transitions** between those system states.

An extended version of Table 6.1 – see Table 6.11 – is used to calculate the overall 3D FP counts for an application taking account of each of the three dimensions.

6.7.4 Function points for highly constrained systems (HCS)

An attempt has been made to extend Symons FPs to deal with 'highly constrained systems' (HCS) which include real time and telecommunications systems (UKSMA, 1993).

The completion of the transaction must also leave the system, particularly the database, in a consistent state.

A general problem with extending FPs to real time systems is that of **granularity**. A unit is recognized as a 'transaction' for FP counting if it is initiated by an end-user and returns some message back to the user. In the case of a real time system, there will often not be a human user initiating the transaction. In the HCS FP approach, a transaction receives inputs from beyond the system boundary and returns outputs back over it, not necessarily to a human operator.

The HCS FP counting method has been influenced by the Jackson Structured Design (JSD) methodology (Jackson 1982). The system (or **realm** in the terminology employed) is seen as a number of communicating **processes** each

Table 6.11 *3D FP complexity multipliers*

External user type	Multiplier		
	Low	Average	High
External input type	3	4	6
External output type	4	5	7
Logical internal file type	7	10	15
External interface file type	5	7	10
External inquiry type	3	4	6
Transformations	7	10	15
States	n/a	1	n/a
Transitions	n/a	1	n/a

accessing and updating a single entity type, whereas in the basic Symons method, a transaction can access many entity types.

The method calls for counts of the following:

(a) the **input messages** to each process from outside the realm, or from other processes (*imt*);

(b) the individual **data item types** in each of the messages identified in (a) (*iat*)

(c) the **messages** output from the realm (*omt*);

(d) the individual **data item types** in each of the messages identified in (c) (*oat*);

(e) **entity accesses** that do not modify any attribute values (*ea*).

The five counts are summed (*imt*+*iat*+*omt*+*oat*+*ea*) to get an overall score for the realm. No weightings are applied to the different types of count – instances of each type of feature are assumed to have similar impacts on system size.

Our own experience of trying to apply this method is that when applied to an existing system, considerable effort is needed for the analysis of the system into processes and the identification of the individual data items involved. While the processes might be seen as 'logical' they are still internal to the application and require considerable effort to unearth.

We also found that the concept of entity types was not understood by many real time programmers.

6.7.5 COSMIC full function points

The COSMIC full function point method is based on full function points (FFPs) associated with two interlinked research groups in Québec, Canada. The developers have been at pains to stress that this method is an *extension* of the IFPUG approach which allows real time applications to be sized more conveniently. The impression given is that the groups have made every effort to ensure that the conventional IFPUG community does not feel threatened by the proposals.

As in the case of 3D FPs, it is argued that conventional FPs adequately capture

The two groups are the Software Engineering Research Laboratory at Université du Québec á Montréal and the privately owned Software Engineering Laboratory in Applied Metrics (SELAM).

Full details of COSMIC-
FFP can be found in
Oligny (1999).

the work content of business-oriented information systems because in these applications the size of the internal procedures is very closely and consistently related to the number of externally apparent features. In real time applications, however, the amount and complexity of internal processing can vary considerably from one transaction to another. The originators of FFPs suggest that this additional complexity has to be captured by considering processes in real time application at a lower level. It is also argued that the kind of standing data structures recognized by the IFPUG counting rules as internal logical files (ILFs) and external interface files (EIFs) do not cater for all the types of data structure that are commonly found in a real time control system.

The original work on full function points has been expanded in scope by the formation of the Common Software Measurement International Consortium (COSMIC) which involves not just the developers of FFPs but also Charles Symons, the originators of Mark II FPs. To remedy the perceived shortcomings **data groups** are identified, that is groups of data items used the systems to control the behaviour of the physical part of the application (for instance, a heating system for an office block).

Four new transactional function types have been proposed as listed below:

- **Entries** (E) which are sub-processes that execute the movement of data into the system from outside the application's boundary;

- **External control exit** (X) which are sub-processes that transmit data beyond the application's boundary;

- **Reads** (R) which are sub-processes that move, but do not alter, a group of data from storage into an area where it can be processed;

- **Writes** (W) which are sub-processes that move a group of data into storage.

Exercise 6.11 Identifying COSMIC full function points

A small computer system controls the entry of vehicles to a car park. Each time a vehicle pulls up before an entry barrier, a sensor notifies the computer system that a vehicle is waiting. The system examines a count that is maintained of the number of vehicles that are currently in the car park. If it is less than the maximum, the vehicle is allowed to enter and the count of the number of vehicles is incremented. When a vehicle leaves the car park, a sensor detects the exit and reduces the count of vehicles.

Identify the Entries, Exits, Reads and Writes in this application.

The overall COSMIC full function point count for an application is calculated by simply adding together the counts of Entries, Exits, Reads and Writes. This can be objected to on the grounds that counts of different types of entity cannot be validly added together. However, the COSMIC standard lays down that separate counts of functional processes, data groups, Entries, Exits, Reads and Writes be maintained and recorded, which would allow the impact of individual counts to be analysed.

6.8 Object points

The first thing that needs to be made clear about the object points referred to here is that they have little or nothing to do with object-oriented systems.

In Section 6.2.1, two main reasons for measuring system size were suggested. The first was to gauge productivity and the second was to predict development effort. If productivity measurement is the key motivation then we want to have a consistent and recognized method that is used over a wide range of projects so that we can compare productivity over a wide range of environments. If, on the other hand, the driving force behind measurement is effort prediction, you would want to restrict the collection of data to your own organization as the past performance of your own projects is the best guide to future performance.

If you are really sure that you only want to collect size and effort data to assist effort prediction, then you will be better off counting the occurrences of the system characteristics that are most easily recognized in your environment. These should be the ones that you know are most likely to have an impact of development effort. The system characteristics that are easiest to count will depend, among other things, on the analysis and design method used and the case tools employed.

Object points can be seen as an example of this approach. Object points were devised at the Leonard N. Stern School of Business, New York University. The method has similarities with the FP approach, but takes account of features that are more readily identifiable if you are building a system using a high-level application building tool.

The reason why object points have attracted interest is that the influential COCOMO II programme, described in the next chapter, has recommended object points as a way of getting a preliminary estimate of the development effort for business oriented information systems. What is frustrating is that the method does not appear to have any easily obtainable detailed counting rules. We therefore present it as essentially an example of a more general approach which is similar to that championed by Watts Humphrey (1995). The general approach is to use counts of significant **objects** in the application: in the specific case of object points these are counts of the screens, reports and 3GL components. Each object has to be classified as either:

A more detailed description can be found in Banker *et al.* (1993). This differs in some aspects from the method described in the COCOMO II definition manual (*CSE*, 1997).

- simple;

- medium;

- difficult.

Tables 6.12 and 6.13 show the scheme used in the case object points to make this classification. The numbers of objects at each level are multiplied by the appropriate complexity weighting shown in Table 6.14. The weighted sub-totals are then summed to get an overall score for the application. We stress that we present these tables of how this has been done in one environment. You would need to make your own judgements about the relationships that apply in your own environment.

Some of these objects may not need to be developed as there are already existing components that can be utilized. The object point score can be adjusted to take this into account. Say that in an application containing 840 object points, 20% can be supplied by using existing components, then the adjusted score would be:

new object points (NOP) = $840 \times (100 - 20)/100 = 672$

Table 6.12 *Object points – for screens*

Number of views contained	Number and source of data tables		
	Total < 4 (<2 servers <3 clients)	Total < 8 (<3 servers 3 to 5 clients)	Total > 7 (>3 servers > 5 clients)
<3	simple	simple	medium
3 to 7	simple	medium	difficult
>7	medium	difficult	difficult

Table 6.13 *Object points – for reports*

Number of sections contained	Number and source of data tables		
	Total < 4 (<2 servers <3 clients)	Total < 8 (<3 servers 3 to 5 clients)	Total > 7 (>3 servers > 5 clients)
<2	simple	simple	medium
2 or 3	simple	medium	difficult
>3	medium	difficult	difficult

Table 6.14 *Object points complexity weightings*

Object type	Complexity weighting		
	Simple	Medium	Difficult
Screen	1	2	3
Report	2	5	8
3GL component	10	10	10

Finally a productivity rate (PROD) has to be identified. It would be best if the estimator could use details of past projects to derive this. As an example, the developers of object points produced the details in Table 6.15 to calculate PROD. In the situation where this information was gathered, as the CASE tool's features were improving with successive releases, so the experience of the developers with the tool was growing too. Given the very specific situation in which these productivity rates were gathered, they can hardly be said to merit the name 'industry averages' and would need to be used with extreme caution.

Table 6.15 *Object point productivity ratings*

Developer's experience and capability	Very low	Low	Nominal	High	Very high
ICASE maturity and capability	Very low	Low	Nominal	High	Very high
PROD	4	7	13	25	50

An estimate of the person-months needed to carry out the project is then calculated by dividing PROD into NOP. For example, given the 672 new object points above and a development environment where productivity was 'nominal', then the estimated effort for the project would be 672/13 = 51 months.

The format of the tables used in object points has been influenced by the format used by the FP method. We have already pointed out, with regard to FPs, the inconsistent results that conversions using such tables can generate. We would strongly recommend anyone building their own model to use simple counts of the significant features, which can then be weighted to reflect their relative influence on development effort.

6.9   Functional size of object-oriented applications

It has already been pointed out that the object points mentioned in the last section have little or no bearing on object-oriented design. The question remains whether the FP approach can be applied to systems constructed using OO. In theory, there is no reason why FPs should not be counted for systems constructed using the OO paradigm as FPs are supposed to relate to the externally apparent features of the application. The functional transactions, such as external inputs, external outputs and external inquiries, seem to be very similar in conception to **use cases** in OO (Armour, Catherwood *et al.* 1996). A use case defines the complete process initiated by an event in the system's environment. It may involve several inter-linked methods being executed which are associated with a number of different classes of object. Having said that, the IFPUG approach, in particular, uses a model of the internal data structures of the system (with Files, Records and Data Element Types) that does not map conveniently from the OO way of seeing things. The advantage of persevering with and applying the FP approach, even though the collection of the details needed might not be easy, is that it allows a common size indicator to be derived that allows productivity to be compared across OO and non-OO developments.

To confuse things further, Harry Sneed (1996) has devised something called 'object points' which *are* related to OO concepts.

There is room for considerable research to establish the link between the OO metrics described in Chapter 5 and development effort. There has been an attempt to develop 'predictive object points' (POPs) which are OO-specific (Teologlou 1999). Like so many of the 'measurements' discussed in this chapter, this is really an effort model. The proposed model uses *estimates* of Weighted Methods per Class, Number of Children and Depth of Inheritance, plus the number of Top Level Classes (TLC) to produce an effort index. The techniques by which such estimates can be derived are suggested, but the fact that they are only estimates needs to be stressed.

6.10 Conclusions

Our first conclusion is that the concept of software size is a very nebulous one because software does not have the physical bulk of the kinds of object that are usually subjected to measurement in engineering. The closest to a 'real' measurement of software size would probably be the number of bytes of internal storage occupied. However, this is not very useful because it does not reflect very accurately the size of the 'problem' that a piece of software to be developed represents. We would contend that 'size' in most practitioners' minds is associated with the idea of difficulty that tends to manifest itself as the effort needed to develop the software.

We have attempted to distinguish carefully between size and complexity, noting that many researchers and practitioners have confused the two. However, because larger systems have the potential to be disproportionately more complex than smaller ones, the two attributes are very closely associated and both contribute to the difficulty of completing the development task.

When counting the features of a piece of software, rather than measuring the dimensions of the software, what we are really doing is measuring various effort drivers. What people claim to be functional size measurements, such as function points, are invariably really effort models. Anywhere that weightings are used to give different degrees of importance to different elements, it is a good bet that those weightings are thought to reflect the relative difficulty (and thus the effort) of their implementation. FPs can be seen as an index indicating the relative amount of effort that might be expected to develop a particular application. The actual amount of effort would, of course, vary considerably because of differences in productivity – reuse, for example, might reduce the actual amount of effort needed to a small fraction of what the FP count might suggest.

Despite the imperfections with FPs that have been noted, they still represent the practical way that any cross-organizational productivity comparisons can be made. If this is your main motivation then you will have to adopt FPs. You would then be able to compare the productivity of your organization or projects with other organizations and project across the globe, using for example data sets and reports produced by the International Software Benchmarking Standards Group (ISBSG). If you decide to adopt the FP approach we would strongly recommend that you record and store past project details at the lowest and most detailed level of aggregation. In other words, try and record the individual counts of the different elements of individual transactions, rather than simply recording the final FP counts for individual projects. Holding this base data will allow you to carry out your own analyses to find the best predictors of effort in your development environment. It might be, for example, that counts of records and data types on the data base of an application turn out to be reasonable indicators of the development effort. Knowing this will allow you to get a good initial idea of the effort required to deliver a system at quite an early stage of the development life cycle without having to do a full FP analysis.

If you plan your data collection cleverly, you might find that you are not irrevocably committed to one particular FP method. You might be able to use the same base data to calculate FPs in different ways for different purposes.

6.11 References

Abran, A. and Robillard, P. (1994), 'Function points: a study of their measurement processes and scale transformations', *J. Systems and Software*: 25, 171–184.

Abran, A. and Robillard, P. (1996), 'Function points analysis: an empirical study of its measurement processes', *IEEE Transactions on Software Engineering*: 22(12), 895–910.

Albrecht, A. J. and Gaffney, J. R. (1983), 'Software function, source lines of code and development effort prediction', *IEEE Transactions on Software Engineering*: 9(6), 639–648.

Albrecht, A. J.(1979), 'Measuring application development productivity', *Proceedings IBM Applications Development Joint SHARE/GUIDE Symposium*, Monterey, CA, 83–92.

Armour, F., Catherwood, B. and Furey, S. (1996), 'Experiences measuring object oriented size with use cases', *Proceedings of 7th European software control and metrics conference*, Wilmslow, UK, 101–114.

Banker, R. D., Kauffman, R. and Kumar, R. (1993), 'An empirical test of object-based output measurement metrics in a computer-aided software engineering (CASE) environment', *J. Management Information Systems*: 8(3), 127–150.

Behrens, C. A. (1983), 'Measuring the productivity of computer system development activities with function points', *IEEE Transactions on Software Engineering*: 9(6), 649–658.

Betteridge, R. (1992), *Uses and Abuses of Function Point Analysis*, The IT Office, Inland Revenue, Telford, Salop.

Betteridge, R., Fisher, D. and Goodman, P. (1990), 'Function points versus lines of code', *Systems Development*: August, 4–6.

Dreger, J. B. (1989), *Function Point Analysis*, Prentice-Hall, Englewood Cliffs.

Heemstra, F. J. and Kusters, R. J. (1991), 'Function point analysis: evaluation of a software cost estimation model', *European Journal of Information Systems*: 1(4), 229–237.

Henry, S. and Kafura, D. (1981), 'Software metrics based on information flow', *IEEE Transactions on Software Engineering*: 7(5), 510–518.

Humphrey, W. S. (1995), *A Discipline For Software Engineering*, Addison-Wesley, Reading, MA.

IFPUG (1999), *Function Point Counting Practices Manual: Release 4.1*, International Function Point Users Group, Westerville, Ohio, USA.

Jackson, M. A.(1982), *Systems Development*, Prentice-Hall, Englewood Cliffs.

Jeffery, D. R. and Stathis, J. (1993), 'Specification-based software sizing: an empirical investigation of function points', *Proceedings NASA-Goddard Software Engineering Workshop*, Greenbelt, MD.

Jones, T. C. (1986), *Programmer Productivity*, McGraw-Hill, New York.

Jones, T. C. (1987), *A Short History of Function Points and Feature Points*, Technical Report, Software Productivity Research Inc.

Kemerer, C. F. (1987), 'An empirical validation of software cost estimation models', *CACM*: 30(5), 416–429.

Kemerer, C. F. (1993), 'Reliability of function points: a field experiment', *CACM*: 36(2), 85–97.

Kitchenham, B. A. (1992), 'Empirical studies of assumptions that underlie software cost models', *Information Systems and Technology*: 34(4), 211–218.

Kitchenham, B. A. (1995), 'Using function points for software cost estimation: some empirical results', in Fenton, N., Whitty, R. and Iizuka, Y (eds.) *Software Quality Assurance and Measurement: A Worldwide Perspective*, International Thomson Computer Press, London.

Kitchenham, B. A. and Känsälä, K. (1993), 'Inter-item correlations among function points', *Proceedings First International Software Metrics Symposium*, IEEE Computer Society, Los Alamitos, CA, 11–14.

Kitchenham, B. A., Pfleeger, S. L. and Fenton, N. (1995), 'Towards a framework for software measurement validation', *IEEE Transactions on Software Engineering*: 21(12), 929–943.

Low, G. C. and Jeffery, R. D. (1990), 'Function points in the estimation and evaluation of the software process', *IEEE Transactions on Software Engineering*: 16(1), 64–71.

Oligny, S. (1999) (ed) *COSMIC-FFP Measurement Manual Version 2.0*, Common Software Measurement International Consortium, available from http://www.cosmicon.com.

Park. R. E. (1992), 'Software size measurement: a framework for counting source statements', Report no CMU/SEI-92-TR-20, ESC-TE-92-20, Software Engineering Institute, Carnegie Mellon University, Pittsburgh, PA.

Rule, P. G. (1992), 'Technical complexity as a size driver', *Proceedings of Third European Software Cost Modelling Meeting*.

Rule, P. G. (1998), 'Compliant, correct, consistent and complete: UKSMA's improvement plan', *Proceedings IFPUG Spring Conference*, Washington, DC.

Sneed, H. M. (1996), 'Estimating the development costs of object-oriented software', *Proceedings of 7th European Software Control and Metrics Conference*, Wilmslow, UK, 135–152.

Symons, C. R. (1988), 'Function point analysis: difficulties and improvements', *IEEE Transactions on Software Engineering*: 14(1), 2–11.

Symons, C. R. (1991), *Software Sizing and Estimating MkII FPA (Function Point Analysis)*, John Wiley and Sons, Chichester.

Teologlou, G. (1999), 'Measuring object-oriented software with predictive object points', *Proceedings of 10th European Software Control and Metrics Conference/6th Conference for the European Network of Clubs for the Reliability and Safety of Software,* Herstmonceux, UK Shaker Publishing, 227–236.

UK Software Metrics Association (1993), *Function Point Counting Practices for Highly Constrained Systems: Release 1.0*, St. Clare's, Mill Hill, Edenbridge, Kent, TN8 5DQ.

Verner, J. M., Tate, G., Jackson, B. and Hayward, R. G. (1989), 'Technology dependence in function point analysis: a case study and critical review', *Proceedings 11th International Conference on Software Engineering,* 375–382.

Whitmire, S. A. (1992), '3D function points: scientific and real-time extensions to function points.' *Proceedings of 1992 Pacific Northwest Software Quality conference*, 137–153.

6.12 Additional questions

1. A software application comprises twelve software modules.

   (a) What is the maximum number of possible links between modules?
   (b) What metrics discussed in previous chapters attempt to capture the actual complexity of the relationships?
   (c) What practical steps can a system designer take to reduce the number of actual relationships between modules?

2. A time-tabling system for a college uses the following files:

   - a file of personnel details of teaching staff that is copied from the college's personnel records system;

   - a file of room details that is accessed from an existing premises database;

   - a database of existing courses and the students enrolled on each course – this is currently used to hold assessment and progression details

   - a file that is created by the time-tabling application and which holds the details of each teaching activity that has been time-tabled, the staff responsible for that activity, the courses undertaking that activity and its location and time.

   Software components will be needed to set up and amend time-tabling details and to create and print time-tables for staff and students.

   (a) Illustrate how you would use the Albrecht FP method as a basis for producing an estimate for this system.

    (b) You will have to make lots of assumptions (or in real life, seek out further information). List these assumptions.

    (c) What difference might making the full IFPUG method make?

3. A small application maintains a telephone directory. The database for the application contains the following data types:

- staff reference;
- surname;
- forenames;
- title;
- department code;
- room number;
- telephone extension;
- e-mail address;
- fax number.

Transactions are needed which:
    (i)   set up new entries;
    (ii) amend existing entries;
    (iii) delete entries;
    (iv) allow enquirers to list on-line the details for a particular member of staff;
    (v) produce a complete listing of the telephone directory entries in alphabetical order.

    (a) Use this scenario to produce an estimated Mark II FP count. List all the assumptions that you will need to make.

    (b) Another requirement could be to produce the listing in (v) in departmental order. In your view should this increase FP count and if so by how much?

4. An application has been counted as having 650 FPs and the technical complexity factors are rated as shown in Table 6.16.

    (a) Calculate the adjusted FP count using the Albrecht/IFPUG method.

    (b) Calculate the adjusted FP count using the Mark II method – treat the additional five technical complexity factors as all being average, except for third party access which is non-existent.

    (c) It has been suggested that the original fourteen factors could be reduced to six. What might these six characteristics be?

5. Table 6.17 is a list of past projects with their sizes in FPs and the effort needed to implement them in staff-days.
    Based on these figures:

    (a) provide an estimate for a new project estimated as having a size of: (i) 50 FPs; (ii) 460 FPs; (iii) 800 FPs.

    (b) what cautions would you give about the estimates in (i) and (iii)?

Table 6.16 *Technical complexity factors for Question 4*

Factor	Rating
Data communications	3
Distributed functions	4
Performance requirements	4
Heavy hardware configuration usage	4
High transaction rate	3
On-line data entry	3
End-user efficiency	5
On-line update	3
Complex processing	3
Reusability requirements	5
Ease of installation	2
Operational ease (for technical staff as opposed to end users)	0
Multiple sites	3
Ease of modification	3

Table 6.17 *Project sizes for Question 5*

FPs	Staff-days
321	32
127	15
450	39
427	36
211	20
68	15
457	40
499	43
443	42

6. In an experiment, five systems analysts are asked to produce, without consulting each other, FP counts for the same specification. In addition, four FP counters from a central audit unit in the organization also produce individual FP counts for the same application. These are listed in Table 6.18.

   (i) Demonstrate how you would measure the level of agreement in each of the two groups over the FP count.

Table 6.18 *FP counts for Question 6*

Systems analyst	FP count	FP auditor	FP count
a	700	w	510
b	710	x	550
c	692	y	525
d	730	z	600
e	650		

(ii) The systems analysts and FP auditors clearly disagree in general terms about the FP count that applies to this application. What factors might you consider if you were asked to investigate the reasons for the differences between the groups?

7. If you are familiar with Microsoft Access,

(i) identify the types of 'object' you might distinguish and count if you wanted to use an object point type of approach;

(ii) explain how you would measure the comparative size of each instance of each type of object?

Chapter 7

How to estimate software development effort

OBJECTIVES

When you have completed this chapter you will be able to:

☐ distinguish the different types of estimating methods

☐ take account of the wide range of factors that influence software development effort

☐ evaluate the effectiveness of effort estimation methods

☐ take advantage of local knowledge and expertise

☐ use the COCOMO family of models

7.1 Introduction

The last chapter on system size has been a preparation for this one. A major motivation for assessing size is to estimate development effort. In this chapter we will review the different techniques for forecasting development effort. In addition to size, there are other characteristics that will lead to a software development task requiring more or less time.

The wide variety of estimation techniques forces us to step back and measure the effectiveness of the effort estimation process itself in order to select those methods that will be effective in our environment. We cannot, for example, assume that constructing a complicated statistical model will necessarily be better than asking local experts for their opinions.

It is possible either to use an existing model, such as COCOMO, to derive estimates or to build your own model. We will look at COCOMO in this chapter and examine building a do-it-yourself model in the next.

7.2   The real nature of effort estimation

A real estimate of effort is one that is formulated *before* the work to which it applies has been done. This obvious point is emphasized as much research work has tried to identify retrospectively which method *would* have produced the most accurate estimate. As a project progresses, so more accurate information about the nature of the project emerges and more accurate estimates can be produced (DeMarco 1982, pages 20–21; Boehm 1984). Hence the point at which an estimate was made in the development cycle should be considered (Boehm and Wolverton 1980). Also, estimates should be done throughout a project, ideally in different ways at different stages.

An estimate, if known to the developer, will become a target (Boehm 1981) and might thus become a self-fulfilling prophecy. With over-generous estimates 'Parkinson's Law' (Northcote Parkinson 1957) that '*work expands to fill the time available*' will come into effect and productivity could fall (Abdel-Hamid and Madnick 1986). Estimating can thus become an intensely 'political' activity where higher level management may press to reduce estimates in order to boost productivity or to make proposed projects seem cost-effective (Lederer and Prasad 1991). Underestimates, on the other hand, can cause the quality of work to suffer with early design and analysis work may be completed on time but at the cost of poor quality and prolonged testing.

Exercise 7.1 Measuring the quality of targets

An over-generous estimate is likely to cause work to take longer than otherwise and estimates that do not allow adequate development time are likely to lead to poorer quality work. Based on these assumptions, suggest how the quality of development effort *targets* could be measured.

An extreme example of this would be a look-up table of LOC and effort for previous projects, which is then 'validated' by looking up the LOC for a past project and extracting the effort figure.

Sometimes, estimates are produced retrospectively in order to evaluate a particular estimating method. Thus they have not been used as targets by developers, and might thus appear less effective. On the other hand, where someone is attempting to build a model that explains effort, it can be tempting to show off how good the model is by demonstrating it 'predicts' the effort for projects used to build the model in the first place. In addition, the real estimators, when creating their estimates might have to use information that later changes – a problem that retrospective estimates do not face.

7.3   Classification of estimating methods

Barry Boehm suggested the following classification (Boehm 1984) of estimating methods.

Algorithmic models – which use 'cost drivers' reflecting the important characteristics of the target system and the implementation environment.

Expert judgement – where the advice of knowledgeable staff is solicited.

Analogy – where a similar, completed, project is identified and its actual cost is used as a basis for the estimate for the new project.

Parkinson – which uses the available resources to derive an 'estimate'.

Price-to-win – where the 'estimate' is a figure that appears to be low enough to win a contract.

Top-down – an overall estimate is formulated for the whole project which is then broken down into the effort required for component tasks.

Bottom-up – component tasks are identified and sized and these individual estimates are aggregated.

Strictly, the 'Parkinson' method is not an effort prediction method, but a way of setting the **scope** of a project. This could be the perfectly acceptable engineering practice of **design-to-cost** (Gilb and Finzi 1988). Similarly 'Price-to-win' is a **pricing** technique, not a prediction method. Therefore these can be rejected as *prediction* techniques although they could have some value as *management* techniques.

Often, the question is not 'how much will this functionality require in effort?' but 'how much functionality can be achieved with this amount of effort?'

To understand the logic of the 'price-to-win' tactic, you have to realize that although customers want one figure, a true estimate is a range of figures clustered around the most likely value. This can be illustrated by considering the case of my going to work on my bicycle. A sensible way of estimating how long it might take me to go to work is to examine past instances of this journey. What we would find is that there is no one exact time that it always takes me. We could plot all the times on a graph and get something like Figure 7.1.

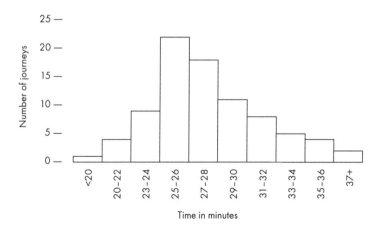

Figure 7.1 *Frequency of different journey times to work.*

From Figure 7.1, we can see that the most common duration was 25 or 26 minutes, although we can also see that on most occasions I took longer than this. We can also see that the more time I allow myself to get into work, the more likely I am to meet that target.

Exercise 7.2 Estimate probabilities

(i)   Convert the graph in Figure 7.1 so that the percentage of journeys in each time band are shown.

(ii) What is the percentage chance that I complete my journey time in 26 or fewer minutes?

(iii) If I wanted to give myself at least an 80% chance of getting into work on time, how much time would I allow myself?

Planning tools often allow you to specify a range of task durations.

With system development, it can be seen that managers bidding for work have a range of estimates to consider. They can either select an 'aggressive' target knowing that there is an increased risk of not meeting it or go for a bigger estimate and risk losing the business to a competitor.

Bottom-up approaches can be product oriented, where individual software components are identified, or task-based where tasks are identified, or a hybrid.

There is considerable overlap among the remaining five categories in the Boehm list. In practice it is difficult to distinguish between algorithmic techniques and top-down ones. The top-down or bottom-up approaches can be combined with algorithmic models, analogy or expert opinion. Further, expert opinion can be used to a greater or lesser extent with any of the other methods – after all, the expert could use any of the other methods. The bottom-up approach, where each component of the software task is sized individually, for instance, requires information from knowledgeable staff.

Boehm suggested that the strengths and weaknesses of the methods tended to balance each other so that algorithmic modelling complemented expert judgement while the top-down approach complemented the bottom-up. A sensible approach would therefore be to use a combination of techniques and to compare the results.

To what extent are the different methods used? Heemstra and Kusters (1991) surveyed practice in software development projects in Dutch organizations and produced the analysis shown in Table 7.1. Note that organizations could use more than one method. The finding that the analogy method was used by 60.8% of organizations but only 50% kept performance details on completed projects suggests that the information about comparable projects was often held in the memories of the estimators – a finding supported by a survey of American IS practitioners (Lederer and Prasad 1993). The Dutch researchers concluded that of the organizations that produced estimates (and 35% did not), 62% based them on intuition while only 16% used formalized estimation methods.

Table 7.1   *Proportion of use of each estimating method (after Heemstra & Kusters)*

Estimating method	Percentage of use
Expert judgement	25.5%
Analogy	60.8%
Capacity problem (i.e. 'Parkinson')	20.8%
Price-to-win	8.9%
Parametric models	13.7%

7.4   Basic components of effort models

7.4.1 Factors to be considered

Most estimating methods need information about similar past projects. The factors that need to be considered include:

- project scope;

- work size;

- complexity;

- technical requirements;

- non-functional (or quality) requirements;

- productivity.

7.4.2 Project scope

It is often forgotten that however accurate an estimating technique is, if the scope of the work has been wrongly defined then the estimate is bound to be wrong. This is a particular problem where an application is modified as this needs a knowledge of the existing code and how it will have to change.

7.4.3 Work size

There must, as detailed in the last chapter, initially be an assessment of the size of the application to be delivered to the client.

You might think that, in simple terms, the bigger the task, the more effort is needed. However, many estimating models take account of **diseconomies of scale**, the tendency for larger projects to be less productive than smaller ones. Typically this is dealt with by introducing exponentiation ('to the power of ...') into effort models in the general form:

$$Effort = (size \times (productivity\ rate))^{exponent} \qquad \text{(Equation 7.1)}$$

Figure 7.2 shows the difference between a linear effort model and one where an exponent of 1.5 has been introduced. Note that the equations used have just been made up to illustrate the shape of the curves.

(i) Identify factors that might contribute to *economies of scale,* that is, things that would tend to make larger projects more productive.

(ii) If there are diseconomies of scale, an obvious thing to do would be to break down large projects into smaller ones. Why might this not be effective?

Exercise 7.3 Economies of scale

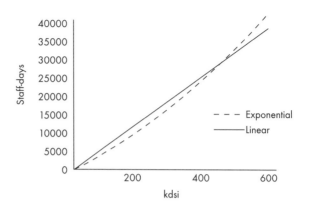

Figure 7.2 *Exponential versus linear functions.*

7.4.4 Complexity

Two applications might have the same size when measured in terms of function points but one might be more difficult for developers to build because of procedural complications. In the last chapter, the tendency to consider this as part of size was noted.

7.4.5 Technical complexity

Albrecht identified 'on-line data input' as a technical complexity factor. On-line input would now be seen as the norm.

We saw this in connection with function points. There might be requirements that are not directly related to size but deliver benefits to the user. The installation of the application at a large number of sites might, for example, generate work. Technical complexity needs to be considered separately from size and 'ordinary' complexity, because technological advances can simplify individual technical issues.

7.4.6 Quality requirements

These overlap with the technical complexity factors noted in 7.4.5. The argument for distinguishing between the two is that generally recognized lists of quality attributes have been produced and specialized methods of measuring their presence exist. A system needing high reliability will require more effort than one with a low reliability requirement. Where high reliability is needed, for example, you might employ **n-version programming** where the different versions of the same functionality are created by independent teams. The different versions of the software can then be run in parallel and the results can be cross-checked. While this will lead to a very reliable system, the development will be extremely costly.

7.4.7 Productivity

The factors so far influence task size. Development effort will also depend on the productivity characteristics of the development environment including the tools and methods used, the amount of component reuse and, most importantly, and staff experience. Two particular influences on productivity will now be dealt with briefly.

Learning curves can affect both individuals and organizations. A trainee will normally be less productive than an experienced system developer and when estimating effort for individual development tasks, account must be taken of the relative experience of the staff involved. Our own experience of trying to take account of individual experience has shown that it presents several difficulties. One is that the effect of lack of experience is not uniform over all sizes of software development task. Curtis *et al.* (1979) suggested that there are significant differences between the ability needed to grasp the logic in a small software module and that needed to understand software comprising many subroutines or logical modules. Lack of experience is likely to be less of a handicap when dealing with smaller sections of code.

Kemerer (1992) has a useful summary of the issues concerning learning curves.

At the organizational level, there will typically be a difficult period when a new technology is adopted. Many of the great IT development project disasters have occurred in these circumstances. Estimating effort when new technologies are adopted is difficult as past project experience is no longer relevant. This causes many managers to be conservative in their approach to new technical development. It might be better to risk being less productive than have a catastrophic IT failure.

A development project might be assessed as needing five people for twelve months. Higher management might then decide that it wants the project completed in a shorter time and allocate ten people for six months. **Schedule compression**, as this shortening of the duration of a project is called, requires additional effort overall. For example, additional management will be required in designing work packages for more staff and there will be increased overheads caused by the need for additional coordination.

7.5 How to evaluate estimating methods and models

7.5.1 Introduction

An effort model is in essence an algorithm that, given certain input parameters such as the size of the software and the productivity rates to be expected, will predict the effort needed. To be effective, the model must have a sound calculation procedure and also be 'tuned' properly for the current development environment. However good the estimation algorithm might be, it will not work properly with the wrong productivity rates. There are a number of model-building methods which can be used to build models for particular environments. We might therefore in some cases be evaluating how well a certain *model* produces accurate estimates in a particular environment. Sometimes, however, we may wish to evaluate how well a *model-building method* produces models, each of which should be effective, to a greater or lesser extent, in its own sphere.

7.5.2 Mean magnitude of relative error

Estimation models are usually compared using **mean magnitude of relative error** or **mmre** as a measure of effectiveness (Conte *et al.* 1986):

$$mre = \text{absolute}(actual - estimated)/actual \qquad \text{(Equation 7.2)}$$

$$mmre = \text{average}(mre) \qquad \text{(Equation 7.3)}$$

Exercise 7.4 Calculation of mmre

Below is a table of estimated and actual effort, in staff-hours, for modules in an application developed by the XYZ organization. Calculate the mean magnitude of relative error.

estimated	actual		estimated	actual
461	321		1681	1639
365	358		1406	1506
445	693		5828	5747
461	723		350	370
389	408		11920	11936
660	300		4602	4680
728	618			

Using absolute values of (*actual − estimated*)/*actual* means that underestimates do not compensate for overestimates.

Chapter 2 described how medians are calculated.

While *mmre* has the advantage of wide acceptance, it should be treated with caution. It is effectively an average of the percentage errors for individual predictions. Individual percentages that use different bases cannot be legitimately added together, quite apart from what subsequent processing might take place (Reichmann 1964). Magne Jørgensen (1995) suggested using **the median magnitude of relative error** to overcome this objection.

Exercise 7.5 Calculation of median mre

Calculate the median magnitude of relative error for the data set in Exercise 7.4.

A 10% error on a small task accounts for fewer hours than on a large one. Thus *mmre* can penalize methods that work better on larger tasks. This could be significant: it has been observed that uncertainty in productivity is less with larger projects (Symons 1991, page 142). A manager might be happy with a method that is unreliable with small projects, where financial risks are low, if it is reliable with the larger projects where risks are higher. *mmre* obscures these considerations.

That *mmre* does not allow underestimates to compensate for overestimates seems reasonable. However, care must be taken if lower level estimates (say for individual functions) are aggregated into higher ones (say for a project). One strength of 'bottom-up' estimating is the tendency of errors in one direction to cancel errors in the other (Tausworthe 1980).

7.5.3 Balanced relative error

mmre also tends to conceal the effect of underestimates (Miyazaki *et al.* 1991) because the measurement has an upper bound approaching 1 when dealing with underestimates compared to an unlimited upper bound when dealing with overestimates. Look at Table 7.2 for an example of how this might work in practice.

Table 7.2 *mre for under and overestimates*

Actual effort	Estimated effort	mre
100 staff-hours	200 staff hours	0.50
200 staff hours	100 staff hours	1.00

An underestimate can be more serious than an overestimate as it might cause a software supplier to make commitments, perhaps of contractual nature, that they cannot fulfil. Miyazaki (1991) proposes a measurement of relative error as follows:

$$balanced\ relative\ error = \text{absolute}(actual - estimated)/$$
$$\text{min}(estimated/actual) \qquad \text{(Equation 7.4)}$$

What would be the balanced relative error for the data set given in Exercise 7.4?

Exercise 7.6 Balanced relative error

This appears to involve two different measurements. One of these is *mmre*, the variation of the estimate from the actual. The other is the variation of the actual effort from the estimate. A project manager is often aware of the effort estimate for developing a piece of software from an early stage and treats that estimate as a target. A measurement (*estimated − actual*)/*estimated* seems to be a truer reflection of the project manager's viewpoint. We have named this '**variation from estimate**' or *vfe* with *mvfe* as 'mean variation from effort'. It is not proposed that *mvfe* should replace *mmre* as a measurement of estimating effectiveness, but should complement it.

7.5.4 Percentage of estimates within 25% of actual (pred(25))

It is common for the **pred(25)** measure to be used to complement *mmre*. This is the proportion of predictions that is within 25% of the actual values. The higher this is, the better. It gives a better picture of the true effectiveness of an estimating method where a very small number of 'outliers', estimates that are grossly wrong, have distorted the *mmre* figure.

Calculate the pred(25) figure for the data set given in Exercise 7.4 above.

Exercise 7.7 Pred(25)

7.5.5 Squared correlation between estimates and actuals

Another widely accepted measure is the squared correlation between predictions and actuals – R^2 (for example, Albrecht and Gaffney 1983, Conte *et al.* 1986, Kemerer 1987). This measure can reveal that a method is good at generating larger predictions for data points with larger actuals and *vice versa*, while its *mmre* is poor because it is not calibrated correctly (Kemerer 1987). For example, if it is known that predictions are consistently 20% too high, appropriate adjustments can be made.

These measurements relate not to a prediction method, but to a method in conjunction with a particular data set. It would be wrong to compare *mmre* figures for different methods which came from tests on different data sets.

7.6 Supporting the estimation process

7.6.1 Effort estimation as a negotiated management process

Effort estimation exemplifies the practical nature of software measurement. To be really practical, we need to consider the environment of the busy development staff who actually produce estimates. Measurement and model-building techniques should be designed to support them.

This use of only limited amounts of information and over-simple 'rules of thumb' in decision-making also occurs in software engineering (Silverman 1985).

Software effort estimation can be seen as a special case of decision-making in organizations. As Keen (1981) noted, computer specialists tend to overestimate the importance of information in managerial decision-making. Generally, managerial decision-making processes are simple and based on what seems to have previously worked well. Under pressure there is a tendency to *reduce* the information used in order to make the problem of manageable proportions. As Keen observes, negotiation, habit, rules of thumb and 'muddling through' seem to have a larger role than any formal analysis of quantified information.

Exercise 7.8 Decision-making

The use of only limited amounts of information and over-simple 'rules of thumb' in decision-making might seem to be poor practice. Put forward a case *in favour* of this approach, such as a manager might make.

Personal estimates, as Boehm (1981) suggested, are subject to various biases. People tend to underestimate the time they themselves need to do a task (DeMarco 1982). However, while people typically underestimate the time needed to do easy-seeming tasks, they overestimate the difficulty of doing the less easy ones (Peters and Waterman 1982). Self-regard seems to encourage an optimistic view with smaller tasks, but larger tasks cause a sense of insecurity.

FPs allow estimators to have evidence to support their estimates and thus resist political pressures to reduce them.

Expert opinion can be sensitive to political manipulation. One survey (Lederer and Prasad 1991) suggested that in Information Systems (IS) environments, developer-estimators were the least likely to shrink estimates. Independent estimators would tend to produce lower estimates than developers because they did not have direct responsibility for meeting deadlines. IS management was even more likely to shrink estimates, perhaps because it sees the estimate as a productivity target for developers. Given the opportunity, user management would be likely to produce even smaller estimates.

The potential bias of the various parties involved led DeMarco (1982) to recommend the setting up of **independent estimating groups**. He argued that estimating groups could accumulate more estimating experience than individuals within project teams, even though developers are more likely to accept targets they themselves have had a hand in formulating (Peters and Waterman 1982).

The validity of the independent estimating group hinges largely on the precise meaning of 'experience'. With software maintenance and enhancement, the 'experience' needed to do an estimate is of the base system to be modified. This would seem to call for the more detailed familiarity with the base system that is likely to exist within the development team.

When an independent estimating group produces a top-down estimate for a project, subsequent detailed planning would still require low level estimates for individual activities. Again, this would call for the participation of people with detailed knowledge of the system to be implemented. In particular, the partitioning of a project into manageable proportions is inextricably tied up with actual design and cannot be purely a management process.

7.6.2 Expert judgement and the estimating of software maintenance effort

Costing models tend to assume that software is being developed from scratch. However, it is suggested that at least 80% of software costs are maintenance (Lano and Haughton 1994).

An estimate of the effort needed to change a piece of software requires an understanding of its current structure and of the consequences of changing it. This would also be the case when a change is actually being made. The initial thought processes of a software engineer sizing a change and actually executing a change are therefore likely to be similar.

Protocol analysis gets programmers to 'talk through' how they do a task as they do it. Such research has led to the hypothesis (Letovsky 1987) that the software specialist constructs a mental model of the software that comprises:

The specification the goals of the system as would be perceived by the users,

The implementation a description of the software modules and data structures that have been physically implemented,

Annotation how the goals in the specification relate to the components in the implementation.

The software specialist employs both specification-to-implementation questioning ('*How* is that implemented?') and implementation-to-specification questioning ('*Why* is that done in the implementation?') to gain an understanding of the system and the way it could be modified to meet the new requirements.

Exercise 7.9 Protocol analysis

Write a description of how you would debug a piece of code. Describe how you would do this in practice, not the theoretically proper way. Pay particular attention to how you would locate and correct errors.

If possible this could be an exercise done in pairs where one person takes notes as another person actually carries out a debugging task.

There is also evidence (Silverman 1985) that software engineers, when confronted with a problem, if unable to recall the solution to a similar previous problem, will analyse the problem into sub-problems until components are found which match cases experienced before. This suggests that the analogy method of effort estimation would be a particularly suitable approach.

7.6.3 How estimators do estimates

This is based on work described in detail elsewhere (Hughes 1996).

In this subsection we will briefly discuss how a group of actual estimators said they produced estimates. We want to emphasize that quantitative analysis in software development *has* to rest upon a solid foundation of *qualitative* analysis. You must understand the system and the environment where you are going to measure things. You have to talk to the actors involved to get an understanding of the processes and issues. Say you wanted to apply measurement to evaluate the effect of variable and procedure naming standards on the reliability and maintainability of applications. First, you would need to establish, qualitatively, what constitutes good variable and procedure naming. Effective naming is essentially a problem of communication between people. The issues to be considered can therefore only be properly identified by talking to the parties involved. Quantitative analysis can then confirm or discard the theories that have been generated by this preliminary qualitative investigation. It is our view that, for example, an investigation described in Pfleeger *et al.* (1994) that tried to establish the influence of standards on software reliability was unsuccessful because of the lack of this preliminary groundwork.

'XYZ' is a pseudonym to protect company confidentiality.

To gain an understanding of how 'expert judgements' about estimates were formed, a survey was conducted of software estimators working in the XYZ organization which develops real-time control systems for telephone exchanges. The work at XYZ was characterized by there being base products that were modified to satisfy the needs of particular customers. The organization had a well-defined management process model where estimates were done and reviewed at pre-set stages of the project life-cycle. The two most important estimates were when the initial feasibility study for a new or modified product was done and when the more detailed system proposal was produced.

Some idea was needed of what was meant by the term 'experience' in relation to estimating expertise. In general terms, it might seem that people could be considered as estimating experts if they:

- had already worked in the application area to which the estimate related;

- had supervisory experience of other people actually doing the work;

- were experienced in doing estimates (not necessarily in the application area).

In fact, experience of having done similar work was the most important reason for asking someone to do an estimate: estimators should know the likely duration of a task because they had done similar tasks previously.

The estimators were asked the amount of time estimating took. There was a wide range of times given – they varied from five minutes to four weeks for an average estimate. Follow-up interviews showed that this was mainly caused by differences in the perception of estimating. Some included the time taken analysing the problem, considering alternative solutions and investigating the impact of the requirements on existing software, while others just thought of the actual allocating of effort to the tasks thus identified. As one estimator commented *'the [feasibility study] takes one month but the estimating half an hour'*. Within this range, many gave the typical time to do an estimate as about an hour.

With estimating, the estimator can stop at any point and one can speculate that this happens when the person's attention tends to flag. It is argued that in some cases the replies do not refer to a real information source but to an intermediate product in the estimation process. The estimators surveyed were asked what information they used to produce estimates, giving a rating in the range 1 to 6 for the importance of each source. Table 7.3 shows the results.

It was not surprising that 'design requirements' got a high rating, but there was surprise that 'resources available' ranked so highly. This highlighted a concern of

Table 7.3 *Information used when producing estimates*

Information used	Summed rating
1. Design requirements	84
2. Resources available	30
3. Base product/source code	28
4. Software tools available	16
5. Previous history of the product (e.g. previous changes)	16
6. Size/complexity of the new function	9
7. Similar previous implementations	8
8. Documentation impacted	7
9. Amount of modified v. new code	6
10. Test site availability	5
11. Bug reports in the software to be amended	4
12. Deadline pressure	4
13. Customer for the product	4
14. Reusability requirements	3
15. Expected life-time of the product	3
16. Quality requirements	2

estimators that was apparent in later interviews: they had to give work-hours for tasks, but did not know who would actually be doing the work – it might be someone who was very experienced or the newest trainee. Clearly this could have a big effect on the actual time.

This echoed the findings of Kemerer (1992) with regard to the adoption of CASE tools which we noted above.

The fourth rated type of information was 'tools used'. The organization constructed different applications using different programming languages and the 'power' of the language had an impact on productivity. The introduction of new tools and techniques brought considerable problems for the estimator: the productivity improvement of a new development approach would be at first uncertain and this would be complicated by the time allowances needed for learning the new techniques and tools.

Estimators were asked what information they would like to be able to use that they currently did not have. '**Rules of thumb**' got the highest rating. This meant things like average productivity rates (such as lines of code/day) and the usual distribution of effort between different phases of a project. '**Data on past projects**', that is, previous changes to a system and the associated estimated and actual effort, was also highly rated. '**Administrative overheads**' were also frequently mentioned and referred to the work-hours that were added to a project for managerial, review and other support activities. The ability to distinguish this from the 'core' effort was important because it allowed an estimator to compare accurately his or her original estimates with the actual effort recorded by the organization's project accounting system.

Estimators were asked how they produced the estimates, especially how they used their sources of information. A considerable part of the process was impact analysis – trying to identify what parts of the existing code would be affected by the new requirements. Estimators then tried to imagine how long it would take them to do the task. This seemed to involve a mental rehearsal of the activities based on recollections of similar tasks in the past, that is, the use of **analogies**.

Some mentioned using an analogy approach to help validate their estimates. Rather than seek for similar past projects and then look at the their actual effort, the reverse happened. They looked for previous projects whose actual effort was about that estimated for the new one and then compared the characteristics of those projects with the current one to see if they had about the same content.

The point of this survey was to suggest how estimating might be improved at XYZ. While only a small number of estimators at a single site were questioned, it illustrated that software effort estimation, especially in a maintenance environment, required knowledge that statistically based models cannot capture by themselves.

The general impression of the estimators' information needs was similar to a list produced by Silverman (1985) after a survey of software engineers working for NASA and the US Military. While NASA, as might be expected, had repositories of all kinds of project data, the software engineers still felt that they lacked needed information. The problem would appear to be getting that information to the engineers in a convenient and usable form.

Expert judgement is far from incompatible with the statistically-based analytical approaches to the estimating problem, and the estimators interviewed seemed to appreciate how a careful analysis of previous projects could help them. The builders of software cost models need to consider how those models can be integrated into the work of the estimating experts. The concept of decision support systems assisting experts in other fields is well developed and the idea of extending this principle to software costing should hardly be controversial.

7.7   COCOMO: a parametric model

It will be recalled that an effort model is simply an algorithm that derives an estimate of effort from the values of effort drivers that are presented to it. In Chapter 8, we will describe how we created models tailored to the specific XYZ environment. However, the instinct of managers is to use 'tried and tested models'. We will therefore first describe the best-known of these, COCOMO (Boehm 1981, 1984) which really refers to a group of models.

Boehm originally based his models in the late 1970s on a study of 63 projects. Of these only seven were business systems and so they could be used with applications other than information systems. The basic model was built around the equation

Because there is now a newer COCOMO II, the older version is now referred to as COCOMO81.

$$(effort) = c(size)^k \qquad \text{(Equation 7.6)}$$

where *effort* was measured in *pm* or the number of 'person-months' (units of 152 working hours), *size* was measured in *kdsi* (thousands of delivered source code instructions), and *c* and *k* were constants.

The first step was to derive an estimate of the system size in terms of *kdsi*. The constants, *c* and *k* (see Table 7.4), depended on whether the system could be classified, in Boehm's terms, as **organic**, **semi-detached** or **embedded**. These related to the technical nature of the system and the development environment.

- **Organic mode** – this would typically be the case when relatively small teams developed software in a highly familiar in-house environment and when the system being developed was small and the interface requirements were flexible.

Generally, information systems were regarded as organic while real-time systems were embedded.

- **Embedded mode** – this meant the product being developed had to operate within very tight constraints and changes to the system were very costly.

- **Semi-detached mode** – this combined elements of the organic and the embedded modes or had characteristics which came between the two.

The exponent value *k*, when it is greater than 1, means that larger projects are seen as requiring disproportionately more effort than smaller ones. This reflected Boehm's finding that larger projects tended to be less productive than smaller ones because they needed more effort for management and co-ordination.

Table 7.4 *Basic COCOMO constants*

System type	c	k
Organic	2.4	1.05
Semi-detached	3.0	1.12
Embedded	3.6	1.20

Exercise 7.10 Basic COCOMO

The figures used here are from Kemerer (1987)

Apply the basic COCOMO model to the lines of code in Table 7.5 to generate estimated work-months of effort, assuming an organic mode. Compare the calculated figures with the actuals, by calculating the *mmre*.

Table 7.5 *Estimates for Exercise 7.10*

Project	KDSI	Actual work-months
1	263.8	287.00
2	40.50	82.50
3	450.00	1107.31
4	214.40	86.90
5	449.90	335.30
6	50.00	84.00
7	43.00	23.20
8	200.00	130.30
9	289.00	118.00
10	39.00	72.00
11	254.20	258.70
12	128.60	230.70
13	161.40	157.00
14	164.80	246.90
15	60.20	69.90

As well as the intermediate model, a further, detailed, COCOMO model attempts to allocate effort to individual project phases.

Boehm in fact found basic COCOMO, by itself, to be a poor predictor of the effort required when applied to new projects and went on to develop the **intermediate** version of COCOMO which took into account 15 cost drivers. In the intermediate model, a **nominal effort** estimate, (mm_{nom}) was derived in a similar way as for the basic model, except that different weightings were used – see Table 7.6.

Table 7.6 *Intermediate COCOMO constants*

System type	c	k
Organic	3.2	1.05
Semi-detached	3.0	1.12
Embedded	2.8	1.20

The nominal estimate was then adjusted by a **development effort multiplier** (*dem*):

$$(mm_{est}) = (mm_{nom}) \times (dem) \hspace{4cm} \text{(Equation 7.6)}$$

where (*dem*) is calculated by taking into account multipliers based on the effort drivers in Table 7.7.

Table 7.7 *COCOMO81 intermediate effort drivers*

Product attributes	RELY	required software reliability
	DATA	database size
	CPLX	product complexity
Computer attributes	TIME	execution time constraints
	STOR	main storage constraints
	VIRT	virtual machine volatility – degree to which the operating system etc. changes
	TURN	computer turnaround time
Personnel attributes	ACAP	analyst capability
	AEXP	application experience
	PCAP	programmer capability
	VEXP	virtual machine (operating system etc.) experience
	LEXP	programming language experience
Project attributes	MODP	use of modern programming practices
	TOOL	use of software tools
	SCED	required development schedule

These multipliers include influences on productivity such as the capability of the staff carrying out the work. Boehm found that a programming team fully conversant with the programming language could reduce the effort required by up to 20%. In general, Boehm suggested, the biggest influence on productivity was the capability of the implementation team.

For example, an organization might decide to use the following multipliers for assessing the effect of analyst capability (ACAP).

Very low	1.46
Low	1.19
Nominal	1.00
High	0.86
Very High	0.71

If the analysts involved in a project, taken as a group, generally possess above average talent and productivity then the estimator might rate the ACAP as high and use a multiplier of 0.8, effectively reducing the nominal estimate by 20%.

The overall *dem*, a single combined multiplier, is the product of the multipliers selected for the effort drivers in Table 7.8.

Table 7.8   *COCOMO81 Development effort multipliers*

Attribute	Very low	Low	Nominal	High	Very high	Extra high
RELY	0.75	0.88	1.00	1.15	1.40	
DATA		0.94	1.00	1.08	1.16	
CPLX	0.70	0.85	1.00	1.15	1.30	1.65
TIME			1.00	1.11	1.30	1.66
STOR			1.00	1.06	1.21	1.56
VIRT		0.87	1.00	1.15	1.30	
TURN		0.87	1.00	1.07	1.15	
ACAP	1.46	1.19	1.00	0.86	0.71	
AEXP	1.29	1.13	1.00	0.91	0.82	
PCAP	1.42	1.17	1.00	0.86.	0.70	
VEXP	1.21	1.10	1.00	0.90		
LEXP	1.14	1.07	1.00	0.95		
MODP	1.24	1.10	1.00	0.91	0.82	
TOOL	1.24	1.10	1.00	0.91	0.83	
SCED	1.23	1.08	1.00	1.04	1.10	

Exercise 7.11
Intermediate COCOMO

In a development environment, most of the systems that are developed are technically similar so that the product, computer and project attributes, as listed in Tables 7.7 and 7.8 do not normally change from one project to another and are given a nominal multiplier of 1.0. All the project can be considered as 'organic' in the COCOMO terminology. Personnel attributes differ from one project to another.

On a new project, the analyst is regarded as being of exceptionally high quality. The programmers are of high quality but have little experience of the particular application area and are going to use a programming language that is new to them. They are however familiar with the operating system environment and thus can be rated as high on VEXP. In this project, schedule compression is high meaning management hope to implement the project in less elapsed time by committing more staff to it.

What would the *dem* for this project? If initial estimate of delivered source code instructions for this project were 15 kdsi, what would be the final estimate?

A new family of models, COCOMO II, is currently (2000) being refined by Barry Boehm and his co-workers. Various multipliers and exponents have had values set initially by experts. However, a database containing the performance details of executed projects is being built up and periodically analysed so that the expert judgements can be progressively replaced by values derived from actual projects. The new models take into account the wider range of process models in common use for software development projects compared to the late 1970s and early 1980s. Estimates are required at different stages in the system life cycle and COCOMO II has been designed to accommodate this by having models for three different stages.

Details of COCOMO II can be found in CSE (1999).

Application composition – where the external features of the system that the users will experience are designed. Prototyping will typically be employed to do this. With small applications that can be built using high-productivity application-building tools, development can stop at this point.

Early design – where the fundamental software structures are designed. With larger, more demanding systems, where, for example, there will be large volumes of transactions and performance is important, careful attention will need to be paid to the architecture to be adopted.

Post architecture – where the software structures undergo final construction, modification and tuning to create a system that will perform as required.

To estimate the effort for **application composition**, the counting of object points, which was described in Chapter 6, is recommended by the developers of COCOMO II.

At **early design** stage, FPs are recommended as the way of gauging a basic system size. An FP count may be converted to a LOC equivalent by multiplying the FPs by a factor for the programming language that is to be used.

The following model can then be used to calculate an estimate of person-months.

$$pm = A(size)^{(sf)} \times (em_1) \times (em_2) \times \dots (em_n) \qquad \text{(Equation 7.7)}$$

Where *pm* is the effort in 'person-months', *A* is a constant (currently, that is, in

2000, 2.45), *size* is measured in KLOC (which might have been derived from an FP count as explained above), and *sf* is exponent scale factor.

The scale factor is derived thus:

$$sf = 1.01 + 0.01 \times \Sigma(\textit{exponent driver ratings}) \qquad \text{(Equation 7.8)}$$

Exercise 7.12 Maximum scale factor

What are the maximum and minimum values that the scale factor (*sf*) can have given that there are five exponent drivers and the maximum rating for an individual driver is five and the minimum is zero?

The qualities that govern the exponent drivers used to calculate the scale factor are listed below. Note that the less each quality is applicable, the bigger the value given to the exponent driver. The fact that these factors are used to calculate an exponent implies that the lack of these qualities will increase the effort required disproportionately more on larger projects.

- **Precedentedness** – this is the degree to which there are precedents, or similar cases in the past, for the project that is being planned. The greater the novelty of the new system, the more uncertainty there is and the higher the value given to the exponent driver.

- **Development flexibility** – this is the degree to which the requirements can be met in a number of different ways. The less flexibility there is the higher the value of the exponent driver.

- **Architecture/risk resolution** – this is the degree of uncertainty there is about the requirements. If they are not firmly fixed and are liable to change then this would lead to a high value being given to this exponent driver.

- **Team cohesion** – this reflects the degree to which there is a large dispersed team (perhaps in several countries) rather than a small tightly knit team.

- **Process maturity** – Chapter 9 on software quality explains the process (or capability) maturity model. The more structured and organized the process by which the software is created, the lower uncertainty and the lower the rating will be for this exponent driver.

Exercise 7.13 Calculating a scale factor

A specialist software house is bidding for a contract to carry out a project for an external customer. The type of project is very similar to the usual project that the software house deals with and is thus given a rating of 2 on this account for precedentedness. Development flexibility is high to the extent that this generates a 1 rating, but requirements may change radically and so the risk resolution exponent is rated at 4. The team is very cohesive and this generates a rating of 1, but the software house as a whole tends to be very informal in its standards and procedures and the process maturity driver has therefore been given a value of 4.

What would be the scale factor (*sf*) that would be applicable in this case?

In the COCOMO II model the **effort multipliers** (*em*) are similar in nature to the development effort multipliers (*dem*) used in the original COCOMO. There are seven of these multipliers that are relevant to early design and sixteen that can be used at the post architecture stage. Table 7.9 lists the effort multipliers for Early Design and Table 7.10 for Post Architecture. As with COCOMO 81, each of these multipliers will, for a particular application, be given a rating of very low, low, nominal, high or very high. Each rating for each effort multiplier has a value associated with it. A value greater than 1.00 means that development effort is increased, while a value less than 1.00 causes effort to be decreased. The nominal rating (1.00) means that the multiplier has no effect on the estimate. The intention is that the ratings and other values used in COCOMO II will be modified and refined over time as details of actual projects are accumulated.

Table 7.9 *COCOMO II Early Design effort multipliers*

Code	Effort multiplier
RCPX	Product reliability and complexity
RUSE	Required reusability
PDIF	Platform difficulty
PERS	Personnel capability
PREX	Personnel experience
FCIL	Facilities available
SCED	Schedule pressure

The COCOMO models do not, remove the need for expert intervention. In some areas for example, an estimate of the lines of code in a potential application will be needed. Deciding at what level to set various drivers requires some subjective judgement, especially as these ratings need to be assessed according to industry standards and not just the range of factors that might locally. Not surprisingly many, such as Kemerer (1987), have stressed that without proper **calibration** for the local environment, estimates produced by COCOMO can be out by several hundred percent. As calibration would require gathering size and effort details for past projects, one might wonder whether it would not be easier to build one's own model as described in the next chapter.

7.8 Conclusions

This chapter has used the previous chapter on system size as a basis for discussing development effort estimation. We have looked at the wide range of approaches that are available. We have been at pains to stress the importance of expert advice and opinion even when using models such as COCOMO. The message that is

Table 7.10 *COCOMO II Post Architecture effort multipliers*

Multiplier type	Code	Effort multiplier
Product attributes	RELY	Required software reliability
	DATA	Database size
	DOCU	Documentation match to life-cycle needs
	CPLX	Product complexity
	RUSE	Required reusability
Platform attributes	TIME	Execution time constraint
	STOR	Main storage constraint
	PVOL	Platform volatility
Personnel attributes	ACAP	Analyst capabilities
	AEXP	Application experience
	PCAP	Programmer capabilities
	PEXP	Platform experience
	LEXP	Programming language experience
	PCON	Personnel continuity
Project attributes	TOOL	Use of software tools
	SITE	Multisite development

stressed is that quantitative models need to be based on a thorough qualitative understanding of the subject area.

7.9 References

Abdel-Hamid, T. K. and Madnick, S. E. (1986), 'Impact of schedule estimation on software project behaviour', *IEEE Software*: 3(4), 70–75.

Albrecht, A. J. and Gaffney, J. E. (1983), 'Software function, source lines of code, and development effort prediction: a software science validation', *IEEE Transactions on Software Engineering*: 9(6), 639–648.

Boehm, B. W. (1984), 'Software engineering economics', *IEEE Transactions on Software Engineering*: 10(1), 4–21.

Boehm, B. W. and Wolverton, R. W. (1980), 'Software cost modeling: some lessons learnt', *Journal of Systems and Software*: 1(3), 195–200.

Boehm, B. W. (1981), *Software Engineering Economics*, Prentice-Hall, Englewood Cliffs.

CSE (1999), *COCOMO II Model Manual*, obtainable from http://sunset.usc.edu/COCOMOII/cocomo.html.

Conte, S., Dunsmore, H. and Shen, V. Y. (1986*), Software Engineering Metrics And Models*, Benjamin Cummings, Menlo Park, CA.

Curtis, B., Shepperd, S. and Milliman, P. (1979), 'Third time charm: stronger prediction of programmer performance by software complexity metrics', *Proceedings of the 4th IEEE International Conference on Software Engineering*, 356–360.

DeMarco, T. (1982), *Controlling Software Projects* , Yourdon Press, Prentice-Hall, Englewood Cliffs.

Gilb, T. and Finzi, S. (1988), *Principles of Software Engineering Management*, Addison-Wesley, Wokingham.

Heemstra, F. J. and Kusters, R. J. (1991), 'Function point analysis: evaluation of a software cost estimation model', *European Journal of Information Systems*: 1(4), 229–237.

Hughes, R. T. (1996), 'Expert judgement as an estimating method', *Information and Software Technology*: 38(3), 67–75.

Jørgensen, M. (1995), 'Experience with the accuracy of software maintenance task effort prediction models', *IEEE Transactions on Software Engineering*, 21(8) 674–681.

Keen, P. G. W. (1981), 'Information systems and organizational change', *Communications of ACM*: 24(1), 24–33.

Kemerer, C. F. (1987), 'An empirical validation of software cost models', *Communications of ACM*: 30(5), 416–429.

Kemerer, C. F. (1992), 'How the learning curve affects CASE tool adoption', *IEEE Software*: 9(5), 23–28.

Lano, K. and Haughton, H. (1994), *Reverse Engineering and Software Maintenance*, McGraw-Hill, Maidenhead.

Lederer, A. L. and Prasad, J. (1991), 'The validation of a political model of information system cost estimating', *ACM Transactions on Computer Personnel*: 9(9), 47–57.

Lederer, A. L. and Prasad, J. (1993), 'Information systems software cost estimating', *Journal of Information Technology*: 8, 22–33.

Letovsky, S. (1987), 'Cognitive processes in program comprehension', *Journal of Systems and Software*: 7, 325–339.

Miyazaki, Y., Takanou, A., Nozake, H. and Okada, K. (1991), 'Method to estimate parameter values in software prediction models', *Information and Software Technology*: 33(3), 239–243.

Northcote-Parkinson, C. (1957), *Parkinson's Law*, John Murray, London.

Peters, T. J. and Waterman, R. H. (1982), *In Search Of Excellence: Lessons From America's Best-Run Companies*, Harper Collins, New York.

Pfleeger, S. L., Fenton, N. and Page, S. (1994), 'Evaluating software engineering standards', *IEEE Computer*: September, 71–79.

Reichman, W. J. (1964), *Use and ABUSE of Statistics*, Pelican, Harmondsworth.

Silverman, B. G. (1985), 'Software cost and productivity improvements: an analogical view', *IEEE Computer*: May, 86–96.

Symons, C. R. (1991), *Software Sizing and Estimating: Mk II FPA*, Wiley and Sons, Chichester.

Tausworthe, R. C. (1980), 'The work breakdown in software management', *Journal of Systems and Software*, 1 171–80.

7.10 Additional questions

1. A software developer is asked to produce an estimate of the effort required to implement a particular set of user requirements as software. She goes about this by comparing the requirement to previous ones that have been implemented as code by her team. She finds one or two that seem to be similar in some respects. Unfortunately, any effort figures for these past jobs have been lost, so she uses the lines of code figures from these modules as input parameters to a version of COCOMO in order to get an estimate. To check how accurate the resulting prediction is likely to be, she takes the lines of code from some more recent jobs where the effort is known and feeds the lines of code into the COCOMO model to see how the estimated effort compares with the actual. The version of COCOMO that she is using seems to underestimate the true effort by 50% so she doubles her original estimate for the new requirement. Finally, she shows her estimate to some of her fellow software developers to see if they think it is reasonable.

    Using Boehm's classification as a starting point, identify the estimating methods that have been used in the above description.

2. (a) Plot the details in Table 7.11 on a graph so that it can be seen whether the software environment in question is displaying economies or dis-economies of scale.
    (b) Discuss possible reasons for the actual pattern that is found.

Table 7.11 *Details for Exercise 2*

Module	Lines of code	Staff-days effort
A	2459	60
B	6300	147
C	4300	96
D	7400	172
E	3000	71
F	2030	51
G	4430	98
H	8450	206
I	5010	114
J	2400	59
K	8300	202
L	4900	111

3. Table 7.12 shows the estimate staff-days for a number of projects and the actual effort that was recorded for each one. Calculate:

(a) the mean magnitude of relative error;
(b) the median magnitude of relative error;
(c) the mean balanced relative error;
(d) the mean variation from effort;
(e) pred(25).

Table 7.12 *Details for Exercise 3*

Estimated staff-days	Actual staff-days
600	290
81	82
1115	1100
500	200
100	80
310	135
580	305
250	230
370	350
350	550

4. Two experts were asked to produce effort estimates for each module within a particular application. Table 7.13 shows their estimates and also the actual effort figures that were recorded.

(a) Compare the accuracy of the two methods using mean magnitude of relative error, median magnitude of relative error, mean balanced relative error, mean variation from estimate and pred(25).
(b) What conclusions can be drawn about the relative estimating skills of A and B.

5. (a) Use the COCOMO81 basic model, assuming that all the modules belong to a 'semi-detached' application, to the lines of code listed in AQ7.2.
(b) Calculate the mean magnitude of relative error and pred(25) for these estimates.
(c) Explain how the COCOMO basic model results could be calibrated to produce more accurate estimates in this instance.

6. A software development group uses the COCOMO81 intermediate model. A particular application that it is about to develop has a very high reliability

Table 7.13 *Estimates for Exercise 4*

Module	Expert A estimates (days)	Expert B estimates (days)	Actual effort (days)
a	260	310	300
b	390	450	425
c	260	260	320
d	890	400	1100
e	2100	2200	2700
f	650	1100	645
g	740	800	695
	200	245	240

requirement and high execution and storage constraints. Both the analysts and the programmers on the project have a high capability, but have no experience of the type of application that is to be developed and are thus rated very low in that respect. All other characteristics of the proposed project appear to be normal.

(a) Calculate the development effort multiplier (*dem*) that should be adopted in this instance.
(b) Apply this to the calculation of estimated effort for the lines of code in Question 2.

7. The software development group that was mentioned in Question 6 has decided to try out COCOMOII. The effort multipliers it uses are the same as those in Question 6. For the exponent scale factors, weightings of 3 are used for each of five characteristics except for development flexibility where because of the constraints of the project, a rating of 1 is applied.

(a) Apply this model to the lines of code listed in Question 2.
(b) How does this model compare to the one derived in Question 6 in terms of mean magnitude of relative error and pred(25)?

Chapter 8

How to build a software development effort model

OBJECTIVES

When you have completed this chapter you will be able to:

☐ use statistical regression techniques to build simple effort models

☐ understand some other methods of building effort models, especially the use of neural networks and rule induction

☐ understand and use the analogy and case-based reasoning approaches to effort estimation

---

8.1 Introduction

The models so far have been rather theoretical. In this chapter we are going to explain how we built real effort models for a real software development environment. This was the XYZ organization that we have already come across in Section 7.6.3 when discussing how estimators do their jobs. It might be recalled that one of the pieces of information that the estimators wanted were 'rules of thumb' that could be used to calculate effort using various factors. At XYZ our response was to produce an 'effort model'. This chapter explains how this can be done using statistical regression techniques. It also describes how other computer-based techniques can be used such as the construction of artificial neural network models, and the use of induction and case-based reasoning techniques.

8.2 The organizational and project setting

8.2.1 The organization

The XYZ organization built automatic telephone exchange equipment and developed software to control that equipment. The organization had a very well-developed and well-documented project management method. However, in terms of the Capability Maturity Model (which will be explained in Chapter 9), the

The organization has subsequently moved to a higher Capability Maturity level.

organization had been rated at only level 1. Relatively small teams of, say, five or six people worked on the projects with which we are concerned. Both low- and high-level versions were used of a programming language that the company had developed specially for its applications.

8.2.2 The identification of effort drivers

The first step was to identify the features that could be possible size drivers in the subsystems that XYZ was developing. The application area was one with which most telephone users will be familiar, the interface between the user of the telephone and the exchange. This supplied such services as call diversions, 'call waiting', which allows you to switch to a later caller when you are already speaking to an earlier one, and 'ring back' when an engaged line becomes free.

The size drivers, with two exceptions, were features of the software that would be apparent to the users of the software. These users could be 'operators' who managed the system on behalf of the service provider or the 'subscribers' who made calls via the telephone system. The two exceptions to this, signals and correction area, were other factors that the local experts felt had an important bearing on effort. The study dealt with two closely related subsystems, which we will call system X and system Y, which were felt to be technically similar.

The putative size drivers were:

    (i)   commands,
    (ii) printouts,
    (iii) input subscriber procedures,
    (iv) enquiry subscriber procedures,
    (v)   announcements,
    (vi) timers,
    (vii) signals,
    (viii)correction area.

Each of these will now be described in turn.

Commands A command is an instruction typed in by an operator at an exchange. It might be a request for the system to give a subscriber access to a particular facility – for instance 'immediate diversion' where a call to a subscriber's number can be diverted. The format of the command line would be:

$$\text{<command>} \quad \text{<parameter}_1\text{>, <parameter}_2\text{> ... <parameter}_n\text{>}$$

The items counted included the number of parameters for each command.

Printouts are items printed on the operator log. Often the print-out records a command that the operator has issued and confirms that the system has successfully completed the required action.

Input subscriber procedures (abbreviated to 'insubs' for convenience) are where subscribers, by dialling a code, send instructions to the exchange which change data within the system. For example, they might request that calls be diverted to a second number.

Enquiry subscriber procedures (or 'outsubs') are very similar to insubs except no system data is altered. Outsubs were originally distinguished from insubs in order to conform to the distinction in Feature Points (see Chapter 6) between 'Inputs' and 'Enquiries'. Subsequently, the distinction was maintained as the outsub processing was usually more simple.

In the case of both insubs and outsubs, parameters can be identified and it is counts of these that were used as effort drivers.

Announcements are messages that are relayed to subscribers – to give subscribers details of the last call to their number, for example. A count of the number of parameters was taken for each announcement. Since some announcements had no parameters it was decided to use the parameter count plus one.

Timers The size drivers so far described have all related to inputs and outputs. 'Timers' and the following one, 'signals', reflect the internal complexity of the software. A timer allows the system to measure the time between two events. A software procedure might automatically call a chosen number. A timer might then be set so that call is abandoned if there is no response after a certain time. Single timers do not present real problems to the software designers, but requirements to deal with several different ones simultaneously can create difficulties.

Signals are messages that are passed between blocks. Unlike the other types of inputs and outputs, signals relate to the internal architecture and will be influenced by the structural decisions made by designers.

Correction area is anomalous as it does not influence the actual amount of functionality that is delivered to the users. With continuously operating systems, it is not always practical to stop to reload revised and recompiled code. Instead 'patches' are made to the software without recompiling it when minor changes are needed. The changes have to be written in machine code, but a high-level language version of the changed procedure is written and reviewed along with the change documentation. When a new version of the software is released, the changes are incorporated into the main code. The incorporation of these patches as proper code when there is a new release is part of the project and is thus counted, but not the earlier maintenance.

8.2.3 Productivity drivers

Because the development environment was always the same, we could assume that most of the influences on productivity would be constant. However, as our earlier survey of estimators suggested, developer experience was an important factor and the months of experience of each software developer were collected in order to assess this.

8.3   Functional versus architectural structures

The part of the development life-cycle of interest here started with a **function system design** of how the system would look externally, including the structure of any new commands or printouts.

The actual software was created as **blocks** by the process of **block system design**. One block might carry out services for several functions and one function might call upon the services of several blocks. In the final stage, the unit of interest would once more become the function when **function testing** was carried out. Table 8.1 illustrates the type of relationship. Function *Fa* calls blocks *B1*, *B3* while function *Fb* is implemented in blocks *B1* and *B2*, and so on. The relationship between functions and blocks is approximately analogous to that between use cases and classes in an OO environment.

Table 8.1   *Functions versus blocks*

functions	Blocks			
	B1	B2	B3	B4
Fa	×	—	×	
Fb	×	×	—	
Fc	×	—	×	×
Fd	—	—		×

Effort was collected for each of the three stages. For function system design and function testing it was collected by function while for block system design it was collected by block. This immediately caused problems. You want to be able to estimate effort at the beginning when you are still thinking in terms of functions. You would like to get, if possible, an overall estimate of the effort that is likely to be incurred for each function. To do this you need to have figures of past work based on functions, but block design effort is collected by block and not function. To solve this problem requires some way of re-allocating block effort to individual functions, which can call for some nice judgements. This illustrates some of the problems that have to be overcome with real world measurement and modelling.

8.4   Time reporting

Project team-members typed details of time spent on tasks, which had been approved by a line manager, into an on-line time recording system. 'Pick lists' were presented to the users from which they could select a project, block or function, and an activity type against which to record hours of work. However, it was possible, rather than allocating hours to a specific function or block, to allocate hours to a 'general' heading. The line managers' primary concern was that hours were booked to the correct project so that they were not especially worried by the lack of precision about functions or blocks.

Another, less common, problem was that at the early stages of a project administrators might not have set up the requisite framework of project, function and block details on the accounting system, so the designers might have to book hours to some temporary 'sink' heading.

We would recommend that a time reporting system defaults automatically to the function or block to which a designer is currently assigned. If there were some work of a genuinely general nature, the designer could consciously over-ride this default. This, however, did not avoid the need to recover somehow the situation where the damage had already been done. The practical steps that were taken by the project support staff within the organization were to use local knowledge where possible to transfer the general hours to particular blocks and functions.

Many who have been involved in practical software measurement note that the accurate recording of effort is more problematic than collecting size details.

What checks could be made on the probable correctness of a timesheet?

Exercise 8.1 Checking timesheets

8.5 Techniques used

This section gives an explanation of some of the statistical techniques used. It builds on and expands some of the points that were made in Chapter 2.

8.5.1 Descriptive data analysis

Descriptive data analysis was conducted to obtain indicators such as the mean, median and standard deviation. It will be recalled from Chapter 2 that these can indicate the statistical procedures that will be most effective. Where data does not conform to a normal distribution then reliance will have to be placed on non-parametric techniques. In fact the figures for none of the drivers were normally distributed.

Bache and Bazzana (1994) noted that they had *never* found a software measurement data set that was normally distributed!

8.5.2 Analysis of correlation coefficients

The **correlation coefficient** indicates the degree to which one variable can account for the variation in another, so that, for example, a small value in one is matched by a small value in the other and *vice versa*. A correlation coefficient of 0.0 would show that there was no pattern at all in the way one variable moved in relationship to the another. 1.0 would indicate that there was a rigid 'lockstep' relationship between the two.

The correlation cross-reference tables were used to identify:

(a) **independent variables** (that is, variables that might eventually be used as input parameters to an estimating model) which were so closely correlated

−1.0 would indicate that there was a very precise and rigid negative relationship where small values in one variable are matched by large values in the other and vice versa.

that if one were measured the other could be forecast from it, suggesting that the values of only one of the variables need to be collected. This problem of **multicollinearity** has already been discussed in Chapter 6 in connection with Albrecht/IFPUG FPs.

(b) independent variables that had a significant correlation with the **dependent variable** (that is, the variable which the model would be trying to predict, in this case 'work-hours') and were therefore good candidates as input parameters to the model.

Table 8.2   *Correlation coefficient cross-tabulation for system X*

	Effort	Commands	Insubs	Outsubs	Announcements	Printouts	Signals	Times
Commands	0.748							
Insubs	0.682	0.871						
Outsubs	0.507	0.702	0.870					
Announcements	0.785	0.599	0.698	0.490				
Printouts	0.650	0.944	0.818	0.725	0.442			
Signals	0.570	0.433	0.374	0.196	0.678	0.264		
Timers	0.755	0.529	0.432	0.181	0.826	0.294	0.787	
Correction area	−0.231	−0.122	0.037	0.277	−0.363	0.088	−0.510	−0.718

To create a rank correlation, values are ranked, so that the highest is given a rank of 1, the next highest a rank of 2 and so. The correlation between the rank values is calculated.

The **Pearson product moment technique** for generating correlation coefficients is an example of a parametric technique that assumes that the data conforms to a normal distribution. Where the data is highly 'skewed', this can produce misleading correlation coefficients. An alternative measurement of **rank correlation coefficients** might be more appropriate in this case, but even here some caution is needed where the same value occurs more than once for the same variable. Table 8.2 shows the rank correlations for a project that added functionality to system X. The values in the table will be discussed in Section 8.7.

Exercise 8.2 Calculating correlation coefficients

For this exercise you will need a spreadsheet package such as Microsoft Excel. Calculate the correlations, both Pearson and rank, for the variables in Table 8.3. What conclusions might you draw from this?

Table 8.3 *Data for Exercise 8.2*

Inputs	Outputs	Database accesses	effort (hours)
2	10	2	24
10	3	4	43
5	5	2	42
3	12	2	28
20	6	4	45
8	16	3	38
5	10	3	33
3	12	3	34
40	4	5	60

8.5.3 Regression analysis

The next stage of the investigation was to attempt to identify an equation in the form:

$$work\text{-}hours = x + (y_1 \times param_1) + (y_2 \times param_2) + \dots (y_n \times param_n)$$

(Equation 8.1)

where $param_1$, $param_2$ and so on are various parameters such as 'commands' and 'input subscriber procedures'. Statisticians have developed standard procedures to carry out this **regression analysis** which allow statistical software packages such as Minitab (the one used in this exercise) and SPSS to do the calculations.

Microsoft Excel also has a more basic facility for doing regression analysis.

The quality of any equation thus produced is usually measured by two indicators. The first is the **goodness of fit** or squared correlation (R^2) between the actual values of the dependent variable and those predicted by the equation. Once again, the closer the number is to 1.00, the better the prediction. However, the apparent goodness of fit of an equation can be 'improved' by simply adding more independent variables as predictors. In fact, given data for N observations, then $N-1$ predictors will produce an equation with a perfect correlation. For example, if lines of code by themselves are used as a predictor of days of development effort, then there is one predictor. If you draw a graph showing relationship between lines of code and effort, then if there were only two data points you draw a straight line on the graph which implies a perfect correlation. However, this equation is unlikely to be effective in predicting new cases. Another indicator (p) is needed which takes into account the number of 'observations' (N) and measures the probability that results are the outcome of chance. The practice is to accept a probability of 5% or below. A note of caution needs to be expressed. The correct calculation of p assumes that the **residuals**, that is, the differences between the actual values and the predictions, have a normal distribution.

There are statistical procedures to solve this problem – see, for example, Hair *et al.* (1987).

One technical problem that can occur is **heteroskedasticity**. Ideally, the value of residuals should be of about the same absolute size regardless of the magnitude of the actual and predicted values of observations. If they are not then doubts will be raised about the validity of the model.

8.6   Evaluating regression models

One basis for model evaluation is a comparison of the predictions made by the model with a simplistic estimate that uses the *average* of the actual dependent variables.

In Figure 8.1, a skeleton graph is shown with some data points, representing actual values found, and some vertical lines from the data points to the average. The improvement in prediction that an equation gives can be measured by the degree to which the sum of the squares of the lengths of these lines is reduced – see Figure 8.2 in which the regression line represents the values a prediction model would give. (The numbers are squared so that negative differences have the same weight as positive ones.)

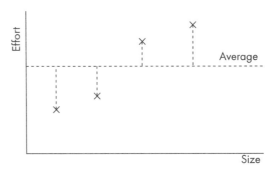

Figure 8.1   *Comparing data points and the average.*

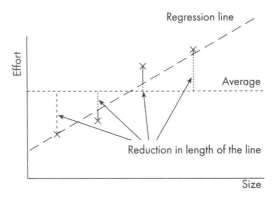

Figure 8.2   *Comparing actual data points and the prediction line.*

The degree of improvement in prediction can be measured by summing the squares of the differences between the actual work-hours and the prediction. The more points on the graph, the bigger the sum of differences is going to be anyway and so the average sum of differences is used.

When a new model is devised, the investigator might want to see how much smaller the sum of squared differences is compared to the previous best model. Two things can affect this, apart from the veracity of the models themselves. One is the number of independent variables used by the model compared to the number of cases. As noted above, a model with N terms ($N-1$ terms and a constant) can always be found to predict the scores of N cases with zero deviance. **Degrees of freedom** (DF) is the number of subjects being analysed less the number of dependent variables and, in general, the higher this is, the better.

In the case of an improvement between two models, the investigator wants to show that the difference is so big that it is well outside the range that could be put down to chance. In general the bigger the ratio between the average sum of squared differences for two models the less likely it is to be chance, but what makes a satisfactory ratio in a given set of circumstances depends on the degree of freedom. Using the ratio and the degrees of freedom, statistical tables have been devised which give the probability that the reduction in the difference between the actual and estimated values is a chance occurrence. Hence the p value that is given with the regression equation is the probability that the difference between the values predicted by the model and the average is based on pure chance. Statistical software tools such as Minitab will work out p for you. A value of 0.05 or less is normally acceptable.

Given the information above, attempts can be made to improve a model. First, **outliers** can be identified, specific instances where there are large residuals (that is, differences between the actual values and those predicted). These can be scrutinized to see if they are anomalies that can be discarded from the analysis. Secondly, any grounds for dividing the data set into sub-sets for analysis can be considered.

Using the details provided in Exercise 8.2:

Exercise 8.3 Building a simple model

(i) draw up a graph showing the effort for each function on one axis and the number of inputs on the other;

(ii) by examining your graph estimate the relationship between effort and inputs in terms of what you would need to multiply the number of inputs by to get an approximate estimate of effort (you might want to add on a constant amount, so that every function requires, for example, two days' set up time regardless of how big it is);

(iii) explore the features in your spreadsheet package which allow you to do regression analysis and try it out on the data we have here.

8.7   Applying the statistical techniques in practice

As has already been noted above, the descriptive analysis of the XYZ data sets revealed that the variables were not normally distributed so that only non-parametric techniques should be used. In the case of correlation coefficient analysis, this meant that rank correlations (see Table 8.2) were used but because of the large number of ties this had to be treated with caution as well. Looking at Table 8.2, subscriber input procedures ('insubs') and subscriber enquiry procedures ('outsubs') appear to be highly correlated. High correlations can also be identified between printouts and commands and also between timers and announcements. While discussing this with the software developers it became apparent that enquiry transactions and update transactions were often linked as the update ('insub') would be used to switch a service on or off while the enquiry would be used to see whether a particular service was currently active or not. Similarly printouts and commands also tended to be linked as a print-out often confirmed that a command had been successful. The correlation between timers and announcements remained a mystery and could be an example of correlations that emerge by chance. With each of these pairs of variables, the correlation suggests that either one or the other should be used as an independent variable but not both.

Examining the relationships between the independent variables and the dependent variable (work-hours), several quite high correlations could be identified, in particular with announcements, timers, signals and, to a lesser extent, commands. Also of interest was a negative correlation between correction area and work-hours, which seemed counter-intuitive as it implied that the more changes to incorporate corrections there were, the less effort needed. Further exploration of the meaning of the effort drivers suggested a partial explanation: most of the work designing the modified code had already been done before the current project had started.

Regression analysis was started by creating an equation using signals as the independent variable as these had the highest correlation with the dependent variable, work-hours. Each of the remaining dependent variables was added to the equation in turn to see whether its predictive power could be improved. As can be seen in Table 8.4, adding commands considerably improved the equation and a further, but less dramatic, improvement was made by adding announcements.

Exercise 8.4 Adding a second predictor

See if you can improve the equation in Exercise 8.3 by adding a second predictor to the model you created in Exercise 8.3 (iii).

The resulting equation in the XYZ environment was:

$$\text{work-hours} = 258 + 17.1 \text{ signals} + 574 \text{ commands} + 83 \text{ announcements}$$

$$(\text{Equation 8.2})$$

Table 8.4 *Multiple regression analysis*

Independent variables	R^2	p
Signals	0.70	<0.05
Signals, commands	0.87	<0.05
Signals, commands, announcements	0.90	<0.05

According to the model represented by Equation 8.2, what would be the work-hours if a function had 5 signals, and two commands but no announcements?

Exercise 8.5 Using a model to make a new prediction

There were two 'warnings' issued by Minitab, the statistics package used: one related to the exceptionally large size of a function which might have an undue influence on the equation and the other to a large 'residual' (or difference between an actual value and its predicted value). Removing the exceptionally large function and then recalculating the equation did not materially affect the results of regression analysis. The function that had the biggest absolute discrepancy did not in fact belong to the same system as the others but had been added to the data set because it happened to be available. It was agreed that this one could be discarded.

Doing this changed the equation to

$$work\text{-}hours = 270 + 15.9\ signals + 238\ commands + 137\ announcements$$
$$\text{(Equation 8.3)}$$

where R^2 was 0.998 and p was <0.05.

The revised model still produced over-estimates for functions a and f – see Table 8.5. This could be partly explained as the staff carrying out the work had been highly experienced and productivity would be expected to be high. This issue of the effect of experience on productivity was subsequently explored in more depth – see Section 8.8. The model had also produced under-estimates for c and d. These could be partly explained by the fact that problems had emerged with these functions in testing because of difficulties with the base code.

Create a graph, similar in format to Figure 8.3, for the model that you have created in Exercise 8.3. Also produce a table in the same format as Table 8.5. Can you identify any outliers?

Exercise 8.6 Model evaluation

A second way in which a model can be improved, it will be recalled, is to try to identify sub-sets within the set of observations that might need to be treated separately. For instance, in the case of the XYZ projects two distinct sub-sets of

Table 8.5 *Estimated hours v actual, excluding one outlier, and using*
Equation 8.3

Function	Estimated	Actual	Difference	% difference
a	461	321	140	44
b	365	358	7	2
c	445	693	−248	−36
d	461	723	−262	−36
e	389	408	−19	−5
f	660	300	360	120
g	728	618	110	18
h	1681	1639	42	3
i	1406	1506	−100	−7
j	5828	5747	81	1
k	350	370	−20	−5
l	11920	11936	−16	0
m	4602	4680	−78	−2

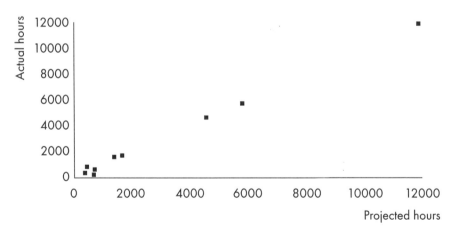

Figure 8.3 *Actual hours v Projected hours using Equation 8.3.*

functions could be distinguished: those which had only signals as inputs or
outputs, and those that had other types of inputs and outputs as well. The form of
the 'signals-only' functions would be very dependent on design decisions while
the 'interface functions' would be more directly influenced by specification
requirements. A decision was therefore made to analyse the two data sub-sets

separately resulting in two distinct equations. This had mixed results: the model for one of the resulting sub-sets was an improvement on the one above while the other was rather worse.

Figure 8.3 and Table 8.5 make this prediction model look quite effective. However, we are simply showing that the equation seems to explain the known pattern of effort in an existing project. The model was actually built using the details from that project so we cannot really say the model has 'predicted' the results in any meaningful way. We need to use the model on a totally new project to find whether it predicts effort accurately. In fact there was a follow-on project that we could try the model out on. Gratifyingly, the model predicted an effort estimate that was only 4% out from the actual effort. It has to be said that the model was not as accurate with other, later, projects. Effort models have a definite shelf-life: over time factors in the development environment will change. Staff will come and go and techniques and methods will evolve. These changes need to be tracked by those developing and maintaining effort models.

8.8 The effect of experience on project effort

As we have seen, there is general agreement that the experience of the staff carrying out a software development project is a key influence on productivity. Essentially, experienced staff should work more quickly and use less effort. The models that we had developed so far had not taken this into account. Our experience should serve as a warning of how models can produce unexpected results.

For each function, three activities were involved: function design, block design and function testing. It was decided that experience was unlikely to be a key influence on function testing. The months of experience of the staff carrying out the function design and block design were, however, recorded individually. We had also, by this time, developed separate models for new development work and for work which involved enhancing existing software.

See Section 8.3 for an earlier discussion of the project phases in this environment.

Regression analysis showed that the experience of the person doing the function design for new software had a *negative* effect on the effort needed. In other words, the more experienced someone was, the less effort was used. This would be exactly what one would expect. However, with block design, the experience of the block designer had a *positive* effect on effort – this was the case with both new and amended software development. Furthermore, a *positive* relationship between experience and effort was found with the function design for new software. In these latter cases, the implication was that the more experienced staff were less productive. There was much speculation about the possibilities of developer 'burn-out', but the most probable explanation was that managers would allocate the most technically tricky tasks, which needed most effort, to the most experienced staff. In the case of the initial design of new software, it would not be clear which functions were the most difficult and so the manager was not able to allocate staff on this basis.

This illustrates how software development systems are essentially human activity systems and how the simple analogies to the measurement and modelling of physical systems can be inappropriate.

There were later projects that were analysed where the software developers had very little or even no previous experience at all. Here inexperience did tend to increase the effort needed. It did not, however, have a uniform effect. With small software tasks, lack of experience did not seem to make much difference, but with larger tasks it did. As Curtis *et al.* (1979) have suggested, there are probably significant differences between the ability to grasp the logic in a small program and that needed to understand software comprising many components.

8.9   Alternative machine-based prediction methods

8.9.1 Perceived limitations of least squares regression

So far, the technique that has been used to create effort models has been least squares regression (LSR). While a mature and well-understood method, it does have some recognized limitations. It assumes that the relationships between the independent and dependent variables are linear. This means that, where there is a positive relationship, as values of the independent variables increase so do the values of the dependent variable. Thus more lines of code will mean more effort. LSR can also deal with negative relationships where more of one thing leads consistently to less of something else: this was the relationship we were hoping to detect between experience and effort. What it cannot deal with is where the relationship itself can change with different values of the variables. For example, there is some evidence that as projects grow in size, so productivity increases until a certain point where management overheads start to make themselves felt and productivity begins to fall off. LSR cannot deal with this pattern of rising and falling.

More detail on the topic may be found in Hughes *et al.* (1998).

In the sections that follow, artificial neural networks, learning by induction and estimating by analogy and the principles behind them will be explained in turn. It should be noted that each 'approach' describes a group of similar techniques.

8.9.2 Artificial neural nets

One way that has been suggested for avoiding the problems associated with LSR has been the use of artificial neural networks (ANNs). With these, an algorithm can be 'taught' through examples to recognize certain patterns in a set of inputs which are linked to certain outcomes. Figure 8.4 illustrates the general features of a single cell of a **neural net** (Page *et al.* 1993).

The **axons** provide inputs to the cell: these could be sensors, for example, that measure the degree of black/whiteness in individual pixels in an image. Alternatively, they could be outputs from one or more other cells. Each input value is multiplied by a **weighting** and the results are summed. The result may be scaled in some way (the reason for the offset or **bias** of w0 shown in Figure 8.4) and then processed by an **activation function** that converts the signal to an output. This output might, for example, be a binary switch indicating whether the image scanned by the sensors is recognized as a certain pattern.

The real power of ANNs comes from the way that such cells can be put together in interacting layers – see Figure 8.5.

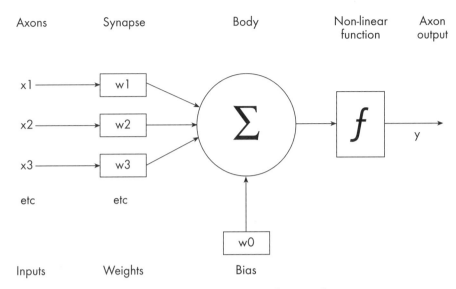

Figure 8.4 *A single 'cell' of an artificial neural network.*

We tried out ANNs on the XYZ project data to see whether they could produce more accurate estimates. In this case, the axons were the size drivers described in 8.2.2 and the project hours were the outcomes.

One of the ANNs we used was BKP (Howlett 1992). This neural network model has to be 'trained' in order to get the best values for the weightings. These weightings are initially set to arbitrary values. A set of inputs is then read and the output that is generated is compared to the desired output. The difference between the actual and the desired outputs is then fed back so that the weightings are adjusted to produce a more accurate outcome. The process is then repeated with the next set of inputs.

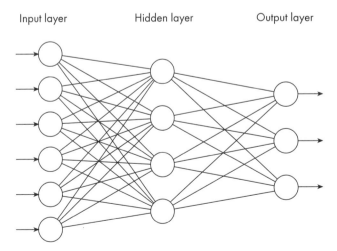

Figure 8.5 *An example of a multi-layer network.*

8.9.3 Estimating by analogy

One of first structured
approaches to using
analogy for estimating was
Cowderoy and Jenkins
(1988).

Reasoning by analogy has already been touched upon in Chapter 6. It requires the
selection from an historical database of one or more **source** cases that appear to be
similar to the **target** case under consideration. To forecast the effort for a new
function, the previous function that has the closest independent variable values to
the new function is identified. The effort figure from the source case may be
adjusted to take account of differences between the source and target case. Strictly
speaking, **analogical** problem-solving accommodates the identification of
analogies from different domains (for example, an engineer might use an analogy
from the animal world to solve a problem of mechanics), while **case-based**
reasoning draws analogies from the same problem domain (Vicinanza *et al.* 1990).

In the case of the XYZ organization, we investigated the effectiveness of the
ANGEL package (Shepperd and Schofield1997) which automates the
identification of analogies. The ANGEL approach does not adjust the attribute
value taken from the source case in order to take account of differences between
the source and target case, in contrast with an alternative tool ESTOR (Vicinanza
et al. 1990), which applies rules to do this.

There are some objections
to the ANGEL method
from the point of view of
measurement theory.

Say that you have two source cases and you want to identify which one is
'closest' to a third, target, case. If you want to do the comparison using more than
one attribute then ANGEL does this by calculating the **Euclidean distance**
between each source and the target. For example, the two attributes might be the
size, measured in thousands of lines of code (*kloc*), and staff experience, measured
in months (*exp*). Let us say that we want to calculate the distance between two
cases *a* and *b*. This can be done as shown in Equation 8.4.

$$distance = \text{square root of } ((kloc_a - kloc_b)^2 + (exp_a - exp_b)^2) \qquad \text{(Equation 8.4)}$$

It can be seen that the Euclidean distance is calculated using a method which is
analogous to the way that length of the hypotenuse is derived, in geometry, for a
right-angled triangle according to Pythagoras' theorem. Because different
attributes may be measured in different units, ANGEL 'normalizes' the values so
that the highest value for an attribute is set at 1 and all the other values are scaled
down from this.

Having worked out the distance between one source and the target, you can then
work out the distance between the other source and the target to see which one is
the smallest.

**Exercise 8.7 Calculating
Euclidean distances**

Work out the Euclidean distance between source case A and the target and source
case B and the target shown in Table 8.6. Do not forget to normalize the values
involved first.

ANGEL selects the best independent variables for use in the comparison
process by evaluating every possible combination of independent variables as

Table 8.6 *Source case data for Exercise 8.6*

	Kloc	Experience (years)	Work days
Source case A	5	2	152
Source case B	2	4	49
Target	3	6	?

potential predictors. This is done by calculating the average percentage difference between the actual and predicted effort for all the cases in the data set. The independent variables which give the lowest average error are selected as the most effective predictors.

8.9.4 Learning by induction

Learning by induction is a family of techniques that attempts to form generalizations from examples by using **inductive inference** (Patterson 1990). This involves identifying classes and sub-classes in a data set which have particular characteristics in common. In the case of software effort estimation these would be characteristics of projects or functions such as size, programming language, staff experience and effort figures. The outcome from this analysis would be a decision tree (see Figure 8.6).

A number of different techniques have been developed to do this. The **ID3** method, developed by Quinlân (1983) has been used to identify potentially problematic software modules that require high development effort or are liable to a large number of faults (Selby and Porter 1988), while the **Optimized Set Reduction** (OSR) technique has been used on the COCOMO and Kemerer data sets and achieved better effort estimates than least squares regression, or indeed the original COCOMO (Briand *et al.* 1992). The **CART** algorithm (Breiman *et al.* 1984) has also been used on the COCOMO and Kemerer data sets (Srinivasan and Fisher 1995). CART stands for Classification and Regression Tree.

The CART algorithm is easy to grasp intuitively. It splits a data set that is ordered by a particular independent variable so that the **variance from the mean** for the *dependent* variable is minimized in the two sub-sets of data.

To calculate the variance, the mean has to be calculated first. For example, the mean of the effort (staff-days) in Table 8.7 is 10.2.

The deviation of each value in the set from the mean is then calculated as the difference between it and the mean. The differences are then squared, and the mean squared deviation is the variance. If we break the table into two sub-sets, first into function *a* on its own and *b* to *e,* and then *a* to *b* and *c* to *e* and so on, then we could work out the variance for each of the sub-sets. The grouping which gives the lowest total variance would suggest itself as the most natural way of breaking the table into sub-sets – see Table 8.8.

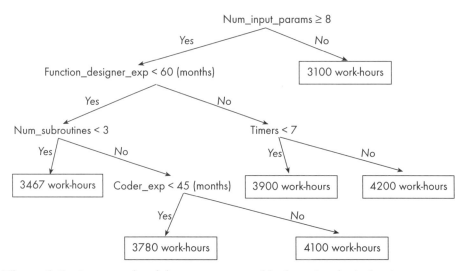

Figure 8.6 *An example of the output created by learning by induction.*

Table 8.7 *Lines of code and effort*

Function	Lines of code	Effort (staff days)	Deviation	Deviation squared
a	250	3	−7.2	51.84
b	270	4	−6.2	38.44
c	1000	15	4.8	23.04
d	1200	14	3.8	14.44
e	950	15	4.8	23.04
			Mean squared deviation	30.16

Table 8.8 *Identifying the lowest total variance*

First sub-set	Variance	Second sub-set	Variance	Total variance
a	0	b to e	74.89	74.89
a to b	44.89	c to e	16.43	61.32
a to c	138.46	d to e	18.49	156.95
a to d	205.93	e	0	205.93

From Table 8.8, it can be seen that the lowest total variance comes from the split between a–b and c–e. This can be used to create a simple rule:

IF lines of code ≤ 270 THEN effort = 3.5 days
ELSE Effort = 14.7

where the effort is the average for the respective sub-set.

The process can then be repeated on the sub-sets to produce further, lower-level, sub-sets and so on. The value of the dependent variable for a new case can then be estimated by identifying the sub-set to which the case belongs.

The method we tried out was a modified ID3 algorithm. This works in a similar way to CART but uses a more sophisticated criterion, based on information theory, for splitting into sub-sets (see Patterson, 1990, for further details).

8.10 Evaluating alternative approaches

In Chapter 7 we discussed some of the measures of effectiveness, such as *mmre*, *mmbre*, and *mvfe*, that could be used to assess the quality of an estimating method. In the methods that we are looking at now, there is a need for two sets of data to be employed. One set of data, which includes values for both the effort drivers and the actual effort sustained for a set of projects or software components, is the **training set** which is used to 'tune' a model. The second set of details is the **evaluation set** that is used to assess how well the model can accurately predict effort for a new set of details.

An alternative approach is **jack-knifing**. Each data point (relating to an implemented software function or a project) is removed in turn from a single data set. The remainder of the data set is then used to generate a model that predicts the estimated effort for the absent data point. In the case of the artificial neural network analyser, for example, the data set, less the dropped observation, is used as a training set and the dropped observation is then used to test the resulting model. This data point is then returned to the data set, another is withdrawn, and the neural net analyser is rerun to create a new model which is tested on the data point that has been removed. The process is repeated for each data point in the set. The result is an estimated effort figure for each data point that can be compared to the corresponding actual figure. It should be noted that this technique evaluates the model building technique and *not* a particular model.

We found that jack-knifing can produce results that are better than would be the case with 'live' estimating. When the effort needed in a new project is being estimated, the group of tasks under consideration may form a cluster with many system-related and environmental factors in common. As such, it may be distinct from previous groups of project data. When an estimating method is being evaluated, jack-knifing will predict the effort for the function that has been 'held out' using the remaining functions. This includes the cluster to which the function belongs. In a real estimating exercise details from that cluster (for example, other components in the same system) would not be available. Jack-knifing is therefore more effective where each observation in a data set represents a project rather than an implemented function.

We compared the estimating methods by dividing software development tasks from five different projects into two groups relating to systems X and Y.

Table 8.9   *System X jack-knife prediction results*
              (order of accuracy in brackets)

Method	%error	mmre	pred(25)	mvfe	mmbre	R^2	adj R^2
LSR	10% (2)	0.32 (2)	0.64 (2)	0.25 (1)	0.36 (1)	0.85 (1)	0.84 (1)
ANGEL	−25% (3)	0.30 (1)	0.71 (1)	0.34 (2)	0.42 (2)	0.78 (2)	0.76 (2)
BKP	9% (1)	1.63 (4)	0.00 (4)	1.05 (3)	2.11 (4)	0.00 (4)	−0.08 (4)
Rule induction	44% (4)	0.57 (3)	0.14 (3)	1.36 (4)	0.48 (3)	0.77 (3)	0.75 (3)

The tendency for *mmre* to be soft on underestimates was discussed on Chapter 7.

In Table 8.9, the traditional least squares regression (LSR) approach has done well in predicting the effort for tasks relating to system X. The neural network based method (BKP) has worked least well. ANGEL seems to have a tendency to underestimate: this might be because it optimized the selection of effort drivers on *mmre* which is 'soft' on underestimates.

Table 8.10 shows a similar analysis to the one above but using the System Y data set. This illustrates how the effectiveness of a method can vary depending on the data set used. The neural network approach was much better here and on some indicators outperformed LSR which fared worse than with the preceding data set. ANGEL worked consistently well with this data set, almost regardless of the measure of effectiveness used.

Table 8.10 *System Y jack-knife prediction results*

Method	%error	mmre	pred(25)	mvfe	mmbre	R^2	adj R^2
LSR	-4% (2)	0.45 (3)	0.32 (4)	0.48 (3)	0.62 (3)	0.56 (3)	0.53 (3)
Angel	-9% (4)	0.28 (1)	0.58 (1)	0.38 (1)	0.43 (1)	0.87 (1)	0.86 (1)
BKP	2% (1)	0.41 (2)	0.53 (2=)	0.46 (2)	0.58 (2)	0.68 (2)	0.67 (2)
Rule induction	5% (3)	0.47 (4)	0.53 (2=)	0.61 (4)	0.77 (4)	0.41 (4)	0.38 (4)

Table 8.11 shows the analysis of results using a combined data set. This shows that more is not necessarily better with data sets. A larger data set might effectively

be composed of data from disparate sub-sets that cause confusing variations when combined. Using *mmre* as the measure of effectiveness, LSR seems least able to cope with a larger, but perhaps less homogeneous, data set, but even here LSR produces estimates that are best in terms of *mvfe*.

Table 8.11 *Results from using a combined data set*

Method	%error	mmre	pred(25)	mvfe	mmbre	R^2	adj R^2
LSR	2% (2)	0.92 (3)	0.24 (4)	0.37 (1)	0.80 (2)	0.73 (4)	0.51 (4)
Angel	-21% (4)	0.37 (1)	0.52 (1)	0.64 (2)	0.69 (1)	0.82 (2)	0.66 (2)
BKP	-1% (1)	0.55 (2=)	0.36 (2)	0.71 (3)	0.92 (3)	0.87 (1)	0.76 (1)
Rule induction	-9% (3)	0.55 (2=)	0.30 (3)	0.75 (4)	0.92 (3)	0.67 (3)	0.43 (3)

Looking at the other measures, although ANGEL generally does very well, we found that if you were to use analogy and then aggregate all the individual estimates the result would be a 20% underestimate and any of the other methods would give a better forecast.

8.11 Qualitative evaluation

8.11.1 A note of caution

We should not draw too many conclusions from the quantitative evaluation as it is based on relatively small data sets and some analysis techniques might work better on larger ones. However, sets of project data are likely, at least initially, to be small. Indeed many of the publicly available data sets commonly used by researchers are quite small – for instance. Albrecht and Gaffney (1983) have 24 projects; while Kemerer (1987) has only fifteen.

Some of the model building techniques need a considerable degree of tuning and improved performance might be possible with different calibrations. Experts in the methods might be able to calibrate the tools more effectively. However, if a method is not robust outside the hands of an expert it will not transfer easily to an 'industrial' environment.

8.11.2 Least squares regression

LSR analysis is a well tried and documented method supported by most statistics packages. The circumstances that can reduce the validity of the method, such as the existence of heteroskedasticity and collinearity are well-known and documented. The models produced are in the simple form of equations that can be applied 'by hand'.

The major disadvantage found in relation to the current data sets was the lack of robustness. This was particularly apparent when applying the jack-knife technique where the withdrawal of a particular observation could significantly change the model. Some modifications to the approach have been developed which can reduce these problems, for instance the use of **least median squares** (Rouseeuw and Leroy 1987) to identify outliers which may distort the model.

LSR identifies linear relationships. Relationships that are not linear can be catered for, but this must be done by 'pre-processing' which transforms the non-linear data into a linear form for analysis (for example, by taking logarithms), but this often requires some intuition by the researcher. Matson *et al.* (1994) provide a good example of how this was done in analysing the Albrecht data set.

8.11.3 Artificial neural networks

It has been suggested that some of the problems with least squares regression can be avoided by the creation of neural networks. It is argued that there is no need to develop an intuitive preliminary model and non-linear relationships can be identified with only limited prior knowledge about the structure of the processes that created the data (Page *et al.* 1993, Samson *et al.* 1997). However, we found that some procedures used with LSR analysis, such as the elimination of collinearity and obvious outliers, could be useful when building ANNs (Gray and MacDonell 1996).

The artificial neural network technology has not reached the maturity of least squares regression and the potential user is presented with a variety of tools and is also often presented with a number of parameters to adjust in order to optimize performance (Samson *et al.* 1997). Exploratory trials can be very time-consuming and doubt will remain about whether the best parameters have been chosen. The BKP package was quite efficient in execution, but there are reports of the considerable amount of execution time required to train a network: for example, that training runs using the 63 observations in the COCOMO data set took 6 to 7 hours (Srinivasan and Fisher 1995).

Different training runs using the same training data set can produce different models because in the training phase the initial weightings are set randomly before the optimization phase is executed. It would be prudent for users to build several models using the same data set in order to gauge the variation in the estimates.

A final drawback of the use of neural networks is that specialist software is needed not only to build the model but also when using the model to produce estimates.

8.11.4 Analogy

This approach in many cases produced the best estimates. The way the results are derived is transparent – in contrast with the opaqueness of neural networks – and technical concerns about such matters as heteroskedasticity and collinearity are less important. The machine-generated estimate can be easily validated and modified by a practitioner with a knowledge of the environment. The analogy approach is also useful for diagnostic purposes: where an individual estimate seems high or low, the previous cases most pertinent to it can be identified for comparison. We found that practitioners with knowledge of the software development environment almost invariably agreed that intuitively the matches identified seemed valid ones.

One consideration relates to the selection of the best parameters with which to select analogies. This is done currently in ANGEL by a brute force calculation of the mean magnitude of relative error (*mmre*) of every possible combination of parameters. As has been shown, *mmre* tends to favour under-estimates and there seems to be some empirical evidence in our results that this is the case.

Another seeming problem with analogy was that of ties. In the data sets used in this investigation, several observations had values for the parameters selected by ANGEL which were identical – in one case seven observations had the same values. The effort figures could vary considerably for the analogous observations and the correct way of combining these to produce an estimate for a particular case was not clear: should they be averaged, for example?

Is special software needed? If the selection algorithm used by ANGEL is required, the identification of Euclidean distances can be done with a little effort using a spreadsheet. More difficult is the selection of the best parameters to be used and this does appear to need a more substantial software tool.

A more general question that ANGEL posed was whether it was more effective at picking analogies than domain experts of the human kind. We did some practical tests which were described in Hughes *et al.* (1998). Our overall conclusion was that ANGEL was capable of outperforming human experts at picking analogies where all the pertinent size drivers were present and no novel factors affected the effort requirements. Where there were novel factors, then the human estimators might be able to identify these while ANGEL would not.

8.12 Conclusions

Techniques that successfully use an analysis of past project data to build models capable of making effort forecasts need to:

- identify the most effective drivers of effort (this might be seen as a 'vertical' selection of data);

- identify and eliminate 'outliers', that is cases that are untypical in some way (this might be regarded as a 'horizontal' selection);

- calculate the nearness of new cases for which predictions are required to the most appropriate existing cases.

The use in regression analysis of a 'step-wise' approach where first a single parameter is identified as having the most consistent relationship with the dependent variable, and then combinations of other parameters with the first are evaluated is an example of driver selection. In contrast, the ANGEL package, as has been noted above, uses a 'brute force' approach where all possible combinations of effort drivers are evaluated. The construction of neural networks does not address this element directly, but may give low weightings to the more spurious candidate drivers.

The calculation of the proximity of new cases to existing ones is the feature which appears to differ most. A successful modelling method has to balance the need to reflect the patterns detected in the data set with the need to avoid giving undue attention to variations which can be attributable to 'noise'. This can also be seen as attempting to obtain the correct trade-off between the **generality** of the model which might make it applicable to a wide range of instances and its **specificity** where the estimates reflect more closely particular circumstances. Regression analysis attempts to produce the most general model, based on identifying linear relationships, whereas analogy is the most specific in identifying an existing actual case. Ironically, the methods that are less specific are often the ones that were found to be less robust when the details in the data set are modified.

The general conclusion is that reliance should not be placed on any one method. For practitioners, the following points are emphasized.

- Software engineering data sets are almost by nature bound to be statistically messy with many outliers and a lack of homoskedasticity. It is not necessarily true that adding more data points will lead to better results if this is done by adding data for projects belonging to radically different environments and application areas.

- the measures of estimating effectiveness used in the research literature (e.g. *mmre*) and the methods used to obtain them (e.g. jack-knifing) may not give a realistic picture of the effectiveness of a method in a true estimating situation.

- When evaluating methods, it would be wise to look at other 'outputs' as well as the estimates themselves. For instance, does the method enhance the understanding of the developers of the nature of the project to be undertaken? LSR and ANGEL did do this in different ways: LSR was able to draw attention to the effect of particular influences on productivity; while ANGEL was able to identify comparable tasks that had been executed in the past.

8.13 References

Albrecht A. J. and Gaffney, J. E. (1983), 'Software function, source lines of code, and development effort prediction: a software science validation', *IEEE Transactions on Software Engineering*: 9(6), 639–648.

Bache, R. and Bazzana, G. (1994), *Software Metrics for Product Assessment*, McGraw-Hill, Maidenhead.

Briand, L. C., Basili, V. R. and Thomas, W. M. (1992), 'A pattern recognition approach for software engineering data analysis', *IEEE Transactions on Software Engineering*: 18(11), 931–942.

Brieman, L., Friedman, J., Olshen, R. and Stone, C. (1984), *Classification and Regression Trees*, Wadsworth International, Belmont, CA.

Cowderoy, A. J. C. and Jenkins, J. O. (1988), 'Cost estimation by analogy as a good management practice', *Proceedings of 2nd IEE/BCS Conference on Software Engineering*.

Curtis, B., Shepperd, S. and Milliman, P. (1979), 'Third time charm: stronger prediction of programmer performance by software complexity metrics', *Proceedings of 4th IEEE International Conference on Software Engineering*, 356–60.

Gray, A. R. and MacDonell, S. (1996), *A Comparison of Model Building Techniques to Develop Predictive Equations*, Department of Computer and Information Science, University of Otago, Dunedin, NZ.

Hair, J. F., Anderson, R. F. and Tatham, R. L. (1987), *Multivariate Data Analysis*, MacMillan, London.

Howlett, R. J. (1992), 'A multiprocessor associative memory classifier for image processing', *Transputer Loan Reports Volume XI SERC/DTI Transputer Initiative*, Rutherford Appleton Laboratory.

Hughes, R. T., Cunliffe, A. and Young-Martos, F. (1998), 'Evaluating software development effort model-building techniques for application in a real-time telecommunications environment', *IEE Proceedings: Software*: 145(1), 29–33.

Hughes, R. T., Young-Martos, F. and Cunliffe, A. (1998), 'A comparison of manual and machine analogy-seeking' in Kusters, R., Cowderoy, A., Heemstra, F. and Trienkens, J. (eds), *Proceedings of 9th European Software Control and Metrics Conference*. 124–132.

Kemerer, C. F. (1987), 'An empirical validation of software cost models', *Communications of ACM*: 30(5), 416–29.

Matson, J. E., Barrett, B. E. and Mellichamp, J. M. (1994), 'Software development cost estimation using function points', *IEEE Transactions on Software Engineering*: 20(4), 275–287.

Page, G. F., Gomm, J. B. and Williams, D. (eds) (1993), *Applications of Neural Networks to Modelling and Control*, Chapman and Hall, London.

Patterson, D. W. (1990), *Introduction to Artificial Intelligence and Expert Systems*, Prentice-Hall, Englewood Cliffs, NJ.

Quinlân, J. R. (1983), 'Inductive inference as a tool for the construction of high performance programs' in Michalski, R. S., Carbonelli, J. G., and Mitchell, T. M. (eds), *Machine Learning: An Artificial Intelligence Approach*, Tioga, Palo Alto.

Rouseeuw, P. J. and Leroy, A. M. (1987), *Robust Regression and Outlier Detection*, John Wiley and Sons, Chichester.

Samson, B. D., Ellison, D. and Dugard, P. (1997), 'Software cost estimation using an Albus perceptron (CMAC)', *Information and Software Technology*: 39(1/2), 55–60.

Selby, R. W. and Porter, A. A. (1988), 'Learning from examples: generation and evaluation of decision trees for software resource analysis', *IEEE Transactions on Software Engineering*: 14(12), 1743–1755.

Shepperd, M. J. and Schofield, C. (1997), 'Estimating software project effort using analogies', *IEEE Transactions on Software Engineering*: 23(11), 736–743.

Srinivasan, K. and Fisher, D. (1995), 'Machine learning approaches to estimating software development effort', *IEEE Transactions on Software Engineering*: 21(2), 126–37.

Vicananza, S., Prietula, M. J. and Mukhopadhyay, T. (1990), 'Case-based reasoning in software cost estimation', *Proceedings of 11th International Conference in Information Systems*, 149–157.

8.14 Additional questions

1. A model has been derived in the form:

   $$effort(days) = 7 + (kloc \times 30)$$

   (i) Calculate the estimates for the following cases.
   (ii) Calculate the effectiveness of the model by calculating *mmre*, *mmbre*, *mvfe*, and *pred(25)*.
   (iii) Use least squares regression to build your own model based on the data set in Table 8.12.
   (iv) Identify potential outliers, and see if your model can be improved by deleting them.

Table 8.12 *Data set for Question 1*

kloc	Actual effort	kloc	Actual effort
24	654	16	538
23	704	24	742
11	289	14	963
8	212	12	441
1	103	2	43
16	504	5	63
16	478	10	308
24	957	8	342
7	180	12	397
5	122	21	789

2. Given the details in Table 8.13:

   (i) calculate the Pearson and rank correlations between each pair of independent variables;

(ii) assess whether the variables conform to a normal distribution;
(iii) identify the independent variables which seem to be the best effort drivers in each case;
(iv) create an effort model using least squares regression;
(v) identify any outliers, eliminate them and recreate the model.

Table 8.13 *Details for Question 2*

Effort	Commands	Insubs	Outsubs	Announcements	Printouts	Signals	Times
3141	32	10	5	21	11	77	7
3062	18	10	3	8	5	2	1
1977	18	9	0	3	1	9	1
1710	0	0	0	6	1	19	4
374	14	2	0	1	6	2	0
421	50	2	1	6	6	9	0
188	26	4	0	0	4	0	0
1167	20	2	1	11	6	13	1
188	4	0	0	0	1	7	0
864	25	0	0	0	12	4	1

3. Apply the model you have created to predict the cases illustrated in Table 8.14. Calculate the *mmre, mmbre, mvfe* and *pred*(25).

Table 8.14 *Cases for Question 3*

Effort (actual days)	Commands	Insubs	Outsubs	Announcements	Printouts	Signals	Times
2030	25	10	0	3	1	12	1
400	14	3	0	2	4	5	0
834	20	0	0	0	14	3	1
1452	13	2	3	8	4	12	1

4. Which of the projects shown in Table 8.15 is closest to the target in terms of Euclidean distance?

Table 8.15 *projects for Question 4*

Module	Insubs	Signals	Timers
a	20	5	1
b	8	10	2
c	8	45	0
Target	4	15	1

5. Create a decision tree that can be used to forecast effort based on the data in Table 8.16.

Table 8.16 *Data for Question 5*

Signals	Timers	Effort (hours)
5	2	934
10	3	988
15	1	220
7	1	180
22	0	750

Chapter 9

How to measure software quality

OBJECTIVES

When you have completed this chapter you will be able to:

☐ define the qualities of good software in measurable terms

☐ design methods of measuring the required qualities of software

☐ monitor the quality of the processes in a software project

☐ use measurement to identify the more error prone components of an application

---

9.1 Introduction

Most people agree that quality is generally 'a good thing'. However, in practice the quality of a computer application can be a vague and undefined concept. We therefore need to define precisely what qualities we require. But this by itself is not enough – we need to be able to judge objectively whether an application meets our quality requirements and this leads to the need for the measurement.

A problem is that waiting until the system finally exists before measuring it is leaving things rather late. Software developers would want to assess the likely quality of the final system while it was still being developed, and also to make sure that the development methods used were likely to produce that quality. This leads to a slightly different emphasis – rather than concentrating on the quality of the final system, a potential customer for software could check that the suppliers were using the methods likely to lead to quality products.

Although various steps can be taken to promote the quality in software products during the various stages of their development, we inevitably end up relying on testing as the final safeguard. Towards the end of this chapter we will consider the role that measurement can play in the management of testing.

9.2   Defining software quality

9.2.1 Quality specification

We need to define carefully what we mean by quality. For any software system, there should be three specifications:

- a **functional specification** describing what the system is to do;

- a **quality** (or **attribute**) **specification** concerned with how well the functions are to operate;

- a **resource specification** concerned with how much is to be spent on the system.

Methodologies such as SSADM primarily produce functional requirements – so how are the required qualities of the proposed system, such as its flexibility when change is needed, to be defined?

There have been several attempts to identify specific product qualities that are appropriate to software. James A. McCall (1978), for instance, grouped software qualities into three sets of quality factors:

- product operation qualities;

- product revision qualities;

- product transition qualities.

The definitions here are those given by McCall, but the reader may come across others.

9.2.2 Product operation quality factors

The ISO 9126 standard presents an alternative set which is described later.

- **Correctness** – extent to which a program satisfies its specifications and fulfils the user's objectives.

- **Reliability** – extent to which a program can be expected to perform its intended function with required precision.

It should be recalled that two qualities may be:
- **indifferent** – the presence of one quality has no effect on the other
- **complementary** – the presence of one quality would suggest the presence of the other
- **conflicting** – the presence of one quality is likely to reduce the presence of the other.

- **Efficiency** – the amounts of computer resources required by the software when executed.

- **Integrity** – extent to which access to software or data by unauthorized persons can be controlled.

- **Usability** – effort required to learn, operate, prepare input and interpret output.

9.2.3 Product revision quality factors

- **Maintainability** – effort required to locate and fix an error in an operational program.

- **Testability** – effort required to test a program to ensure it performs its intended function.

- **Flexibility** – effort required to modify an operational program.

9.2.4 Product transition quality factors

- **Portability** – effort required to transfer a program from one hardware configuration and/or system software environment to another.

- **Reusability** – extent to which a program can be used in other applications.

- **Interoperability** – effort required to couple one system to another.

Look at McCall's list of quality factors. Identify examples of pairs that are: (a) indifferent, (b) complementary and (c) conflicting.

Exercise 9.1 Relationship between qualities

McCall's software quality factors reflect the external view of software that users would have. For instance, usability would be a key concern of users. These quality factors have to be translated into the software characteristics of which the developers would be aware – **software quality criteria** (Table 9.1).

The same software quality criteria often appear for more than one software quality factor. What is the significance of this?

Exercise 9.2 Repeating software quality criteria

9.2.5 Identification of appropriate quality measurements

Defining quality is not enough. If we are to judge whether a system meets our requirements we need to be able to measure its qualities. For each criterion, one or more measures have to be invented which assess the degree to which the quality is present.

As we noted in Chapter 1, any good relative measure must be able to relate the number of units to the maximum possible in the circumstances. The maximum number of faults in a program, for example, is going to be related to the size of the program so a measure of 'faults per thousand lines of code' is more helpful than 'total faults in a program' as a means of judging the quality of a program.

Trying to find measures for a particular quality helps to clarify ideas about what that quality really is. What is being asked is, in effect, 'how do we know when we have been successful?' An answer to this is essential if the quality objectives are to be communicated to a large number of people.

The measures may be **direct** where we can measure the quality directly or they can be **indirect** or **surrogate** where the thing being measured is not the quality itself but an indicator of the degree to which the quality is present. By identifying measures management are setting targets for project team members so care has to be taken that an improvement in the measured quality is always going to be valid. For example, the number of errors found in program inspections could be counted.

In software quality assessment, measures may be: **relative quantity measures** which quantify the presence of the quality, or **binary measures** where the quality is deemed either to be present or not.

Table 9.1 *Software quality criteria*

The same software quality criterion may apply to more than one of the software quality factors.

Quality factor	Software quality criteria
Correctness	Traceability, consistency, completeness
Reliability	Error tolerance, consistency, accuracy, simplicity
Efficiency	Execution efficiency, storage efficiency
Integrity	Access control, access audit
Usability	Operability, training, communicativeness, input/output volume, input/output rate
Maintainability	Consistency, simplicity, conciseness, modularity, self-descriptiveness
Testability	Simplicity, modularity, instrumentation, self-descriptiveness
Flexibility	Modularity, generality, expandability, self-descriptiveness
Portability	Modularity, self-descriptiveness, machine independence, software system independence
Reusability	Generality, modularity, software system independence, machine independence, self-descriptiveness
Interoperability	Modularity, communications commonality, data commonality

This count could, of course, be increased by allowing more errors to go through to the inspection stage rather than eradicating them earlier – which is not quite the point!

In general, the user of software would be concerned with measuring what McCall called **quality factors** while the developers would be concerned with **quality criteria**.

The following should be laid down for each quality:

- **measurement** – the unit of measurement;

- **test** – the practical test of the extent to which the attribute quality exists;

- **worst** – the worst acceptable value;

- **plan** – the value that it is planned to achieve;

- **best** – the best value that appears to be feasible (the 'state of the art' limit) – this would be a level that is known to have been achieved elsewhere;

- **now** – the value that applies currently.

In order to derive these **quality specifications** it might be necessary to break down a quality criterion into further sub-criteria. Take the quality criterion 'communicativeness' which contributes to the quality factor 'usability'. One aspect of this might be the ease of understanding of the menu structure, for example, how easy it is to find the command to carry out some function. Another aspect of communicativeness would be how informative the error messages are, while yet another would be the clarity of the 'help' pages.

Another case is portability where a sub-criterion might be identified that we could call 'ease of installation', the ease with which the software can be installed in a new environment. With some software applications, installation may be complicated, for example, by the need to set various system parameters. A specification for the quality might be in the form:

Quality: Ease of installation

Measurement: Time to install in hours and minutes

Test: The software will installed at three different sites and the times required for installation will be averaged.

Worst: Two hours

Planned: 30 minutes.

Best: Not known.

Now: Not applicable.

One reason for trying to identify the 'best' possible value for the measurement lies in the need to have something against which to compare any measurement taken. For this same reason, it might be better to evaluate more than one application in the same domain so that comparisons between products can make the meaning of the measurement values clearer.

Suggest quality specifications for a word processing package. Give particular attention to the way that practical tests of these attributes could be conducted.

Exercise 9.3 Quality specification

9.3   The ISO 9126 software quality characteristics

Over the years, various lists of software quality characteristics have been put forward such as those of McCall, described above, and of Boehm *et al.* (1978). A difficulty has been the lack of agreed definitions of the qualities of good software. The term 'maintainability' has been used, for example, to refer to the ease with which an error can be located and corrected in a piece of software, and also in a wider sense to include the ease of making any changes. For some 'robustness' has meant the software's tolerance of incorrect input, while for others it has meant the ability to change program code without introducing errors. ISO 9126 standard was published in 1991 to tackle the problem of defining software quality. This 13 page document was designed as a foundation upon which further, more detailed, standards could be built.

A new version of ISO 9126 was issued in 1998

ISO 9126 identifies six software quality characteristics:

- **Functionality** which covers the functions that a software product provides to satisfy user needs;

- **Reliability** which relates to the capability of the software to maintain its level of performance;

- **Usability** which relates to the effort needed to use the software;

- **Efficiency** which relates to the physical resources used when the software is executed;

- **Maintainability** which relates to the effort needed to the make changes to the software;

- **Portability** which relates to the ability of the software to be transferred to a different environment.

ISO 9126 suggests sub-characteristics for each of the primary characteristics. It is perhaps indicative of the difficulties of gaining widespread agreement that these sub-characteristics are outside the main standard and are given in the document for information only. They are useful as they clarify what is meant by the main characteristics.

Characteristic	Sub-characteristics
Functionality	Suitability
	Accuracy
	Interoperability
	Compliance
	Security

Compliance refers to the degree to which the software adheres to application-related standards or legal requirements. Typically these could be auditing requirements.

Interoperability and **security** are good illustrations of the efforts of ISO 9126 to clarify terminology. Interoperability refers to the ability of the software to interact with other systems. The framers of ISO 9126 have chosen this word rather than 'compatibility' because the latter causes confusion with the characteristic referred to by ISO 9126 as 'replaceability' (see below).

Characteristic	Sub-characteristics
Reliability	Maturity
	Fault tolerance
	Recoverability

Maturity refers to the frequency of failure due to faults in a software product, the implication being that the more the software has been used, the more faults will have been uncovered and removed. It is also interesting to note that **recoverability**

has been clearly distinguished from **security** which describes the control of access to a system.

Characteristic	Sub-characteristics
Usability	Understandability
	Learnability
	Operability

Understandability is a pretty clear quality to grasp, although the definition *'attributes that bear on the users' efforts for recognizing the logical concept and its applicability'* in our view actually makes it less clear!

Note how **learnability** has been distinguished from **operability**. A software tool might be easy to learn but might be time-consuming to use because, say, it uses a large number of nested menus. This may be fine for a package that is used only intermittently, but not where the system is used for several hours each day by the end user. In this case learnability has been incorporated at the expense of operability.

Characteristic	Sub-characteristics
Efficiency	Time behaviour
	Resource behaviour
Maintainability	Analysability
	Changeability
	Stability
	Testability

Analysability is the quality that McCall called 'diagnosability', the ease with which the cause of a failure can be determined. **Changeability** is the quality that others have called 'flexibility': the latter name is perhaps a better one as 'changeability' has a slightly different connotation in plain English – it implies that the suppliers of the software are always changing it!

Stability, on the other hand, does not mean that the software never changes: it means that there is a low risk of a modification to the software having unexpected effects.

Characteristic	Sub-characteristic
Portability	Adaptability
	Installability
	Conformance
	Replaceability

Conformance, as distinguished from **compliance**, relates to those standards that have a bearing on portability. The use of a standard programming language common to many software/hardware environments would be an example of conformance.

Replaceability refers to the factors that give 'upwards compatibility' between old software components and the new ones. 'Downwards compatibility' is specifically excluded from the definition.

ISO 9126 provides some guidelines for the use of the quality characteristics. The fact that the relative importance of different quality characteristics will depend on the type of product under examination is stressed. Thus reliability will be of particular concern with safety critical systems while efficiency would be crucial for some real time systems. For interactive end user systems, the key quality would be usability. Once the requirements for the software product have been established, the following steps are laid down:

Quality metrics selection. Measurements which are indicators of the characteristics of each quality have to be identified. No specific guidance is given by the ISO 9126 on the applicability of the various measurements that might be used.

Ratings level definition. The metrics used must be mapped onto scales that indicate the degree to which the requirements have been satisfied. For example, in one application 'time behaviour' in the sense of response time might be important. For a key transaction, actual response times could be mapped onto quality scores as shown in Table 9.2.

Assessment criteria definition. The way that the quality scores are combined or summarized to give an overall view of the product has to be defined. The software product has now to be evaluated by measuring its attribute values, converting them to quality scores or ratings, and summarizing the ratings to obtain an overall judgement. ISO 9126 does not specify how this has to be done, only that some method must be devised.

Table 9.2 *Mapping response times onto quality scores*

response time (seconds)	quality score
< 2	5
2-3	4
4-5	3
6-7	2
8-9	1
>9	0

One approach, for example, recognizes that some quality rating levels should be **mandatory**. If a product fails to reach any of the mandatory rating levels it must be rejected regardless of how good it is in other ways. Other characteristics could be desirable but not essential. For these characteristics it might be possible to give a rating in the range 1–5, say, reflecting how important each one is. Above we have shown in the case of time behaviour how its measurement in a particular product can be translated into a *quality score* on a scale 0 to 5. The importance of each quality can be given due weight by multiplying each one by an importance weighting. These weighted scores can then be summed to obtain an overall score for the product. The scores for various products can then be compared to get a first cut order of preference. For example, the quality of two products might need to be compared on the grounds of usability, efficiency and maintainability. The importance of each of these qualities could be rated as 3, 4 and 2 respectively, out of a possible maximum of 5. Quality tests might result in the following in Table 9.3.

Table 9.3   *Combining quality scores*

		product A		product B	
Product quality	Importance rating (a)	Quality score (b)	Weighted score (a×b)	Quality score (c)	Weighted score (a×c)
Usability	3	1	3	3	9
Efficiency	4	2	8	2	8
Maintainability	2	3	6	1	2
Overall			17		19

Some would criticize this approach by saying that it is invalid to combine totally different attributes in this way. My own view is that what this overall score represents is a **consumer preference**. In choosing any product, the purchaser has to weigh one quality against another and it is this process that is being formalized.

An attempt (Kitchenham *et al.* 1995) was made to use the ISO 9126 standard to define the qualities needed in the software to control systems in an unmanned station in the Antarctic. This was to perform scientific experiments which, during the Antarctic winter, were to be monitored and controlled by satellite link from Italy. One finding was that the qualities required can vary from component to component within the system and that therefore quality definition at the level of the overall system might not be appropriate. The researchers also found that the most important quality for this application was availability which was a mixture of the ISO 9126 top level qualities of reliability and maintainability – separating the two elements was in practice very difficult.

9.4   Practical software quality measures

Below are some ways in which particular qualities can be measured. It is emphasized that the measures are illustrations only and should certainly not be treated as definitive. Each project will need to devise its own measures to meet its own specific needs. The measures described relate to the final software products of a project.

9.4.1 Reliability

This might be measured in terms of:

- **availability** – the percentage of a particular time interval that a system is usable;

- **mean time between failures** – the total service time divided by the number of failures;

- **failure on demand** – the probability that a system will not be available at the time required or the probability that a transaction will fail;

- **support activity** – the number of fault reports that are generated.

Exercise 9.4 Measuring availability

A computer system can normally be accessed by operators from 7.30 am until 6.30 pm from Monday to Friday. Over a four-week period the system was unavailable for one whole day because of problems with a disk drive and was not available on two other days until 12 noon because of problems with overnight batch processing runs.

What were the availability and the mean time between failures of the service?

9.4.2 Maintainability

This is closely related to **flexibility**, the ease with which the software can be modified. The main difference is that before an amendment can be made, the fault has to be diagnosed first. Maintainability can therefore be seen as flexibility plus a new quality **diagnosability** which might be defined as the average amount of time needed to diagnose a fault.

Maintainability can be seen from two different perspectives. The user will be concerned with the elapsed time between a fault being detected and it being corrected, while software development managers will be concerned about the effort involved.

Exercise 9.5 Assessing maintainability

Table 9.4 is an excerpt from a report generated from a help-desk logging system. Assess the maintainability of module AA247 from the point of view of:

(i) the user management;
(ii) the developer management.

Table 9.4 *Excerpt from a report generated from a help-desk logging system*

Module	Date fault reported	Fault corrected	Effort (hours)
AA247	1.4.2000	2.4.2000	5
AA247	10.4.2000	5.5.2000	4
AA247	12.4.2000	5.5.2000	3
AA247	6.5.2000	7.5.2000	2

9.4.3 Extendibility

This is a component of the more general quality of flexibility. It can be defined as the productivity needed to incorporate a new feature into an existing system expressed as a percentage of the normal productivity when developing the software from scratch.

As an example, a software application originally comprised 6000 SLOC and took 400 work-days to implement. An amendment has led to 210 SLOC being added which took 30 work-days to implement, thus:

> Recall that SLOC stands for 'source lines of code'.

     productivity for the original system
        = 6000/400
        = 15 SLOC/staff day

     productivity for the amendment
        = 210/30
        = 7 SLOC/staff day

    extendibility
        = $7/15 \times 100$
        = 47%

A software application of 7 KLOC took 350 days to develop. A later addition to the application comprised 500 SLOC and took 15 days. What, on the basis of the addition, was the extendibility of this application.

> **Exercise 9.6**
> **Extendibility**

9.4.4 Usability

To illustrate how usability can be measured, I would like to use as an example some research that has been done by a colleague, Fraser Hamilton (Hamilton *et al.* 1998). Hamilton has been investigating the establishment of general design principles that if followed should lead to more usable computer interfaces. The identification of putative principles has required an extensive review of the theory in this area. This has led to the measurement work being based on a clear idea of the underlying models that might be applicable. As noted elsewhere, in our view many software measurement exercises have been inconclusive because the factors that are likely to influence the behaviour of the system being subjected to measurement have not been properly thought out.

In Hamilton's research, based on well-established existing theories two possible influences on usability were identified:

- **Taxonomic categorization.** Simplistically, this is grouping fields together in the interface that refer to the same entity. For example, in an application which deals with the ordering of a book which is not in stock in a book-shop when a customer requests it, details belonging to the customer would naturally be grouped together, while details belonging to a specific book would also be clustered.

- **Sequential dependency.** This principle implies that an interface should reflect the order in which operations are logically constrained to occur. In our book-shop example, the customer and the book would need to be identified before the order for the book could be recorded.

To test out the usefulness of these principles, four different interface designs were created for the bookshop ordering application – see Table 9.5.

Table 9.5   *Conditions in interface design evaluation experiment*

Control	A control where neither principle was followed – in other words, a complete mess.
TC	A design which took account of taxonomic categorization, but not sequential dependency.
SD	A design which took account of sequential dependency but not taxonomic categorization.
TC&SD	A design which took account of both principles.

The **control** is effectively a baseline from which the degree to which the other designs vary can be assessed. If the control design performs about as well as, or even better, than the designs that have resulted from systematic design, then this would set the alarm bells ringing. The factors we thought from our consideration of the theory should be influencing the system would not seem to be doing so.

Different groups of ten subjects were asked to operate the four different interfaces in five successive trials and the times they took and the number of errors they made were recorded. The average figures for each of the groups over the five trials are shown in Figures 9.1 and 9.2.

The question is now raised of the extent to which the differences between the measurement values for the four different interface designs are significant or the result of mere chance. It will be recalled from Chapter 2 that we distinguished

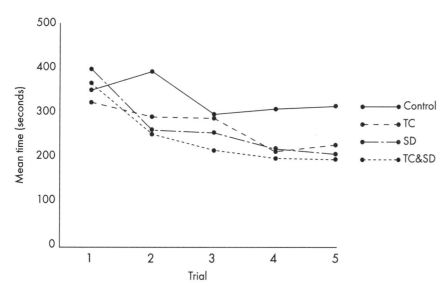

Figure 9.1 *Mean task completion times.*

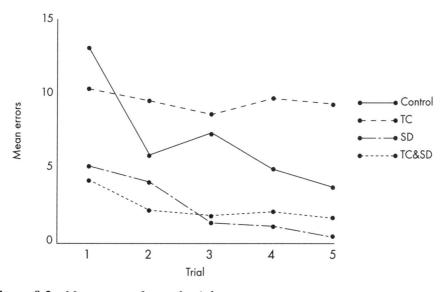

Figure 9.2 *Mean errors for each trial.*

between parametric and non-parametric statistical techniques. We noted that in order for us to be sure that parametric techniques will work correctly the data to be analysed should have a normal distribution. In addition, if there are two or more sub-sets of data, each sub-set should have about the same degree of variance. In details of task durations and error counts collected by Hamilton and his colleagues, the degree of variation between measurements for the same interface design (as measured by the standard deviation) was greater for the sets of details that had higher mean scores. Thus variance was substantially different and non-parametric statistical techniques were called for.

I have found the text by
Hugh Coolican (1994) to
be a relatively easy read
on these matters.

This is similar to the p
value that was produced
as a by-product of least
squares regression in
Chapter 8.

The particular statistical test that was selected was the **Kruskal–Wallis test** which is used to establish the probability that data from different sub-sets belong to different populations rather than all coming from the same population. If they come from different populations, then the differences between the sub-sets have meaning and have not come about purely by chance. The reader who is interested is directed to an appropriate statistics textbook, but the key feature of the method is that it can be applied to three or more **conditions**. In the experiment being described, for example, the four conditions are those listed in Table 9.5. The result of the calculation is the probability (p) that the difference in values for the different conditions was as the result of pure chance. A value of p that is less than 5% ($p < 0.05$) is normally regarded as satisfactory. In the interface evaluation experiment, for example, it appeared that the difference in the results for the first trial could well be the result of chance. It can be speculated that when you are new to a system, you experience a certain amount of floundering around at the start regardless of how well the interface might have been designed. This suggests that you should not rely on a single usability trial but should get the subjects to carry out a series of trials to see how they perform as they become more familiar with the system.

The pattern that emerges from these trials can be seen in Figures 9.1 and 9.2. The subjects using the interface designed with both the sequential dependency and taxonomic dependency principles in mind consistently carried their tasks more quickly and with fewer errors than those using the control design. In the case of the design that took account of sequential dependency but ignored taxonomic categorization, the subjects initially did not do better than those using the control, but by the fifth trial were doing better. This suggests that with practice the users were able to group mentally the scattered fields that logically belonged together.

One of the more general points that emerges is that as with other qualities, usability can be broken down into component sub-qualities. These include the following:

- **Initial ease of use.** This is sometimes referred to as the 'intuitiveness' of the application or even its 'guessibility'. Although we have suggested above that there is a tendency to flounder with any new system, the surface meaning of some interfaces is easier to grasp than those of others. This means that the user will be able to make immediate sense of some interfaces. This quality could be measured by the time it takes to carry out operations the first time the system is used and by the number of errors made on initial use.

- **Ease of learning.** This can be judged, to some extent, by the steepness of the descending curves in graphs like those in Figures 9.1 and 9.2. This gives an idea of how quickly one can learn to use the system effectively. One way of measuring this would be by the amount of time it takes to reach a level of proficiency defined by operation time or error level.

- **Ease of use.** This relates to how easy the system is to use once the operators have got used to it. In some cases users might be prepared to put up with having to take time to learn how to use a system if this means that eventually they can use the system more effectively. This is rather like learning shorthand – this can be time-consuming to learn, but eventually should allow you to save time.

- **Memorability.** This is the degree to which users are still able to use the system effectively if they go away and come back to it later.

To what extent do the sub-qualities we have identified for usability match those sub-characteristics defined in the ISO 9126 standard?

Exercise 9.7 Matching ISO 9126 qualities

9.5 Bridging the gap between internal and external qualities

In the discussion of the McCall model of software quality in Section 9.2, it will be recalled that the **external** qualities of the software (that McCall referred to as **quality factors**) were distinguished from **internal** qualities (or **quality criteria** as McCall called them). The key question is whether by measuring the internal qualities of software, we can predict what the external qualities are likely to be. This has turned out to be a very difficult undertaking that has not been accomplished with complete success.

'Internal' implies that the quality is internal to the product, as it often is. However, 'internal' in this context really means internal to the project. For example, the quality of the interface design is not properly internal to the software product, but it is internal to the project. On these grounds, some might prefer the term **predictive** rather than internal.

One line of attack, as characterized by the work of Geoff Dromey (1995) has been to develop the theoretical links between internal qualities (or **quality-carrying properties** as Dromey calls them) and the external qualities. For example, it is suggested that for software to have the quality of **correctness**, the code, internally, would have to be:

- **Computable** – that is, it should obey the basic laws of arithmetic (and not try to divide by zero, for example);

- **Complete** – all necessary procedural elements needed for correct operation are present;

- **Assigned** – all values used by an operation have been properly assigned;

- **Precise** – variables are defined so that computation is carried out with the required level of precision;

- **Initialized** – assignments to loop variables are correct;

- **Progressive** – each iteration of a loop decreases control variables correctly;

- **Variant** – termination of a loop is carried out correctly;

- **Consistent** – for example, variables are manipulated using operators appropriate for the data type to which they belong.

The SCOPE project, parts of which are described in Bache and Bazzana (1994) attempted to identify measurements of internal attributes that could be used to predict external qualities. The SCOPE project used a 'bottom-up' approach to this problem by looking at existing metrics and seeing how they could be applied. They commented: '*Ideally, we would like to make predictions of external attributes and use these as a basis for QA or certification. Alas, this is generally not possible.*'

Hamilton's work on the quality of interface design also suggests predictive metrics could be applied here.

Although, as we have seen in the chapters on structural and object oriented metrics, there have been some partial, retrospective, successes in identifying links between certain internal and external attributes, this still remains a problem. We will see in a later section in this chapter that it is possible to predict which software components are likely to have most faults, but this tends to be simply on the basis that the more code there is in a module, the more errors there are likely to be.

Exercise 9.8 Linking external and internal qualities

According to McCall – see Table 9.1 – the external quality of portability is linked to the internal qualities of modularity, self-descriptiveness, machine independence, and software system independence. Discuss how we could measure these external and internal qualities. What problems are there with the links between these qualities as suggested by McCall?

9.6   External standards

9.6.1 BS EN ISO 9001

The British standard for Quality Management systems was previously called BS 5750.

If an organization requires a new IT application, a decision might be made to use an outside contractor to produce the software rather than develop it in-house. A client using the services of an outside contractor would be concerned that the contractor is following the best quality practices. It is now common to include in contracts terms covering the quality management practices that a contractor will use. Various national and international standards bodies, including the British Standards Institution (BSI) in the United Kingdom, have inevitably got involved in the creation of standards for quality management systems. The British standard is now called BS EN ISO 9001:1994, which is identical to the international standard, ISO 9001:1994. Standards such as ISO 9000 series try to ensure that a monitoring and control system to check quality is in place. They are concerned with the certification of the quality of the control process, not of the end-product itself. The ISO 9000 series govern quality systems in general terms and not just those in the software development environment.

The TickIT programme in the UK applies ISO 9001 in software development environment.

Establishing measurement procedures to control the production process in software development takes time and effort and many software suppliers would rather devote their energies to the more immediate tasks of actually writing code. The imposition of a requirement by customers for adherence by suppliers to the ISO 9001 standard or the attainment of a certain level of the Capability Maturity Model, which will be described in the next section, is probably the most likely reason why most software suppliers begin to take measurement seriously.

In order to qualify for ISO 9001 certification, the organization must document all its quality procedures. The procedures must allow the precise quality requirements for a product to be established. When a specific quality attribute of the product is checked, the outcome of this control procedure must be recorded and steps must be taken to ensure that any remedial work then takes place. The ISO 9001 certified organization needs to record these checks and remedial actions, not just for internal control, but also so that it can demonstrate to external auditors if necessary that it is correctly operating its quality management procedures. From a measurement point of view, the importance of ISO 9001 is that this recording of defects and their removal can supply measurement data. Indeed, one ISO 9001 requirement is that the appropriate statistical techniques are used to verify the acceptability of the final product.

9.6.2 Capability process models

Rather than just checking that a system is in place to detect faults, a customer might wish to check that a supplier is using software development methods and tools which are likely to produce good quality software. Even the ISO 9001 recommendations may be regarded as fairly minimal. Customers might feel more confident, for instance, if they knew that their software supplier was using systematic methods. In the United States, an influential **capability maturity model** (CMM) has been developed at the Software Engineering Institute (SEI), a part of the Carnegie-Mellon University. This places organizations producing software at one of five levels of process maturity which indicate the sophistication and quality of their software production practices. These levels are defined as follows.

See H. S. Watts, *Managing the Software Process*, Addison-Wesley, New York, 1989.

- **Level 1: Initial** – the procedures followed tend to be haphazard. Some projects might be successful, but this tends to be because of the skills of particular individuals including project managers. There is no level 0 and so any organization would be at this level by default.

- **Level 2: Repeatable** – organizations at this level will have basic project management procedures in place. However, the way individual tasks are carried out will depend largely on the person doing it. There is probably a tendency to treat the development process as a **closed box**, where the inputs and outputs are known, but not the actual mechanisms by which inputs are converted into outputs. If a new project comes along which is similar (that is, the system characteristics are more or less the same as those for the previous project) then there is a fair chance that the new project can be completed

The SEI originally developed CMM for the US Department of Defense who wanted to be able to assess the capability of contractors from whom they procured software.

successfully. The problem comes when there is a new project that is radically different: perhaps it uses a new software architecture. In these cases, there is a high risk of failure – many of the classic computer disasters have been in these circumstances.

- **Level 3: Defined** – the organization has defined the way that each task in the software development life cycle should be done. At this level the project processes are opened up and individual sub-processes are identified. The linkages between these sub-processes are also identified. This implies a more disciplined approach to development tasks.

- **Level 4: Managed** – the products and processes involved in software development are subject to measurement and control.

- **Level 5: Optimizing** – improvement in procedures can be designed and implemented using the data gathered from the measurement process.

For each of the levels, apart from the default level 1, **key process areas** (KPAs) have been identified as distinguishing the current level from the lower ones. These are listed in the Table 9.6.

Table 9.6 *CMM Key process areas*

Level	Key process areas
1. Initial	Not applicable
2. Repeatable	Configuration management, quality assurance, sub-contract management, project tracking and oversight, project planning
3. Defined	Peer reviews, inter-group co-ordination, software product engineering, integrated software management, training programme, organization process definition and focus
4. Managed	Quality management, process measurement and analysis
5. Optimizing	Process change management, technology innovation, defect prevention

The assessment is done by a team of assessors coming into the organization and interviewing key staff about their practices using a standard questionnaire to capture the information. A key objective is not just to assess, but to recommend specific actions to bring the organization up to a higher level.

A criticism has been made of the approach that it is unrealistic to try and assess an organization as a whole – in reality there will be major differences between the way that individual projects are conducted. **Bootstrap**, which is a European initiative along the same lines as CMM, does allow assessment to be done at a project level.

Bootstrap also caters for ratings between the major levels e.g. at 2.6 which indicates that the project is better than level 2 but not yet up to a level 3 standard.

9.7 Using measurement to improve processes

Without getting bogged down in the particular requirements of the Capability Maturity Model, how can these ideas be usefully applied? To explore this question, let us take a scenario from industry.

9.7.1 The UVW scenario

UVW is a company that builds machine tool equipment that contains sophisticated and extensive control software. This software is produced and maintained by the Software Engineering department. Within this department are separate teams that deal with the software for different types of equipment.

Lisa has been working at UVW for five years and is highly regarded as a software developer and is now a Software Team Leader in the Software Engineering department with a team of six Systems Designers reporting to her.

Her group is responsible for new control systems for a particular line of machine tools and also for the maintenance and enhancement of existing systems for the product line. The dividing line between new development and the maintenance is sometimes blurred as a new control system often makes heavy use of existing software components which are extensively modified to create the new software.

A separate Systems Testing Group test software for new control systems, but are not called in for error correction and adaptive maintenance in systems that have already been released.

A project for a new control system would be under the management of a Project Engineer who would have overall responsibility for both the hardware and software sides of the project. Because the Project Engineer would not primarily be a software expert, however, he or she would make heavy demands on a Software Team Leader, such as Lisa, in an advisory capacity. Lisa can, as a Software Team Leader, be working for a number of different Project Engineers in respect of different projects, but in the UVW organization chart she is always shown as reporting to the Head of Software Engineering.

When there is a new control system to be developed, the Project Engineer will write a software requirement document that will be reviewed by a Software Team Leader, who will then approve the document, usually after some amendment. A copy of the requirements will then go to the Systems Testing Group so that they can start work on creating system test cases and a system test environment. Lisa, if she were designated Software Team Leader, would then write an Architecture Design document which would break the requirements into the actual software components needed. These would then be allocated to Work Packages which would then be carried out by individual members of Lisa's team.

The general practice at UVW is to get the software written as quickly as possible so that it can be loaded onto the hardware platform for both initial hardware and software debugging. At this point, the hardware and software engineers would inevitably have to alter the requirements, and consequently the software, as they find inconsistencies, faults and missing functions. The Systems Testing Group should be notified of these changes, but this can be patchy. Once the system is seen to be in a satisfactory state by the developers, it is released to the Systems Testing Group for final testing before being shipped to the customers.

These are some of the problems that Lisa has:

- The Head of Software Engineering and the Project Engineers do not always liaise effectively leading to the over-commitment of staff to both new systems and maintenance jobs at the same time;

- The initial testing of what is effectively a prototype often leads to new requirements being identified;

- There is no proper control over change requests – the volume of these can increase the demand for software development effort well beyond that originally planned;

- System testing can go on longer than originally planned because of the number of bug fixes, or alternatively forced deadlines might be met by releasing software with known errors.

Looking at this scenario, we can see that there is an awful lot of opportunity for improvements. Indeed, it is very difficult to know where to start. However, approaches like that of CMM help us identify the things that have to be place before others can be successfully introduced. An immediate step to improve matters would be the introduction of more formal project planning and control. This would at least enable us to assess how the big the problems were, even if we cannot yet really get down to solving them. Given a software requirement, the creation of a formal project plan would enable staff work-loads to distributed in a managed manner. More importantly perhaps at this point, the monitoring of the plans would allow managers to see what specific problems were emerging with a particular project. Effective control procedures might make managers more aware of how changes in system scope were increasing the demands for software development effort. In the short term schedules could be adjusted to reflect this. Figure 9.3 represents how this control system could be visualized.

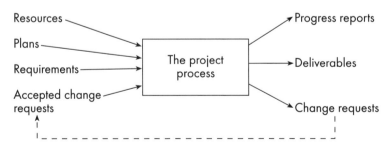

Figure 9.3 *The project as a 'closed box'.*

The next steps to improve the situation would be to carefully define the processes involved in the software development process – see Figure 9.4.

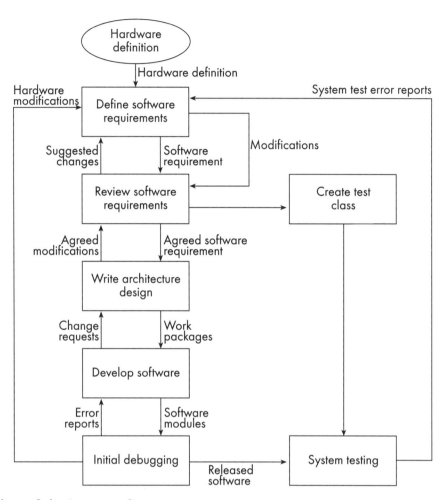

Figure 9.4 *A process diagram.*

The diagram in Figure 9.4 does not show the flows of information needed to indicate how managers could ensure the correct amount of staff time is allocated to the development activities. Amend the diagram to show these flows.

Exercise 9.9 Management information flows

Once this formalized process model has been put in place, the behaviour of the various processes within it can be monitored. We can see, for example, how many change reports are being generated or how many system defects are being detected at system testing phase. Apart from information relating to the products that pass between processes, we can also collect effort information about each process itself. All this will allow more effective remedial action to be taken more speedily when problems are found.

At the final stage of process development, the information collected can be used to improve the process model itself. It might, for example, become apparent that the definition of the software requirement is a major source of defects. Steps could therefore be taken to improve this process. One way of dealing with some of the faults might be to find ways whereby the hardware component of the system could be simulated using software tools. This could help the hardware engineers to produce more realistic initial designs. It might even be possible to build control software and test it against the hardware simulation. This would help to resolve some technical problems at an earlier stage.

9.8   Predicting fault counts and fault density

9.8.1 Faults and failures

It is usual to distinguish between faults and failures. An error might be made by a software developer and this will result in a **fault**. When the software is executed, the fault could make itself apparent because the application does not behave as expected: this is a **failure**. In a classic piece of research at IBM, Adams (1984) showed that not all faults were equally likely to lead to failures. It would appear that faults in heavily used components would tend to be the first to cause failures. Musa (1993) describes how this can be exploited to reduce failure rates by analysing **operational profiles** that identify the most heavily used components and by making sure these are subjected to more demanding testing.

We have our own practical experience in this field. Once again this relates to our work with the XYZ organization. In this case, only faults discovered in function testing were considered. In system testing it is likely that testing will subject each component to approximately equal scrutiny and that the number of faults uncovered will not be significantly influenced by the degree to which they are used operationally

Several studies have noted that smaller modules, while having smaller fault counts, may have larger fault densities than those of larger ones (Hatton, 1997).

Microsoft Excel has a facility which produces these diagrams as one of the Data Analysis tools (not as part of the Chart feature).

Fault counts and fault densities need to be distinguished. A **fault count** is the number of faults found in a component. It will be recalled that at XYZ, the components are blocks. It would be surprising if larger blocks did not have more errors than smaller ones. In order to take account of the differences in size **fault density** is calculated as the number of faults divided by some measure of size, in this case, **volume**, the amount of machine memory occupied by the compiled code.

What would be really useful would be to see if there were a small number of components in an application generating most of the faults or failures. By concentrating our efforts on these, we might be able to decrease failure rates quickly and relatively cheaply. One way of doing this is by drawing up a **Pareto graph**. This is a bar chart where the bars represent the errors in individual components. These are shown in descending order of magnitude. By examining such a graph, Moeller and Paulish(1995) were able to show that in the applications they were studying 10% of the code was responsible for 45% of faults. They counted not just faults found in testing but also failures detected in operational running. They found that smaller modules tended to have higher fault densities.

Ohlsson and Alberg (1996) describe work done at Ericsson aimed at producing a fault prediction model. They present an adapted Pareto diagram which illustrates that, for example, 20% of modules contained 60% of faults. Note that in this case the *number of modules* is used while in the Moeller and Paulish analysis it is the proportion of code. Another important difference is that while Moeller and Paulish count both testing and operational faults, Ohlsson and Alberg count only faults found in system testing. Care has to be taken with interpreting the results at Ericsson as there results might simply mean that larger modules have more errors.

9.8.2 The data set analysed

In our own analysis (Hughes *et al.* 1999) there were details of 63 development tasks relating to the two subsystems, X and Y. The jobs were either the development of new software blocks or the enhancement of existing ones.

The XYZ application was described in Chapter 8.

As is invariably the case with software measurement data none of the variables were normally distributed which made the use of parametric statistical techniques problematic. Tests for rank correlations between variables showed that in particular block size, development effort and fault counts were correlated.

Following the lead of Moeller and Paulish a Pareto diagram was constructed using fault counts and modified volume – see Figure 9.5.

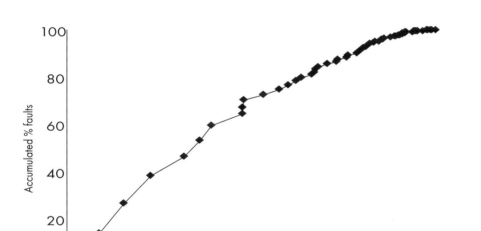

Figure 9.5 *Accumulated faults versus accumulated block size.*

This does not seem to show the same concentration of faults in a small proportion of code that Moeller and Paulish found. Errors seem to be fairly evenly distributed throughout the code. It is possible that the difference between Figure 9.5 and the pattern found by Moeller and Paulish is because the current data set is based on system tests conducted before operational release while the data of Moeller and Paulish includes operational failures. Operational use would mean some components would have more faults recorded because of heavier operational use.

Figure 9.6 shows a Pareto style diagram that follows the Ohlsson and Alberg practice of mapping faults against the number of modules.

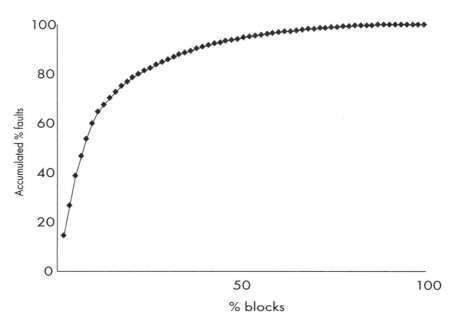

Figure 9.6 *Accumulated faults versus number of blocks.*

Figure 9.6 shows a similar pattern to that presented by Ohlsson and Alberg: 20% of modules contributed 60% of faults. In the current case however the reason for this was simply that the 20% of modules contributing 60% of faults were the larger modules anyway. The advice to developers, based on our findings, to look most closely at larger modules as having potentially more errors cannot be regarded as radical.

9.8.3 Fault prediction models

One interesting outcome was that we could create models similar to those created to forecast effort but in this case to forecast the number of errors. A prediction model to forecast faults was constructed using least squares regression. This produced the equation:

$$FT\ faults = -0.87 + 0.27(block\ signals) + (announcements)$$
$$+ 0.22(commands) + 0.0043(correction\ area) \quad \text{(Equation 9.1)}$$

which had an R^2 value of 87.4% after discarding three outliers.

9.8.4 Fault density versus block size

As indicated earlier, fault counts were closely associated with block size. What would be more challenging would be to try and model the influences on fault density.

Unfortunately, the initial analysis of correlations between variables showed that fault density appeared to have no relationship with other variables with the exception of 'correction area' where there was a Pearson correlation of 0.64 and a Spearman rank correlation of 0.218. With the latter test, the large number of ties could have affected the result.

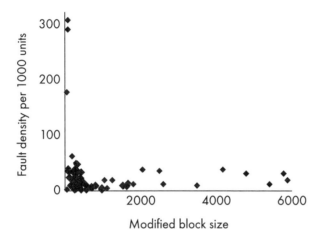

Figure 9.7 *Fault density versus modified block size.*

The relationship between fault density and modified block size is best understood by looking at Figure 9.7. In general fault density seems to be fairly consistent across all sizes of block, but where there are anomalies, these tend to be with the smaller blocks. Three cases stand out as anomalies: these were all blocks that communicated with other systems and were very heavily used operationally. This identification of outliers points to the possibility of producing guidelines to indicate which blocks are most at risk of failure. It is contended that with this set of data high fault densities are *not* generally associated with smaller blocks, but the *risk* of a high fault density is.

9.9 Conclusions

Important points to remember about software quality include the following:

* Quality by itself is a vague concept and practical quality requirements have to be carefully defined;

* There have to be practical ways of testing for the relative presence or absence of a quality;

- Most of the qualities that are apparent to the users of software can only be tested for when the system is completed;

- Ways of checking during development what the quality of the final system is likely to be are therefore needed – but it is often difficult to use internal measurements to forecast external qualities;

- It is possible to construct models that forecast, with some accuracy the number of errors likely to be found in testing components – this is largely because larger components are likely to have more faults;

- The pattern of failures in operational running will be different to that in testing because the volume of use of each component will become an important influence.

9.10 References

Adams, E. (1984), 'Optimizing preventive service of software products', *IBM Research Journal*: 28(1), 2–14.

Bache, R. and Bazzana, G. (1994), *Software Metrics for Product Assessment*, McGraw-Hill, Maidenhead.

Boehm, B. W., Brown, J. R., Kaspar, H., Lipow, M., MacLeod, G. J. and Merit, M. J. (1978), *Characteristics of Software Quality*, TRW Series of Software Technology 1, North-Holland, Amsterdam.

Dromey, G, (1995), 'A model for software product quality', *IEEE Transactions on Software Engineering*: 21(4), 146–162.

Hamilton, F., Johnson, P. and Johnson, H. (1998), 'Task-related principles for user interface design' in van der Vear, G. (ed), *Proceedings of Shaerding Workshop on Task Analysis*.

Hatton, L. (1997), 'Re-examining fault density – component size connection' *IEEE Software*: March/April, 89–97.

ISO (1991), *ISO 9126 Information Technology – Software Product Evaluation – Quality Characteristics and Guidelines for Their Use.*

Kitchenham, B. A., Linkman, S., Pasquinni, A. and Nanni, V. (1995), 'Experiences with ISO 9126', *Proceedings of European Software Cost Modelling Conference*, Rolduc 17–19 May.

McCall, J. A. (1978), 'An introduction to software quality metrics' in: Cooper, J. D. and Fisher, M. J. (eds), *Software Quality Management*, Petrocelli, New York.

Moeller, K-H. and Paulish, D. J.(1995), 'An empirical investigation into software fault distribution' in Fenton, N., Whitty, R. and Iizuka, Y. (eds), *Software Quality Assurance and Measurement: a Worldwide Perspective*, International Thomson Computer Press, London.

Musa, J. D. (1993), 'Operational profiles in software engineering reliability', *IEEE Software*: 10(2), 14–31.

Ohlsson, N. and Ahlberg, H. (1996), 'Predicting fault-prone software modules in telephone switches', *IEEE Transactions on Software Engineering*: 22(12), 886–894.

Watts, H. S. (1989). *Managing the Software Process,* Addison-Wesley, New York.

9.11 Additional questions

1. McCall suggests that simplicity, modularity, instrumentation and self-descriptiveness are software quality criteria, that is, internal characteristics that promote the external quality of testability.

    (a) Explain what is meant by each of the four criteria above.
    (b) Describe possible measures for each of the criteria.
    (c) Describe practical ways in which the measures could be assessed.

2. Discuss how meaningful the following measurements are.

    (a) The number of error messages produced on the first compilation of a program.
    (b) The average effort to implement changes requested by users to a system.
    (c) The percentage of lines in program listings that are comments.
    (d) The number of pages in a requirements document.

3. How might you measure the effectiveness of a user manual for a software package? Consider both the measurements that might be applicable and the procedures by which the measurements might be taken.

4. In a particular development environment, user requirements are obtained by interviewing users. The interviews are initially planned by examining the appropriate organization chart and identifying which staff to interview. A provisional plan is then drawn up of who will be interviewed and when. Once an interview has been completed, interview notes are created. On completion of all the interviews, the notes are analysed to draw up data flow diagrams (DFDs) showing the processes in the application domain, the flows of information between those processes and the data stores that they maintain and access. In parallel with this, data analysts will produce a logical data structure diagram (LDS) showing the main entities of interest to the application, the attributes of these entities and the relationships that link entities together. A process/entity cross-reference table is then drawn up showing which processes in the DFD access which entities in the LDS. As a result of this amendments may be made to either the DFD or the LDS. For each entity on the LDS, an entity life history (ELH) is then created which documents the sequences of system states to which the entity may be subject.

5. Draw up a development process model for the method describe above, similar in style to the one shown in Figure 9.4, identifying the points at which measurements could be taken. Why would measurement be particularly important at this stage of a development project?

6. (a) Explain why the counts of errors recorded by the system testing group in the UVW scenario are more likely to be accurate than the counts of errors found during debugging in the *develop software* process.

   (b) The *system testing* process feeds back error reports to the *define requirements* process rather than the *develop software* process. Why should this be?

   (c) Describe how the quality of *memorability* referred to in Section 9.4.4 might be measured for a particular application?

Answer pointers

Chapter 1:

Exercise 1.1 Qualities of a spelling-checker

These might include effectiveness in: detecting incorrect spellings; suggesting correct spellings; avoiding flagging correct words as misspellings.

Exercise 1.2 Evaluating qualities of a spelling-checker

We *could* construct a questionnaire and ask users of the spelling-checker to provide a rating for each of the three qualities.

   An alternative approach would be to 'test-drive' the spelling-checker by running it on an actual document and counting the number of incidents where:
(a) an incorrect word is correctly identified;
(b) a correct word is incorrectly flagged;
(c) an incorrect alternative is suggested for an incorrectly spelled word.

Exercise 1.3 Practical evaluation of a spelling-checker

Obviously the results here would depend on the document checked and the spelling-checker and dictionary used.

Exercise 1.4 Identifying attributes

The attributes of spelling checker might include: algorithm used; dictionary used; spelling correctness (extent to which words in dictionary are actually correct); completeness of vocabulary (that is, number of valid words known); correcting effectiveness

   The attributes of document writer might include: typing skill; spelling skill; specialisms (for example, legal, scientific and so on).

Exercise 1.5 Error rate for suggested corrected spellings

The error rate for suggested spellings would be $3/18 \times 1000$ or 167 errors per thousand suggestions.

Exercise 1.6 Information lost through aggregation

Aggregation can lose information about the general range and spread of values of attributes in the group of objects being aggregated such as average values and the degree to which individual values can deviate from that average.

Exercise 1.7 Check-digit effectiveness

An estimate might be based on the following reasoning. Given that the check-digit for the reference number being examined is 1, then the chances of a new reference number formed by misreading the old number in some way having the same valid check digit of 1 as well by pure chance is 1 in 11 or 9.1%.

Chapter 2:

Exercise 2.1 User versus IT support staff perceptions of response time

	Option A	Option B	Option C
Option A	n/a	longer than	shorter than
Option B	shorter than	n/a	shorter than
Option C	longer than	longer than	n/a

	19 seconds	20 seconds	21 seconds
19 seconds	n/a	longer than	shorter than
20 seconds	shorter than	n/a	shorter than
21 seconds	longer than	longer than	n/a

There is clearly a difference between the users' perception that Option A takes longer than Option B and the timings taken by the support staff. The actual difference between the 19 and 20 seconds recorded could be minimal, especially if fractions have been truncated so that the figures might originally have been 19.8 and 20.1 seconds, for example. The support staff may have carried out their timings under different conditions, perhaps in a test environment. In an operational environment, the data base may have a different distribution of types of record and the fact that many users may be trying to access the same data base may have an effect on particular response times.

Exercise 2.2 Consequences of and contributors to 'user friendliness'

Among the consequences of a lack of user-friendliness might be:

- more time needed by users to carry out a task;

- more errors made by users when operating a system: note that this could also increase the time needed to carry out an operation as time may be consumed in correcting errors;

- users' feeling of stress and frustration;

- unused system functionality: because users do not understand a feature of the software or the way it is operated.

Among the factors that contribute to user friendliness might be:

- consistent design: this could be assessed by adopting a standard template and counting the number of times an input/output design deviates from that standard;

- consistent terminology: for example that the same terms are used in the interface that the user employs in the surrounding clerical procedures;

- number of key strokes or mouse clicks required to carry out an operation.

Exercise 2.3 life cycle model.

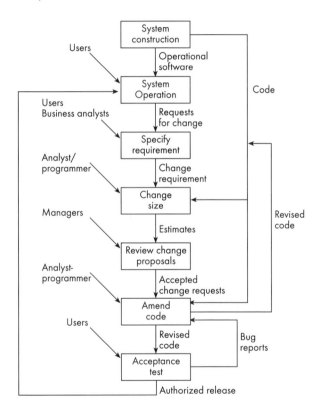

Exercise 2.4 Derived versus fundamental measurements

(i) Derived – number of faults/module size.
(ii) Fundamental or derived – could be derived from the difference between finish and start times.
(iii) Derived – task size/effort, for example, lines of code per day.
(iv) Derived – mean time between failures, for example, as operational time/ number of failures.

Exercise 2.5 Scale types

(i)

order	entry	value	difference from previous	
1	b	1.2		lowest
2	d	1.3	0.1	
3	g	2.1	0.8	
4	f	2.3	0.2	mid-point
5	a	3.5	1.0	
6	e	4.5	1.0	
7	c	7.5	3.0	highest

Ordinal scale.

(ii) mid-point – lowest = f (2.3) – b (1.2) = 1.1
highest – mid-point = c (7.5) – f (2.3) = 5.2
Interval scale.

(iii) When creating boundaries for *restricted ordinal* measurements you may want to group together those instances that seem to be naturally clustered. Putting together b and d as 'low', g, f, d, e, together as 'medium' and c as 'high' is one way that might be adopted.

Exercise 2.6 Drawing a histogram and calculating the average

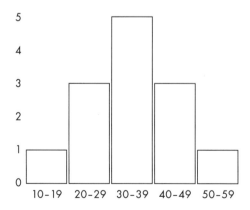

The average for this sequence is 34.8. This is very much in the centre of the middle and most highly populated range of values and suggests that this is a normally distributed set of numbers.

Exercise 2.7 Drawing a histogram – changing patterns

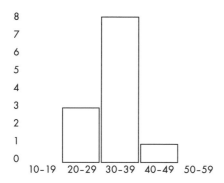

The average of this range of values is 32.8. Although the distribution looks skewed in this graph we can adjust the ranges to reveal its normal distribution – see below.

Exercise 2.8 Histogram with a non-normal distribution

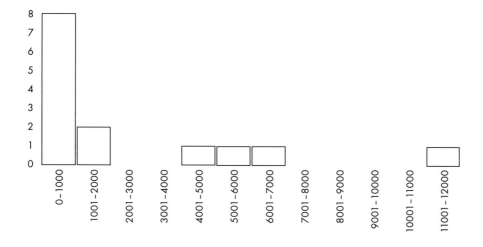

Exercise 2.9 Creating box-plots

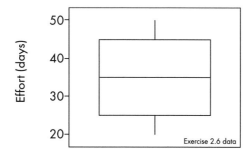

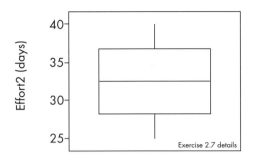

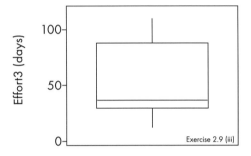

Chapter 3:

Exercise 3.1 Calculating information content

What is the smallest number of bits that it would take to hold the following information?

(i)   yes or no: 1 bit.
(ii) the years in a century: 7 bits.
(iii) the letters of the alphabet: 5 bits.
(iv) the settings on a UK traffic signal (green, amber, red, red and amber): 2 bits.

Exercise 3.2 Assessing the need for additional bits

(a) 36 settings would require an additional bit
(b) four further settings would be available: green and amber, green and red, green and amber and red, no lights at all. You might argue about the wisdom of the no lights signal, but it could mean 'traffic lights not working'!

Exercise 3.3 Measuring uncertainty

The dice: 2.58
The coin: 1.00

Exercise 3.4 Assessing information redundancy

(a) The maximum uncertainty that can be recorded in 8 bits is 8 bits! Upper and lower case alphabetic characters, plus the ten digits, would account for 62 different settings.
$H = \log_2 62 = 5.95$
Redundancy is therefore $(8 - 5.95)/8 = 0.26$

(b) The two ASCII characters would have 2^{16} different combinations that would allow up to the year 65,536. 0 to 99 make up 100 combinations so that
$H = \log_2 100 = 6.44$
The redundancy is therefore $(16 - 6.44)/16$ or 0.60

Exercise 3.5 Drawing a flowgraph

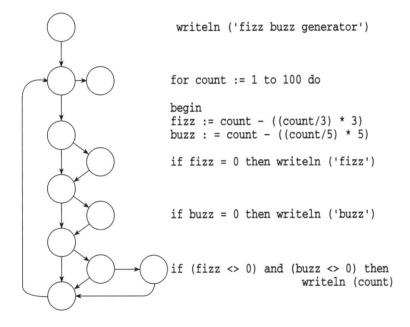

```
writeln ('fizz buzz generator')


for count := 1 to 100 do

begin
fizz := count - ((count/3) * 3)
buzz : = count - ((count/5) * 5)

if fizz = 0 then writeln ('fizz')


if buzz = 0 then writeln ('buzz')


if (fizz <> 0) and (buzz <> 0) then
                    writeln (count)
```

Exercise 3.6 Cyclomatic complexity

$e = 16$ and $n = 12$, therefore $V(g) = 16 - 12 + 1 = 5$

Exercise 3.7 The Prather metric

The Prather metric would be $3 + ((1\times2) + (1\times2) + 1)\times2 + (2\times2) = 17$

Exercise 3.8 Test effectiveness

Statement coverage = $7/8 = 0.88$
Branch coverage   = $5/7 = 0.71$

Chapter 4:

Exercise 4.1: tasks involved in testing

These might involve:

- comprehending the user requirement document;

- isolating individual requirements that will need testing;

- identifying the dependencies between requirements – for example, certain transactions may have to be carried out to set up conditions on a data base which subsequent transactions can report on;

- calculating and recording the expected results for each transaction, or test case, in the set of test data;

- executing the tests;

- checking the results;

- identifying discrepancies between test results and expected results and recording the nature of the discrepancy;

- report the discrepancies noted above to development staff;

- retesting when corrected software has been released by development staff.

Note that different factors will affect the ease with which of the above sub-tasks can be completed. For example, the ease with which the first two tasks can be done will depend in part of the quality of the requirements document.

Exercise 4.2: Possible drawbacks of an initial design

The implied design does not, at the moment, consider the processing efficiency of the proposed software solution. For example, if the set of numbers to be examined was very large, making separate passes through the set for the different sub-processes might be quite time-consuming. We might therefore want to access each number in turn once and carry out all the processing associated with that number just once.

It can also be seen that the preliminary design takes no notice of possible duplication of processing. When calculating the standard deviation, you might wish to calculate the mean as a preliminary step – this depends on the particular algorithm that you use. This will already have been done by the *calculate mean* procedure. It would therefore be convenient if the *calculate mean* function could pass its result over to the *calculate standard deviation* function. However, the designer might not be keen to do this as the *calculate standard deviation* function, as it stands, could be a handily reusable component.

Exercise 4.3: Types of module cohesion

(a) (i) The module has some procedural cohesion as the first three procedures have to be executed before calculate skew procedure, but there is no reason why, for example, calculate mode cannot be executed before calculate mean rather than afterwards.

(ii) All elements operate on the same external data, therefore communication cohesion is high.

(iii) The reason why the order of execution noted in (i) is important is because *calculate mean, calculate mode, calculate standard deviation* all pass their results to *calculate skew*.

(iv) All elements of the module contribute to the output result, *skew*: therefore functional cohesion is high.

(e) (i) This would increase procedural cohesion and sequential cohesion as *calculate mean* would have to be executed before *calculate standard deviation.*

(ii) This would reduce the functional cohesion of the overall module.

Exercise 4.4: Graph impurity metric

(a) $11 - 10 + 1 = 2$

(b) $9 - 8 + 1 = 2$

Exercise 4.5 DateDifference module structure

(a) Yau and his colleagues were primarily interested in control flow data bindings.

(b) (i) The following modules would be affected: DateDifference; CheckDate; DateToDays; DayNumber.

The ripple effect could be reduced by having the date that is input to *DateDifference* changed by that module from DDMMYYYY back to the old MMDDYY format before *CheckDate*, *DateToDays*, and *DayNumber* are called. Of course, this would not solve the year 2000 problem, which, it might be guessed, is why this particular change has been requested. The existence of two different date formats might be confusing to a person coming along at a later date – this would be an example of how maintenance changes could make code more difficult to follow.

(ii) $7 - 6 + 1 = 2$

The above answer is based on the fact that *CheckDate* and *DateToDays* are called from different places, even though in each case it is from the same module. Technically I suppose this makes it an impure tree. For some measurements, duplicate calls are ignored, and if this rule was applied here then the answer would be $6-5+1 = 0$. This illustrates how with software measurements the precise method of application is almost always a problem. We will come across this problem in several more places. It also illustrates a particular weakness with this measurement: *CheckDate* would appear to be a highly reusable procedure and to suggest that the structure would somehow be improved by duplicating the code seems unreasonable.

(iii) Actual data bindings

In the following section, it is assumed that using a variable as a parameter when calling another procedure counts as a 'use'.

(CheckDate, ErrorIndicator, DateDifference)
(DayNumber, Days1, DateDifference)
(AddDaysInYear, Days1, DateDifference)
(DayNumber, Days1, AddDaysInYear)
(DayNumber, Days2, DateDifference)
(AddDaysInYear, Days2, DateDifference)
(DayNumber, Days2, AddDaysInYear)
(AddDaysInYear, Days, DayNumber)
(AddDaysInYear, Days, DateToDays)
(DayNumber, Days, DateToDays)

Control data bindings

(CheckDate, ErrorIndicator, DateDifference)
(DayNumber, Days1, DateDifference)
(AddDaysInYear, Days1, DateDifference)
(DayNumber, Days1, AddDaysInYear)
(DayNumber, Days2, DateDifference)
(DayNumber, Days, DateToDays)
(AddDaysInYear, Days2, DateDifference)
(DayNumber, Days2, AddDaysInYear)

Note:

(AddDaysInYear, Days, DayNumber) does not become a control data binding because examination of the code shows that control is never passed to DayNumber after AddDaysIn Year.

4.6 Fan-in and fan-out for the DateDifference module

First of all, a table can be produced showing the flows of data between the modules as in Table A.1.

From this the Fan-in and Fan-out can be calculated:

Modules	Fan-in	Fan-out
DateDifference	6	6
Checkdate	2	2
DateToDays	3	5
DayNumber	1	1
AddDaysInYear	2	1

Table A.1   *Flows of data between modules*

From	To					
	DateDifference	*CheckDate*	*DateToDays*	*DayNumber*	*AddDaysInYear*	*Calling module*
DateDifference	n/a	Date1, Date2[a]	Date1, Date2	[b]	—	DifferenceInDays ErrorIndicator
CheckDate	ErrorIndicator ErrorIndicator	—	—	—	—	—
DateToDays	Days1, Days2	—	—	Date	Year, Days	—
DayNumber	—	—	—	—	Days[c]	—
AddDaysInYear	—	—	Days	—	—	—
Calling module	Date1 Date2	—	—	—	—	—

a. ErrorIndicator is passed from DateDifference to CheckDate, but as this is a null parameter that only contains a value when control is returned from the call we have not counted it.
b. There appears to be an indirect flow of data between *DateDifference* and *DayNumber* as *Date* is passed via *DateToDays* without *DateToDays* manipulating it. The rules as laid down by Henry and Kafura do not seem, however, to recognize flows over three levels of modules.
c. This is an example of an indirect flow.

Chapter 5:

Exercise 5.1: Classifying OO Metrics

Our suggestion is:

(i)   SS
(ii) CR
(iii) SC

There could be lots of argument over this. For instance it could be that (ii) is related to complexity as well as reuse. What such arguments would illustrate is that a metric could validly be placed in more than one category.

Exercise 5.2: OO system size measurement

Number of classes	10
Number of methods	28
Number of attributes	24

Exercise 5.3: Weighted methods per class

Class	WMC
Holding	4
Loan item	2
Copy item	3
Printed material	3
Recorded material	3
Sheet music	3
Journal article	3
Long loan	2
Short loan	2
Desk loan	2

Note:

In this instance we have given each method the same weighting. In some cases, methods could be weighted according to their relative size, for example according to the lines of code they contain.

Exercise 5.4 Depth of inheritance

Class	DIT
Holding	0
Loan item	1
Copy item	1
Printed material	2
Recorded material	2
Sheet music	2
Journal article	2
Long loan	3
Short loan	3
Desk loan	3

Exercise 5.5 Number of children

Class	NOC
Holding	2
Loan item	2
Copy item	2
Printed material	3
Recorded material	0
Sheet music	0
Journal article	0
Long loan	0
Short loan	0
Desk loan	0

Exercise 5.6 Response for class

Class	RFC
Holding	4
Loan item	7[a]
Copy item	8
Printed material	7
Recorded material	7
Sheet music	9
Journal article	9
Long loan	7
Short loan	7
Desk loan	7

a. Loan item has 1 method that is called via message passing in Figure 5.3.

Exercise 5.7 Lack of cohesion of methods

	m2	m3	m4
m1	dissimilar	dissimilar	dissimilar
m2		similar	dissimilar
m3			dissimilar

Therefore $5 - 1 = 4$

Exercise 5.8(a) method inheritance factor

Class	Inherited methods	New methods	Total
Holding	0	4	4
Loan item	4	2	6
Copy item	4	4	8
Printed material	6	3	9
Recorded material	4	3	7
Sheet music	6	3	9
Journal article	6	3	9
Long loan	7	2	9
Short loan	7	2	9
Desk loan	7	2	9
Totals	51	28	79

Method inheritance factor = 51/77 = 0.66

Exercise 5.8(b) Polymorphism factor

Class	Over-riding methods	New methods (a)	Descendents (b)	a×b
Holding	0	4	9	36
Loan item	0	2	5	10
Copy item	0	4	2	8
Printed material	2	3	3	9
Recorded material	2	3	0	0
Sheet music	2	3	0	0
Journal article	2	3	0	0
Long loan	2	2	0	0
Short loan	2	2	0	0
Desk loan	2	2	0	0
Totals	14			63

Polymorphism factor = 14/63 = 0.22

Chapter 6:

Exercise 6.1 Examples of different types of program

Our suggestions are:

(a) A program which sets up a new occurrence of a record type on a database. This would especially be the case where the record has a large number of data items such as a new insurance policy holder in a insurance records application. This would have a large number of inputs but few outputs. It could be argued, however, that a large number of different types of input would require an equally large number of output error messages.

(b) A program that generates a detailed report of data set up on a database would have few inputs but many outputs.

(c) A program which amends a record on a database might have to display the current content of the record and then allow any of the fields on the record to be altered.

Some general points need to be noted here.

In order to assess the size of software we need to count the different *types* of input and output, not the actual inputs and outputs that occur when a program is executed on a particular occasion. For example, a report program might simply print out staff name, room number and telephone extension for each employee in an organization. On one particular run, the details are printed for 500 employees. The count of types of output would still be 3, not 3 times 500.

Similarly, there could be some outputs that are not always produced. An error message would be a good example of this. The error message would be counted as an output type despite the fact that it is only intermittently produced during actual executions of the software.

The key factor is that the code exists in the software component whether it happens to be used or not. Similarly, the fact that the same code is executed many times to produce lines in a report does not remove the fact that the code only exists once and is thus counted only once.

Exercise 6.2 Effort needed to implement inputs and outputs

The answer would, of course, depend on the precise nature of the software requirements. However, in general you might find that dealing with inputs is more difficult and time-consuming than dealing with outputs.

When dealing with inputs for example, you will need to consider that:

• the operator will need to be solicited for the input;

• the input will have to be received;

• the input will have to be checked to be in the correct format and to be compatible with other variables;

• if there is any discrepancy in the input, an error message will need to be displayed and the operator will need to be asked for a new input;

• if the input is acceptable, it may have to be reformatted for internal storage.

Exercise 6.3 Estimating effort for a new software component

(a) The estimate for the new component could be calculated as follows:

Module	SLOC	Staff-days
A	1200	48
B	750	29
C	2000	86
D	1450	60
totals	5400	223

Average SLOC per staff-day = 5400/223 = 24.21 SLOC per day
The estimate for the new component is therefore 900/24.21 = 37.3 days

(b) The new estimate is based on the assumption that the new component and the resources that are going to be used to produce it are very similar to those for the previous cases. It could, of course, be the case that in fact a new different programming language was going to be used or a different member of staff employed who is a raw trainee and has a low productivity rate as a consequence. The way the estimate is calculated assumes there are no fixed amounts of effort needed: for example, it could be that the developer always needs 5 days' effort at the start to set up the development environment, regardless of the number of lines of code to be written. If you calculate the SLOC/staff-day for each component individually you will see that larger components seem to have lower productivity rates. The method suggested does not take into account the possibility that larger components might need disproportionately more effort.

6.4 Calculating error densities

Module	Faults	SLOC	Fault density per 1000 SLOC
A	54	1200	45
B	33	900	36.6

Exercise 6.5 Comparing productivity using SLOC

The productivity rate in terms of SLOC per day for the Assembler code developer would be 2000/50 = 40 SLOC per day, while for the high-level code developer it would be 800/32 = 25 SLOC per day. This might imply that the Assembler code developer is more productive, although the high-level code developer has produced the equivalent end-product in 20% less time. The problem is of course that Assembler SLOC and high-level language SLOC are very different and do not offer a common basis for comparison.

Exercise 6.6 Calculating Albrecht FPs

The various user function types can be listed as follows:

User function type	Data store/ transaction	Rating
logical internal file	payroll file	average
	salaries table	simple
	tax table	simple
	bank credits	simple
	project accounting details	simple
external interface files	personnel details	average
	bank credits	simple
	project accounting details	simple
external inputs	monthly payroll calculation	complex
	salary/tax code update	simple
external outputs	monthly payslip production	average
	annual pay summary	average

The function points can now be calculated thus:

	Simple	Average	Complex
External input type	1×3		1×6
External output type		2×5	
Logical internal file type	4×7	1×10	
External interface file type	2×5	1×7	
External inquiry type			

This adds up to 74 function points.

It might be noted that under later IFPUG rules, bank credits and project accounting details would not be counted as external interface files but would probably be counted as external outputs.

In the case of the salary/tax code update, it could be argued that there is an implied external inquiry as well as an external input as the details would need to displayed to the user before they could be updated.

Exercise 6.7 FP count for an External Output

The file types would be EMPLOYEE/POSITION and Salary, that is 2 files.

Note: the treating of EMPLOYEE and POSITION as two record types in one file may seem to be rather arbitrary. The distinction between record types and file types seems to stem from flat file organizations and does not seem to be that relevant to modern relational data base systems.

The data items output are: payroll reference, name and address, date of birth, date of joining the company, position reference, start date, end date, salary grade, and current salary, that is 9 data types. Looking up Table 6.5 gives us a rating of 'average' which translates via Table 6.1 into an FP count of 5.

Exercise 6.8 Mark II FP calculation

Inputs: a user request to initiate the transaction that is, 1 input

Entities accessed: EMPLOYEE, POSITION and SALARY, that is, 3 entity types

Outputs: payroll reference, name and address, date of birth, date of joining the company, position reference, start date, end date, salary grade, and current salary, that is 9 data types.

The Mark II FP count would therefore be $(1 \times 0.58) + (3 \times 1.66) + (9 \times 0.26) = 7.9$

Exercise 6.9 Mark II calculation of TCA

Rating technical complexity

Factor	Rating
Data communications	0
Distributed functions	0
Performance requirements	3
Heavy hardware configuration usage	3
High transaction rate	0
On-line data entry	3
End-user efficiency	5
On-line update	3
Complex processing	3
Reusability requirements	3
Ease of installation	3
Operational ease (for technical staff as opposed to end users)	0
Multiple sites	3
Ease of modification	3
Interfaces to other applications	0
Special security features	3
Direct access for third parties	0
User training features	5
Documentation requirements	3

The total of technical complexity adjustment factors would be 43. The adjusted function point count would therefore be:

$$800 \times (0.65 + (43 \times 0.005)) = 692$$

It can be seen that the new 'industry average coefficient' makes a big difference to the adjusted FP count.

Exercise 6.10 Evaluating inter-rater consistency
(a)

system	rater a	rater b	% difference
a	120	135	12.5
b	352	333	5.4
c	190	202	6.3
d	300	394	31.3
e	260	255	1.9
f	600	612	2.0
			9.9

It is usual to say that one should not average percentages and the median difference might be more appropriate. A counter argument is that the attribute being measured here is the judgment of the rater on six different occasions, not the size of the systems as such.

(b)

system	rater b	rater a	% difference
a	135	120	11.1
b	333	352	5.7
c	202	190	5.9
d	394	300	23.8
e	255	260	2.0
f	612	600	2.0
			8.4

(c) mean = 403.3 and standard deviation = 55.27
coefficient of variation = $(55.27/403.3 \times 100) = 13.7\%$

Exercise 6.11 Identifying full function points

Entries (E)	vehicle waiting, vehicle left
Exits (X)	lift barrier
Reads (R)	check count of vehicles
Writes (W)	increase vehicle count, decrease vehicle count

Chapter 7:

Exercise 7.1 Measuring the quality of targets

Our suggestions are:

- over-estimates – measure productivity in terms of, say, days/KLOC or days/ function point and compare this across different activities;

- under-estimates – look at fault density in terms of faults/KLOC or faults/ function point.

A problem could be that low productivity or high fault density could be the result of factors other than the quality of the estimate of development effort. In other words, these measurements would be *loosely coupled* to the attribute of interest.

Exercise 7.2 Estimate probabilities

(i)

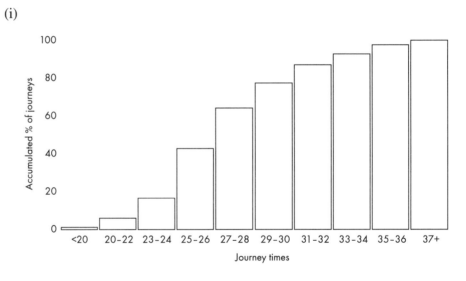

(ii) I have a 43% chance of completing journey in 26 minutes or less.
(iii) 31 to 32 minutes.

Exercise 7.3 Economies of scale

(i)   The following might cause economies of scale:

- Dispersion of start-up effort – at the beginning of a project there are start-up activities to do with planning and organization which often are not in proportion to the size of the project. For example there could be delays caused by the need to get clearance from various authorities to go ahead with the project. These start-up costs can make a disproportionately bigger impact on smaller projects.

- Learning curves – with any new project the staff probably have a certain amount of learning. This could be about the application domain (for example, the meaning of the terms employed by the users of the system), or about the technical domain (for instance the programming languages used). With bigger projects, staff have the opportunity to become quite expert.

(ii) Breaking a large project down into smaller increments is usually very sensible. However it might not be without cost.

- Some start-up costs will be incurred with each increment;

- Some work may have to be repeated – user requirements might have to be reviewed, for example, as they might have changed over time;

- There could be problems of 'software breakage' – later increments might require changes to functionality that was implemented in previous increments.

Exercise 7.4 Calculation of mmre

estimated (e)	actual (a)	difference (d)	mre (d/a)
461	321	140	0.44
365	358	7	0.02
445	693	248	0.36
461	723	262	0.36
389	408	19	0.05
660	300	360	1.20
728	618	110	0.18
1681	1639	42	0.03
1406	1506	100	0.07
5828	5747	81	0.01
350	370	20	0.05
11920	11936	16	0.00
4602	4680	78	0.02
		mmre	0.21

Exercise 7.5 Calculation of median mre

Remember that the median is the midpoint if the values are sorted into ascending (or descending order). In this case it is 0.05.

Exercise 7.6 balanced relative error

estimated (e)	actual (a)	difference (d)	minimum (m)	bre (d/m)
461	321	140	321	0.44
365	358	7	358	0.02
445	693	248	445	0.56
461	723	262	461	0.57
389	408	19	389	0.05
660	300	360	300	1.20
728	618	110	618	0.18
1681	1639	42	1639	0.03
1406	1506	100	1406	0.07
5828	5747	81	5747	0.01
350	370	20	350	0.06
11920	11936	16	11920	0.00
4602	4680	78	4602	0.02
			mbre	0.25

Exercise 7.7 Decision-making

This is a discussion question with no single correct answer. However, points that could be made include:

- In a business environment, decisions have to be made quickly. There is not much time for careful analysis;

- The lack of time means that large quantities of information cannot be examined before coming to a decision;

- Information provided by 'experts' is not always that helpful anyway – different experts give different stories or are reluctant to commit themselves to specific advice;

- There is a question of which information you can trust – it is better to restrict the information to a small sub-set that you know is trustworthy rather than look at a wide range of sources some of which might be ambiguous or unreliable;

- Because the future is uncertain, 'correct decisions' are only identifiable retrospectively – for example the decision to buy shares in a company will be 'correct' if the value of the shares appreciates – but there is a large element of chance in this;

- Making the 'correct' decision is only a small part of being a manager – making the decisions work is more important.

Exercise 7.9 basic COCOMO

Project	KDSI	Actual pm	estimated pm	mre
1	253.7	287	803.06	1.80
2	40.5	82.5	116.96	0.42
3	450	1107.31	1465.83	0.32
4	214.4	86.9	672.97	6.74
5	449.9	335.3	1465.49	3.37
6	50	84	145.93	0.74
7	43	23.2	124.55	4.37
8	200	130.3	625.59	3.80
9	289	116	920.78	6.94
10	39	72	112.42	0.56
11	254.2	258.7	804.72	2.11
12	128.6	230.7	393.47	0.71
13	161.4	157	499.47	2.18
14	164.8	246.9	510.52	1.07
15	60.2	69.9	177.33	1.54
			mmre	2.44

The figures here differ from those in Kemerer (1987) because an organic mode has been assumed in every case.

Exercise 7.10 Intermediate COCOMO

The nominal effort would be $3.2 \times 15^{1.05} = 54.9$ work months. The development effort drivers would be:

Factor	Rating	Multiplier
ACAP	very high	0.71
AEXP	low	1.13
PCAP	high	0.80
VEXP	high	0.90
LEXP	low	1.07
SCED	high	1.04

$dem = 0.71 \times 1.13 \times 0.80 \times 0.90 \times 1.07 \times 1.04 = 0.64$
final estimate $= 54.9 \times 0.64 = 35.3$ person-months

Exercise 7.11 Maximum scale factor

The maximum value for *sf* would be:

$$1.01 + 0.01 \times (5 + 5 + 5 + 5 + 5) = 1.26.$$

The minimum value for *sf* would be:

$$1.01 + 0.01 \times (0 + 0 + 0 + 0 + 0) = 1.01.$$

Exercise 7.12 Calculating a scale factor

The sf in this case would be $1.01 + 0.01 \times (2 + 1 + 4 + 1 + 4) = 1.13$.

Chapter 8:

Exercise 8.1 Checking time sheets

Our suggestions are that you might check:

• Are any totals correctly calculated?

• Does the number of hours worked in a day or a week match the normal hours for these time periods?

• Have any overtime hours been approved? – see note below

• Are the projects referred to recognizable as ones to which the developer is allocated?

• Are the activities recorded those that one would normally expect members of staff to undertake?

• Are the activities ones that are appropriate for the project to which they refer? For instance, one would not expect software coding to be carried during a feasibility study project.

• If there are any hours allocated to a 'general' heading, is there any indication of what the nature of these were?

• What are the reasons for any major differences between this week's time sheet and last weeks?

Note that in many organizations, overtime is not paid. There might therefore be a tendency not to record overtime hours on time sheets. This can lead to misleading productivity rates being derived, which in turn could make the estimation of effort for future projects problematic.

Exercise 8.2 Calculating correlation coefficients

The Pearson correlation coefficient are shown in the table below:

	Inputs	Outputs	Accesses	Effort
Inputs	—	−0.52	0.86	0.90
Outputs	—	—	−0.50	−0.63
Accesses	—	—	—	0.84
Effort	—	—	—	—

Two independent variables, *inputs* and *accesses*, are strongly correlated. This implies that only one of these should be used in any prediction model. *Inputs* are more highly correlated with the dependent variable *effort* than *accesses* are, which suggests that *inputs* would be the better one to use as an input variable to our effort model. *Outputs* are moderately, if negatively, correlated with *effort*. What this can sometimes mean is that modules that have outputs tend to be easier to implement than other modules.

Below is a table showing the rank correlations:

	Inputs	Outputs	Accesses	Effort
Inputs	—	−0.60	0.84	0.93
Outputs	—	—	−0.46	−0.69
Accesses	—	—	—	0.78
Effort	—	—	—	—

Exercise 8.3 Building a simple model

i) and ii)

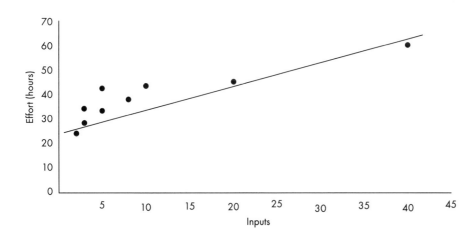

This shows our attempt at drawing a line on the graph that approximates to the relationship between number of inputs and hours of effort. We can argue about this quite a bit! What should be noted in this case is that the largest function at 40 inputs and 60 days of effort could have a disproportionate influence on where the line is drawn.

(iii) If you are using Excel you can go to the **Tools** menu and then select **Data Analysis**. When the list of techniques is displayed select **regression**.
The result of this will be:
effort = 30 + 0.78 × *inputs*
with $R^2 = 0.80$ and $p < 0.05$.

Exercise 8.4 Adding a second predictor

Trying each of the remaining independent variables with inputs we get:

effort = 36 + 0.68 × *inputs* − 0.54 × *outputs*
which has $R^2 = 0.84$

Note:
The negative influence of outputs *could* be because outputs are easier to develop.

effort = 24.1 + *0.58* × *inputs* + 2.62 *accesses*
which has $R^2 = 0.82$

Exercise 8.5 Using a model to make a new prediction

Work-hours would be 258 + 17.1 × 5 + 574 × 2 = 1491.5 work-hours

Exercise 8.6 Model evaluation

estimated	effort (hours)	difference	% difference
32	24	8	32
38	43	−5	−12
34	42	−8	−19
32	28	4	16
46	45	1	2
36	38	−2	−5
34	33	1	3
32	34	−2	−5
61	60	1	2

The first row seems to be a particular anomaly.

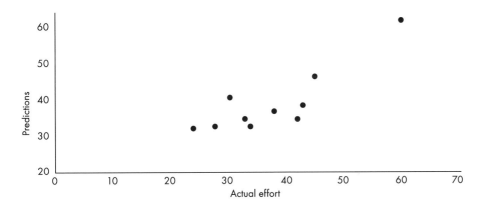

Exercise 8.7 Calculating Euclidean distances

The first stage is to normalize the values.

	kloc	Normalized	Exp	Normalized	Work-days
A	5	1.00	2	0.33	152
B	2	0.40	4	0.67	49
Target	3	0.60	6	1.00	

The 'distance' between A and target is:

$$\sqrt{(1.00 - 0.60)^2 + (0.33 - 1.00)^2} = \sqrt{0.16 + 0.44} = 0.78 \text{ approximately}$$

The distance between B and the target is:

$$\sqrt{(0.400 - 0.60)^2 + (0.67 - 1.00)^2} = \sqrt{0.04 + 0.11} = 0.39 \text{ approximately}$$

Thus B is adjudged to be closer to the target.

Chapter 9:

Exercise 9.1 Relationship between qualities

Indifferent relationships. Usability and reusability would seem to have little bearing on one another in spite of the familiarity of their names.

Complementary relationships. A program that demonstrated flexibility might also be expected to have a high degree of maintainability.

Conflicting relationships. A software application can be highly efficient because it exploits the architecture of a particular type of hardware to the full, but in consequence not be easy to transfer to another hardware platform.

Exercise 9.2 Repeating software quality criteria

The presence of the same software quality criterion for more than one software quality factor would indicate that the software quality factors are complementary.

Exercise 9.3 Quality specification

There are several qualities of a word processing application for which specifications could be produced of which only two examples are given below.

Quality	Ease of learning
Definition	The time needed by a new-comer to acquire enough skill to produce a standard document in a target time
Scale	Hours
Test	Interview subjects to see how much experience of word processing they have. Supply them with a machine, the software and a manual and a set of standard documents. Time how long it takes them to reach a target speed for setting up a document.
Worst	6 hours
Planned	2 hours
Best	1 hour
Now	Not applicable

Quality	Ease of use
Definition	The time for an experienced user to produce a standard document
Scale	Minutes
Test	Time subjects who have experience of the application takes to produce a standard document
Worst	30 minutes
Planned	15 minutes
Best	12 minutes
Now	not applicable

Exercise 9.4 Measuring availability

During week-days, the system should be available from 7.30 am to 6.30 pm, that is 11 hours. For the four week period, the time available should by $11 \times 5 \times 4 = 220$ hours.

It was unavailable for $11 + 4.5 + 4.5 = 20$ hours.

Percentage availability was therefore $(220 - 20)/220 \times 100 = 90.9\%$

Mean time between failures would be $200/3 = 66.66$ hours

Exercise 9.5 Assessing maintainability

Incident	Elapsed time to correct fault (days)	Effort to correct fault (hours)
1	1	5
2	25	4
3	23	3
4	1	2
average	12.5	3.5

Exercise 9.6 Extendibility

Original development productivity: 7000/350 = 20 lines of code per day
Amendment productivity: 500/15 = 33.33 lines of code per day
Extendibility: $33.33/20 \times 100 = 166\%$

Exercise 9.7 Matching ISO 9126 qualities

The idea of *initial ease of use* seems to be captured by the ISO 9126 sub-characteristic of *understandability. Ease of learning* fairly obviously corresponds to *learnability,* while *ease of use* seems to be clearly covered by *operability.* The concept of *memorability* does not seem to be covered by the ISO 9126 framework.

Exercise 9.8 Linking external and internal qualities

Measuring portability. One way of doing this is to measure the amount of effort needed to implement the application in a new environment. This could be normalized by calculating porting effort per KLOC.

Measuring modularity. This was extensively discussed in Chapter 4. A low information flow complexity metric would tend to indicate better modularity.

Measuring self-descriptiveness. A problem with this quality is that it depends on the reader of the code. Some terminology might well be easily understood in a restricted locality, but not more widely. We could test how accurately representative software developers could guess the function of particular procedure or variable purely from their names.

Measuring machine and software system independence. One measure of this could be the percentage of machines on the general market upon which this application could run.

   One problem with linking internal and external qualities in this case is that software system independence looks very much like an external quality in any case. Other questions could be raised about why other internal qualities have been left out like generality and communications commonality. Does the presence of modularity, for example, necessarily have to lead to increased portability?

Exercise 9.9 Management information flows

When the *architecture design* process is taking place which creates work packages, there could be a further output that is an effort estimation for each software component. These could be passed to a management function which allocates staff to the *develop software* process. The *develop software* process would need to pass back information about the actual effort being used as this would allow adjustments to resource allocations to be made as necessary.

Index